# Black & Gold

## The End of the Sixties

Mike Trial

Published by AKA-Publishing
Columbia. Missouri
www.AKA-Publishing.com
www.akayola.com
www.yolandaciolli.com

Library of Congress
Trial, Mike: Black & Gold, the end of the sixties
ISBN: 978-1-936688-17-3

Also available in Trade Paperback
ISBN: 978-1-936688-16-6

AKA-Publishing

# Black & Gold

## *The End of the Sixties*

**Mike Trial**

# Chapter 1

The high-backed wooden booths in the Heidelberg had filled early. Sorority girls in tee shirts emblazoned with greek letters mixed and mingled with fraternity guys. Mark stood at the bar, his hand on a glass of draft Hamm's beer. It was the last Saturday night before classes began for the fall semester 1968.

"DGs, Pi Phis, Tri Delts," someone said into his ear. It was Jeff Cooper smiling his wide, uncertain smile. He was dressed in a preppy uniform—blue blazer, rep tie, yellow shirt, gray slacks, and polished loafers.

"Working the orientation desk?" Mark said. He fumbled change out of his pocket. "We need music."

"Play something good for a change," Jeff called after him. "If I hear you play 'Wild Thing' one more time I'm going to pull the plug on that jukebox."

After Mark returned and "Wild Thing" was playing, he and Jeff raised their glasses. "To senior year." They toasted.

"Did you get moved into the trailer?" Mark, Jeff and Bill Whitten would be sharing a three-bedroom trailer this year.

"Yeah. Met Bill," Jeff said. "Seems like a nice guy. He was already studying."

"He is a nice guy. Studious type, unlike me. He'll finish up his degree in three and a half years."

Jeff raised his glass again and grinned. "Versus your four and a half years, right?"

"Good things should not be rushed."

Dave sauntered over. "Going skydiving tomorrow?"

"Yeah," Mark said. "You?" Dave nodded. He poured his glass full and stared at it. Jeff essayed, "No lecture tonight? Usually by now you'd be on about politics as expounded by the beautiful Carol."

"I'm fed up."

Mark swept the crowd with his hand. "Nonsense. Best time of the year and best year of our…"

"Fed up with Carol. I don't know why I've spent so much time chasing her."

"Because she's beautiful, Dave," Jeff said, incredulous. Dave had been pursing Carol since last spring, even to the point of taking a sublease on an apartment in the same apartment building where she lived. Mark assumed the Triumph TR3 he'd traded his old Chevy for a few months ago was part of the chase.

"I'm looking for something deeper."

"Carol's the smartest person on campus, profs included," Jeff continued. "I read her stuff in the *Columbia Free Press* sometimes. She's brilliant. And beautiful. And you're going to give her up?"

"I never had her, certainly not in the carnal sense." Dave wandered off into the crowd.

Jeff shook his head. "The brooding existentialist Zen philosopher. Have I forgotten any of the other philosophies he's into this week?"

Over four years of college, Dave's major had migrated from business through economics, into political science and now philosophy. Mark suspected Dave's interest in jazz, the beat generation's poetry, and Zen was a bit of a pose—a statement of depth in the face of Mark and Jeff's engineering majors.

Jeff began chatting up a couple of doe-eyed freshman girls with clear eyes, creamy skin, slim bodies, and nervous laughs, whose very innocence exuded sensuality.

A girl materialized beside Mark. She was good-looking in a small town kind of way—short brown hair, a slim body in tight jeans and a plain white tee shirt, entirely different from the sorority look-alikes. She edged over beside Jeff and tried to get the bartender's attention.

Jeff turned his attention to this new target. "Hi there." She ignored him. The freshmen girls drifted off.

"What's your major?" Jeff persisted. She looked around at him. "Mind your own business."

Jeff turned to Mark. "I'm going to the Stephens mixer tonight. Why don't you come along, unless Jennifer's got you on a short leash." Jeff grinned a knowing grin that Mark was beginning to resent.

"I'll meet you there," Mark countered. He didn't really want to go, but he was getting tired of Jeff's insinuations. Mark's friend Grant served the pizza Mark had ordered and scurried off. Mark reached over the bar, filled a glass with beer, and set it in front of the girl beside Jeff.

She smiled at him—pretty, not beautiful, but wonderful big brown eyes.

Jeff slid the pizza tray an inch toward her. "Have some pizza." She ignored him.

Jeff turned to Mark. "Neither you or Dave know how good you've got it, going steady with good-looking women." Mark was secretly pleased.

"Don't envy me too much," Mark said, pointing across the crowd to a girl in a tight pink Tri Delt tee shirt surrounded by a knot of drooling guys. "That's what we all want, right?"

"High maintenance," Jeff said. "Like that Dodge 426 Hemi you and Tim Bryant were always lusting after in high school."

Grant came over. "You want to do some relative work tomorrow?" Since he'd started skydiving two years before, Mark had found he had a natural talent for relative work, moving laterally through the air while free falling to link up with another skydiver falling at the same rate. "Yeah. Let's do."

"Well, I'm going to get going," Jeff told Mark. "See you at the mixer."

Once Jeff was out of earshot, the girl started in on the pizza. "I'm starving," she said, talking with her mouth full. "My name's Debbie."

"I'm Mark."

"What's relative work?" Debbie asked.

"Skydiving," Mark said. "I'm teaching Grant here the finer points of the sport."

Grant snorted. "You're teaching me? See you tomorrow at ten." Somebody put The Turtles on the jukebox. "The MU skydiving club. It's fun," Mark told her.

She eyed him up and down. "Fun? I thought it was sort of macho. Death-defying."

Mark laughed so long and loud that several of the nearer sorority girls eyed him critically. "Sport jumping is about speed and freedom; falling free through the air. It's about life, not death."

She nodded approvingly. "Good, I'm glad you're not the gung-ho military type—I've met too many of those types already." She finished her pizza.

Mark slid some change her way. "Play us some tunes."

She made her way through the crowd to the jukebox and chose "Time Has Come Today."

* * *

Mark looked out the open door of the Cessna at Columbia spread out five thousand feet below him. In the distance was a toy-like Jesse Hall dome on the MU campus, south of Highway 70 slicing the town in two, the shady suburbs, the farmland beyond stretching to the flat horizon. The skydivers sat cross-legged on the bare aluminum floor, swaddled in the meditative roar of the engine and the air rushing by.

At altitude the pilot throttled back, the plane settled into an expectant glide, and Mark followed Dave out into the airstream. They both pushed off and dropped away into silence, surrounded above by a hemisphere of blue and below by one of green. Mark rolled over on his back and contemplated the blue sky, the glare of the sun. He backflipped onto his belly and, guiding the air with his arms and legs, he let the airstream glide him closer to Dave. They linked hands for a moment, then drifted apart. Mark formed his body into an arrow, head down, and glided away. He stabilized just upwind of the orange circle of pea gravel that marked the target landing area. The ground was slowly spreading open to receive him, hypnotically engaging the eye as it expanded, imperceptibly increasing its speed.

Mark pulled the ripcord, his chute slid open and he hung in silence, two thousand feet of clear air below his boots. "Nice jump," Dave said conversationally from above him. Dave had his toggles pulled down, spilling air to drop faster until he was even with Mark.

"Yeah. Perfect air." They sat in silence admiring the unparalleled view of familiar streets lined with elms and oaks. "Our town. Our time," Mark said to himself.

On the ground they tossed their chutes into their cars. Dave idled his TR3 over to Mark's Chevy. "Let's come out again next Sunday."

Mark jumped in his car. The Ozark Airlines flight from St. Louis was just taxiing up to the terminal. "I've got to pick Jennifer up right now. Why don't you meet us for a beer at the Heidelberg around seven?"

Dave and ran a hand through his shock of black hair. "No time for the Berg tonight. You and Jennifer going to live together this year?"

"No."

Mark drove around the hangars to the little terminal's parking lot just as the DC-3's door opened. Jennifer was the third person out, dressed in a blue miniskirt, tanned and slim, long silky black hair parted in the middle. She came down the steps with coltish grace, burdened with a purse, a sweater, a huge red Carnaby Street shopping bag, and a small wooden box. He kissed her, breathing in Chantilly perfume. "Welcome back," he said.

"I've missed you." She handed him a small box containing six Florida oranges. "My parents insisted."

Mark laughed, "Thank them for me. It's thoughtful of them." In the hot front seat of his car their kiss was passionate but familiar.

"I missed you this summer," Mark said. The door closed on the Ozark DC-3, and it pivoted, glinting silver and green in the late afternoon light. "I should have come to visit you in Florida. I thought about you all the time." He looked away. "I used to replay in my mind all the times we spent together, from our first blind date, to the first night we spent together, to…"

She blushed. "I was so…"

"...naïve, in the best sense of the word. We both were; we both are. We made love and we talked about love."

She smiled. "Do we dare say the word 'love' right now, out in public, in daylight?"

He took a deep breath. "Yes. I love you."

"I love you too," she said. The DC-3 passed overhead, glinting in the golden light.

Mark started the car and they drove to Columbia College. "After you get settled into the dorm, let's go get some food and a beer at the Berg."

Jennifer put her hand on his arm. "Not tonight Mark, I have to be in the auditorium at seven for orientation and afterwards there's a get-acquainted session from eight to nine, and I need to unpack my stuff. I should have come back yesterday, but I didn't."

Mark helped Jennifer get her things up to her room in North Hall. Girls filled the halls, meeting and greeting and unpacking.

"See you tomorrow night," Mark said, exiting the chaos.

* * *

Car windows down, Hendrix on the radio, the balmy air rolling in, Mark couldn't keep the grin off his face. What had Dave said? Our time, our turf. He told himself he should do some reading for his first classes tomorrow, but when the light turned green at Conley Street, he found himself turning toward campus, full of anticipation. This was the new age of enlightenment, the Age of Aquarius. Everything was acceptable, and the unexpected was expected. On the streets, students were everywhere. Mark jostled his way through the milling crowd in front of the green door of the Shack, through the boisterous crowd in front of the open door of the Italian Village bar. A jukebox blasted the street with Janis, furtive freshmen darted away from swaggering upperclassmen, foursomes of newly pledged fraternity guys eyed foursomes of newly pledged sorority girls, a miasma of Shalimar and English Leather hovering over them. Mark stepped into the Heidelberg and spotted Jeff. For Mark, and Dave and Jeff, the Berg was their turf, a safe haven for the few last months before they faced the working world, the draft, and the war. The Berg was a time capsule where they knew their undergraduate years would always exist.

And the Berg was also the home of cheap beer: draft Hamm's in ten-ounce glasses for twenty-five cents, fifteen cents during happy hour. Mark poured some from the pitcher.

"Didn't see you at the mixer last night," Jeff said.

"I changed my mind, didn't go," Mark said. ""How'd you do?"

Jeff shook his head, and looked around the room. "Damn.

Here comes Mitchell. That guy's an obnoxious loud-mouth."

Larry Mitchell elbowed through the crowd and shook hands with Jeff and Mark. "Hey guys," too loud even in the noisy bar.

"What's up?" Mark said, handing him a glass of beer. Mitchell was another townie. Loud and brash, he had always seemed to need to demonstrate that he knew more about whatever the subject of conversation was.

"Bad news," he said, drawing up a chair.

Mark and Jeff exchanged glances.

"You guys remember Tim Bryant don't you? Kind of a geeky guy, but nice."

Mark nodded, "Sure. He was in Business and Public Administration, flunked out of MU but got accepted at some diploma mill in Nebraska I think. I knew him pretty well. We used to race slot cars together."

Larry gave Mark a disdainful look.

"I remember Tim," Jeff said. "Always wore black-framed glasses, still had braces on his teeth. Dated Diane what's-her-name all through high school."

Mark nodded. "Yeah, that's him. What about him?"

Larry frowned at his beer. "Well, his parents and mine go to the same church. My parents were talking to them last Sunday. Tim got killed in Vietnam last month."

The statement lay there between them and the bar seemed suddenly silent.

"He flunked out of that college in Nebraska," Larry continued. "Got drafted, shipped to Vietnam…" He shrugged. "Only in-country a few weeks before he got it. Funeral's Wednesday."

## Chapter 2

Dave and Carol stood across the living room of Dave's apartment. "I'm moving," Dave said finally. "I've rented a room in an old house over on Paquin."

Carol pushed perfect blonde hair out of her eyes in that characteristic gesture Dave had been so smitten with when he first met her, but now just found irritating. "Moving into some cockroach-infested dump in the student ghetto won't solve this 'dissatisfaction' you're talking about. You can do so much more by staying involved, working for a political solution…"

"That was last semester. The system is corrupt, it's hopeless trying to change it. Besides, I'm seeking clarity. I need time…"

"Clarity? Is that what it's called? Contemplating your navel rather than doing something about the problems in the world?" Carol's mouth set in a line, her crystal blue eyes flashed. "I thought you were better than that."

She began to pace, irritating Dave further. "Ever since I've known you, Carol, we've done nothing but talk politics, there's more…"

"It's important," she interrupted. "You told me so yourself." Her tone turned conciliatory. "But if you have to meditate you can do it just as easily in a clean place, with good plumbing and a nice kitchen, and air conditioning."

"I want to live simply."

"But you'll keep your sports car?"

He shrugged her off.

"And Transcendental Meditation? It's a fad, Dave, nothing

more." Her eyes lost their sympathy. "It might even be dangerous."

"Zen," Dave corrected, "not TM. And there's nothing dangerous about it."

Carol ignored his remark. "All these self-styled gurus—they're just publicity seekers, it's theater, acting..."

"Like the demonstrators in Peace Park. Half those people you're haranguing are just there to 'make the scene.' It's political theater. To change the world, we need to change ourselves. That's what Buddha said. And that's what Dubcek should be doing, not getting a bunch of people killed throwing rocks at Soviet tanks."

Dave knew Dubcek and Prague Spring were Carol's hot buttons. "Freedom is precious and he's willing to fight for it," she snapped back. "He's a Slovak and a lifelong communist party member. He was legally elected and now he's making significant improvements in Czechoslovakia. Freedom of the press, improvements in the agricultural economy..."

"Jesus, you have to tell everybody everything you know," Dave snapped.

She threw up her hands theatrically. "Well...I'm going. Good luck in your new life." She picked up her purse, shook her head, and was gone.

After the door closed and silence had settled for a time, Dave finished packing a box. "Well, that's that," he said to himself. In twenty minutes he had all his things packed. "... sparkling blue eyes, perfect blonde hair, elegant body," he heard himself muttering. "Always smarter than anybody else in the room, and always seems to have to show it. She's smart, she's effective, but she irritates people. Her family has wealth and position, she moves through campus society effortlessly, admired and respected. Officer of one of the premier sororities on campus, an honor student every semester. Her good looks turn heads everywhere she goes."

He took his sports jackets and slacks out of his closet and laid them across the couch. "Yeah, beautiful Carol." He carefully slid his Getz, Coltrane, and Brubeck records into a box, packed towels around them, and carried them to his car. With the top down, he could move everything in two trips.

* * *

Dave parked his black TR3 in the gravel lot behind the old house and clomped up the narrow stairs to his room on the third floor. The one room apartment had a sloped ceiling on one side, and a view of the gravel parking lot and an old oak tree. He unrolled the futon, threw the sheets and blanket on it, set up the brick and board bookcase and stacked his books on it, then set up the record player near the window and arranged his row of records. He opened a Busch and leaned against the window frame looking at the oak leaves, still in the evening gloom. The streetlight came on. He clicked on a light and rearranged the paperbacks, glancing in Alan Watts' The Way of Zen. He drew a deep breath, listening to the sounds around him, and sat down cross-legged on the mattress. Long slow breaths—*susoku*. The great way is comparable to water. It enriches the world without being attached to anything.

When his meditation was over, Dave stood up on stiff legs, glanced fondly at his records and row of books, then out the window at his black TR3 parked in the weedy parking lot behind the house. Liberated from attachment to things? "Well, not yet," he whispered to himself with a grin. He showered in the grungy bathroom down the hall and dressed in slacks, a pressed white shirt, and a corduroy sports jacket, then headed over to the mixer at Stephens College. He ignored the dull headache that had been throbbing since his second trip up the stairs.

* * *

Her nametag said Susan. She was a buxom girl with short blonde hair, dressed in a beautifully tailored pants suit. A sophomore from Webster Groves, majoring in drama, Jeff thought she'd said. Jeff steered her out onto the terrace away from the music, while couples drifted in and out of the French doors opened to the mild evening.

A haze of cigarette smoke soon hovered in the still air. Couples stood in the dim light talking and laughing with the nervous tones and gestures of those who have just met.

"So," Jeff said, lighting Susan's Pall Mall, "what brought you to Stephens College?"

"Originally the drama department..."

"Going to be an actress?"

"Not any more. Two semesters was enough of that. But I was also working in the wardrobe department and found I really enjoyed costume design, fashion design. That's my major now." She tapped her cigarette artfully into a stone planter box of phlox, trying not to think of her boyfriend, recently departed. Jeff smiled at the gesture.

"What are you smiling at?" she said.

"You may have left the stage behind, but you still know how to act." He touched her arm. "I mean that as a compliment. Acting isn't just artifice, it's good communication."

That's not what Allen used to tell me, she thought. She put an engaging smile on her face, a hand on Jeff's arm, and pulled him into conversation about himself to suppress her recriminations and regrets. Unaware of being maneuvered, Jeff gave this interesting girl a lengthy explanation of electrical engineering as a major and his growing dissatisfaction with it. When he wound down, much more relaxed and confident in himself, she maneuvered the conversation to music.

"Janis Ian?" Jeff said cautiously. "She's...alright. But most folk music is just crap."

"Janis Ian is great," Susan corrected him. "Beautiful voice, good guitar, and lyrics that actually have something to say, not just 'do-wah-diddy'...and most folk music is not crap."

"Well, yes, you're right," Jeff back-pedaled. "I just meant the stuff you hear on the radio...Janis Ian is a good singer, but once you've got the message of "Society's Child," how many more times are you going to listen to it? Same with all the message songs, whether it's folk or rock. The protest stuff is the worst. I sympathize with César Chávez and the migrant workers, but get really tired of hearing 'We Shall Overcome.'"

Susan continued to smile, but Jeff could tell he was offending her. He looked this way and that for a new topic, finding none. From inside the amplifiers bleeped and squealed and the band swung into something meant to be the Classics I.V.'s "Stormy."

"Let's dance," Jeff said. Susan took his arm and they disappeared in the crowd on the dance floor.

* * *

Monday, the first day of class, Mark felt great. He had not read any of his assignments, but liked the feeling of talking about the courses, and the fact that no homework was due and no exams were imminent. His Machine Design course looked great, so did his Electronics and Materials lab course. But Thermodynamics—it was going to be a bitch. He spent forty minutes of agony frantically scribbling down the spew of derived equations that Professor Bradley was writing on the board. He'd fill the board, erase it, and fill it again. When class ended, Mark staggered out into sunshine on the quad and made a beeline for the Heidelberg. Thermo was going to be bad. But, the weather was beautiful, classes were over for the week, and happy hour awaited him.

* * *

Mark slid in through the Friday afternoon crowd at the door of the Heidelberg Bar and Restaurant. Happy hour and the place was packed. "Hey, Mark!" Jeff waved from the crowd. Mark slid his books onto the table, sat down, and helped himself to one of the five glasses of draft beer on the table.

"Want to double date tonight?" Jeff said.

"I have to study tonight," Mark said. He took another long drink of flat beer.

"Look at those two," Jeff said. Two girls trailing a wake of male stares made their way through the crowd. "No bras and miniskirts," Jeff breathed. "These are great days."

"How'd you do at the mixer last night?" Mark asked.

Jeff couldn't hide his grin. "Met a girl there, Susan, from Webster Groves. We're going out to dinner tonight." He glanced at his watch. "Thought you might want to double date."

"Too late for me to get a date," Mark said, sliding a beer glass around on the table.

"But now that Jennifer's back in town…"

"We're not married, you know."

"You'd be crazy to lose a girl like Jennifer. She's great," Jeff said earnestly. "I wish…jeez, here comes Maynard G. Krebs." Dave was making his way through the crowd toward them. At the table he sat down and grabbed a glass of beer.

"I'm surprised Timothy Leary Jr. still drinks beer," Mark joked. Jeff flashed Dave a peace sign.

"Alcohol and meditation are holy fire. Psychedelics are too heavy."

"That beard looks like shit, Dave," Jeff said pleasantly.

"Thanks. It does look good, doesn't it?"

"Where'd you get that shirt? Salvation Army?" Mark added.

Dave finished off the glass of draft Hamm's. "As a matter of fact, yes. You should stop by there yourself, Mark. You wear exactly the same thing every day—Levi's, blue Gant shirt, Weejuns…you look like some J.C. Penney's preppie."

"Thought I saw you at the mixer last night," Jeff said to Dave.

"I was there for a while," Dave frowned around the room. "Those girls aren't my type. Too..."

"...smart?" Mark filled in.

"...suburban," Dave finished unperturbed. "No depth."

"You shouldn't be out prowling around anyway," Jeff said. "You're going to lose the beautiful Carol."

"Not that I ever had her," Dave said, squinting around the room again. "She wants to spend all her time talking politics, organizing protests, writing that damned *One Voice Manifesto*. Yesterday we spent an hour arguing over whether Alexander Dubcek's political coalition is strong enough to reach détente with the Russians in Prague." He grabbed another partial beer and drained it. "I've had it with her. The damned thing is, she's really interesting, she's beautiful, she's usually right in her political assessments. But I want more out of life than political conversation."

"Well..." Jeff leaned in toward Dave, "...if you and Carol aren't going to be at your place tonight, I'd like to borrow your apartment. I'm taking Susan to dinner, and afterward, well, the trailer is too crowded and...we need someplace to go."

"I don't think you'd be very interested in my apartment, not the new one anyway."

Mark and Jeff stared at him.

"I moved out of Tiger Village," Dave said. "No more Carol, no more swimming pool, no more club house. I got a room in one of those old houses on Paquin Street."

Mark was incredulous. "That's going to ruin your man-about-town image. You didn't trade in your TR3 for a VW van did you?"

"Of course not. Women come and go, but you keep your car—that's important. Anyway, I'm going a different direction now, and I don't need that glossy Tiger Village lifestyle. Come by some time. 2210 Paquin. I'm on the third floor, apartment 3C."

"Damn," Jeff said. "I wish you'd told me. I'd have sublet your place rather than the trailer."

Mark gave him a hurt look and set his beer down. "You guys are all wound up over these women. Sue, Carol, what's it matter? Tim's dead. That's what matters."

The three of them sat there and avoided each others' eyes. The color seemed to have drained out of the room.

"I'll see you guys later." Mark made his way to the door.

## Chapter 3

Hypnotized by the Hamm's sign's bilious blue waters endlessly rippling, Mark sat at the bar, an untasted beer in front of him. The I.V. was quiet. Mark went to the pay phone and dropped a dime in the slot. He slowly dialed the first digit of Jennifer's phone number, then the next, then stopped. After a while the phone clicked, his dime dropped into the change slot, and the dial tone whined. If he told her about Tim's death, she would be very caring, but pity and condolence would not ease the restless anger he felt.

When he returned to the bar, there was a girl sitting on the barstool next to his. She gave him a hug, pushing her small breasts against him. "Remember me?"

"Debbie," Mark said.

"You're a skydiver. I want to learn skydiving," she said. She had a cute smile, and brown hair cut so short it seemed boyish, but her body was attractive in a tee shirt and jeans.

"Okay," Mark said. She started to raise her hand to order a beer when Mark stopped her. "Let's get out of here." He pulled her gently along, off the barstool and out the door. He was surprised to see night had fallen while he'd sat nursing a beer.

"What's your hurry?" she said breathlessly as they hurried down the street. At his Chevy, Mark pointed to a tumbled white mass on the backseat. "That is a parachute."

As he drove she leaned over the seat feeling the filmy nylon. Then she slid over to sit right beside him, just like high school. He put his arm around her. "I didn't take time to repack my chute, just threw it in the back seat."

"Isn't it dangerous to leave it tangled up? Will it open right if it's not..."

"I'll straighten it out when I repack." He parked in the big gravel parking lot behind the University Services building, shut of the engine, and tuned the radio to KAAY. There were three other cars there, lights off, spaced far apart. Debbie lit a joint and they passed it back and forth without speaking. When the joint had burned down to a roach, Mark tossed it out the window and took her in his arms and kissed her with angry passion. They clambered over the seat and into the frothy tangles of the parachute and made love. For a while, the warmth of her body eased the chill that had come into him ever since he'd heard Tim was dead.

Mark leaned over the seat and turned the radio off. Debbie got a pack of Winstons out of her purse on the front seat. Her body was white in the darkness.

"Don't smoke back here, you can burn a hole in the nylon."

She put the cigarette away. "Don't talk much do you?" she said.

He stepped out of the car naked, oblivious to other cars nearby, and quickly dressed. She wriggled into her jeans and tee shirt and they sat in the front seat smoking cigarettes.

"You from St. Louis?" Debbie asked, blowing a smoke ring at the stars.

"Columbia," he said, staring at the darkness.

She snorted, "Me too, but not for long. I'm leaving..."

"We're all leaving," Mark muttered. "One way or another."

"What about skydiving? When can I...?"

Mark cut her off. "I've got to get going. Where's your car parked?"

* * *

At the end of Tim's funeral, Mark followed the others out

of the old church and stood on Walnut Street blinking in the sun. The rest dispersed to their cars—friend's of Tim's parents, a handful of high school classmates Mark had lost touch with long ago.

The Indian summer afternoon seemed an illusion, a two-dimensional picture in sepia tones.

Tim's house on Michaelson Drive was like its neighbors, a modest 1950's ranch-style with a blue Buick in the carport and a neatly trimmed lawn. The street was lined with mature elm and oak trees. Impatiens lined the Bryants' driveway. In the over-crowded living room Mark stood for a time, trying to think of something to say, but there was nothing to be said. In the church, the priest's cant had been meaningless and Mark knew his own condolences to Tim's parents were equally so. The stairway door stood open. He made his way down to the rec room in the basement and sat on one of the barstools at the little bar. Conversations upstairs drifted down the stairs in the tone and tempo of funerals, the dichotomy of mimicking normalcy while consoling a great loss.

Tim's slot car track was still set up on the ping-pong table. Mark ran his finger through the dust. At the end of the table were four model car boxes. Mark opened one and took out Tim's beautifully detailed Ford GT40. Another box held a red Mustang with white racing stripes.

He replaced them in their boxes and sat back down at the bar. The leaves on the trees outside made dappled patterns in the melancholy light coming through the high basement windows.

Tim sat on the other barstool, wearing his familiar black-framed glasses. "Remember the old slot car place over on Business 70?" he said softly.

"I remember," Mark whispered. "We had some fun there didn't we? Remember that model Ferrari I had back in high school?"

"Yeah."

"That was the summer we double-dated almost every week. Diane set me up with her friend." Mark grinned. "I remember the night we were driving around in your car. We were always in your car, you kept your Plymouth looking and running perfectly. My old Chevy, well… anyway, remember we drove over to Boonville just for something to do and got into that drag race with those guys in that '55?"

"Yeah," Tim said. He was staring at the pale light coming in through the basement windows. "They beat us pretty bad."

Mark laughed. "I remember afterwards we drove up to that little park on Old Highway 63 overlooking Hinkson Creek…"

"The old makeout spot."

"Yeah," Mark laughed again. "My date and I were in the back seat. I had my shoes off and one foot down alongside the front seat. In the dark, Diane mistook my white sock for her white purse and tried to pick it up."

"Those were good days," Tim said, suddenly subdued. He ran his finger down the vinyl padding at the edge of the bar. "I always liked the long summer evenings here in Columbia, high school days. I'd get home from stocking shelves at Nowell's, take a shower and put on Levi's and a white tee shirt, pick up Diane for a drive-in movie or cruise around town, maybe a hamburger at McDonald's or a root beer at Mugs Up. I wish they'd never ended." Tim's ghost faded into the shadows. The conversations upstairs continued in soothing whispers.

* * *

Mark's spirits lifted when Jennifer came down the stairs of her dorm. She was beautiful. As they walked to his car arm in arm, the scent of her Chantilly took him back through all of their days together. Life was what mattered, the days and hours of our lives, not the words of priest when we die.

"Keith is playing guitar now?" Jennifer said as they drove

down Ninth Street toward the Hofbrau.

Mark nodded. "He said he'd never play for money, and now he's playing down at the Hofbrau once a week." Mark shrugged. "But I don't think it's about the money, not really. His parents are pretty well off. I'm sure they're paying his way through school. Funny thing is, he's kind of a tightwad."

"I remember that time he refused to pay for his date's lunch," Jennifer laughed. "That won't get him many dates."

"I think his parents bought that ratty little trailer for him, so he wouldn't have to pay rent. What a dump."

"It had its uses," Jennifer said coyly.

"Yeah," Mark grinned. "Rednecks outside drinking Old Milwaukee and throwing the cans in the yard, while we're inside talking about Andrew Marvell's poetry, and later, in the bedroom...."

The Hofbrau was crowded, but a booth opened up just as Mark and Jennifer walked in. They ordered bratwurst plates, a draft beer, and a Coke.

"...cups overflow with wine and well-turned words amaze..." Jennifer arched an eyebrow at Mark.

"Gerard Manley Hopkins?"

"Thomas Campion. A distant relative of mine no doubt," she laughed.

"You look great tonight, did I tell you that?" She smiled, embarrassed. Keith made his way between the tables and stepped up on the little dais in the spotlight. His lank yellow hair disappeared in the harsh light, making him look like a balding northwoodsman in his worn jeans, plaid shirt with sleeves rolled up, and hiking shoes. He tuned his Gibson intently. There was a piece of paper taped to the inside top of his guitar case that spelled "thanks" in flower power letters. Jennifer and Mark traded looks.

But his playing was strong, complex and stylish. He covered a handful of folk-rock classics, then some bits of Reinhardt and Les Paul, and slowed the tempo down for a medley of pop tunes. After a pause he played "Suzanne" more beautifully that Mark had ever heard it.

"He could play for a living," Jennifer told Mark as they applauded.

"But he says the chances of making a good living as a musician are miniscule. He wants a sure road to big bucks."

Keith disappeared on break.

"He talks about a Porsche, a glossy apartment, all that stuff, but every once in a while, he'll get this wistful tone in his voice and talk about hitting the road, playing guitar, living the free life, playing what he wants, how he wants." Mark touched Jennifer's hand. "I guess we all dream about unlimited freedom sometimes." She didn't answer.

By the time Keith started his second set, the front tables were full of girls in rapturous silence. At the end of his set, one requested he play "Suzanne" again and he slid into it, slowing it down even more. "Looks like he's acquired a few groupies," Jennifer whispered.

When he'd finished, the applause went on for a long time. Mark assumed he was going to do an encore, but instead he sorted through sheet music in his guitar case until he found what he was looking for. He shaded his eyes in the spotlight. "Let me read you these all too familiar lyrics. 'Greeting, you are hereby inducted into the armed forces of the United States.'" He put the paper down gingerly and stood up slowly. "I've been drafted."

The room went silent. One of the girls said softly, "For real?" He nodded, and suddenly he was surrounded by girls making solicitous sounds. Mark and Jennifer made their way out past the throng of admirers, but Mark caught his eye and told him, "Meet me tomorrow at the Heidelberg."

On the drive back to Jennifer's dorm, Jennifer started a quote, "...the shadow of death...sorry," she said.

But Mark nodded. "But you're right. Another one of us about to enter that valley."

* * *

Thursday afternoon Dave was walking down Ninth Street mentally reliving the discussion just ended in his International Politics class. He chuckled. He'd manipulated the discussion so that he could list some of Milton Freidman's liberal views as to what government should not do: agricultural price controls, minimum wage setting, public housing, the draft. His planning and memorization had paid off. His classmates, and even the grad student teaching the class, could think of no logical argument against his points, and best of all, Dave was sure they thought he had thought them up himself.

"Want to do some acid, man?" somebody said. There was a girl in a burgundy sweater and lush brown hair sitting on the lawn in front of Lowry Hall. She had lush brown hair and her infectious smile made her beautiful in the way plain-featured girls can be.

Caught off guard but propelled by her engaging energy that left him no choice, Dave said, "Sure."

"Well, let's go then." Unasked, she linked arms with him and they walked the four blocks to Paquin Street. Completely off-balanced by this engaging girl with big hair, a big smile, and big breasts he hoped would be pressing close to him, Dave lectured her on politics and Zen. She had a small chip in the corner of one of her front teeth, which he felt was charming.

The old three story frame houses on Paquin had been partitioned into cheap apartments and had recently become the center of the counterculture in Columbia, which some viewed as a disgraceful ghetto, and others viewed as an oasis of forwarding-thinking lifestyles in conservative Columbia.

"Third floor," Dave said, admiring her butt as they made their way up the narrow stairs to his stuffy room. Dave slid a window up. She showed him two tiny white tablets in the palm of her hand. Although Dave did not do drugs any stronger than pot, he took one and swallowed it with a slug of beer from his refrigerator. "Same trip as window pane acid, but not as many hours," she told Dave. "I like it better. More color and less movement."

"I'm Allison Gates," she said. They shook hands.

"Dave Gardner."

Talking with her was easy. Dave was taken with her big laugh, big tits, and hips a little too wide. He tried to look cool and avoid staring at her as she rolled around on the mattress pulling one book after another out of his pile of paperbacks. Her breasts were bouncing around beautifully under her cotton blouse embroidered with the tree of life, its roots spelling Katmandu.

He lit a stick of incense and sat down beside her on the mattress. The sounds of traffic and people drifted in the open window on the Indian summer breeze.

"Let me guess," Dave said. "You're from New Mexico."

She laughed, clapped her hands, and then kissed him unexpectedly. "No, but I'd like to be. When I was in junior high school, back in Moberly, I used to tell my friends my parents had been living in a commune out West when I was born."

"Moberly." Dave did not add the dismissive remark he would have added talking with Carol. "Like to tell stories do you? Make up your life as you go along?"

"I like to live life as I go along," she said. She sat down on his mattress, perfectly at ease, and looking very sexy in her earth-mother way. "Yeah, a farm on Route K east of Moberly."

"What's your major?" he asked.

"I'm not enrolled," she said. "I just sit in on classes that seem interesting. I sat in on an Anthropology class today."

The colors in the old wallpaper were beginning to shift as

the acid started to affect his senses. "You feel it?"

"Yeah," Allison said. "It's neat."

Dave grinned. "Neat?"

She leaned over and hugged him. "Don't make fun."

Dave held her for a moment, intoxicated by her warmth, the scent of her hair, and the warm brown of her eyes. "You are beautiful." And so different from Carol, he thought. He knew his logic could never persuade her of anything.

She pulled back. "Don't give me that. I've got a big butt, a chipped tooth, my hair is uncontrollable..."

"You're beautiful," he repeated slowly as the drug took him along, pulling him into her vortex.

Allison sat in *zazen*, eyes closed, hands on her thighs palms up—a beautiful Buddha, her curly brown hair a halo. "I was thinking about sunrises," Allison said slowly. She opened her eyes and moved to sit across from Dave at the window, one arm on the sill. She picked up a book from his stack. "I read this book, *Journey to the East*. There's this guy Leo, who's been their guide on this journey. He asks if they've become friends and Leo says he doesn't know people at all. He says knowing a dog is better. Easier." She laughed, then stopped. "Sorry."

Then she burst out laughing again, snorted, and they both laughed until tears were running down their cheeks.

After they caught their breath Dave said, "Nothing to be sorry about, you didn't write the book, Hermann Hesse did." They both started laughing again and couldn't stop for a long time.

Allison pulled *Monday Night Class* from Dave's bookshelf. "I went to hear this guy Stephen, the guy who wrote this. He travels around the country teaching people stuff." She paused, seeing something only she could see.

A wave of color washed over Dave unexpectedly. "Colors," he said. "Shades of lavender and purple and chartreuse.

Beautiful." The angular light on the faded wallpaper revealed a rose pattern he had not known was there. He studied the faded roses, the bare wood floor, the old Indian blanket on the mattress. The afternoon light was fading. Moving with infinite slowness he picked up a candle, set it in the plate that served as a candleholder, found some matches, and got it lit.

Allison was talking, "... stuff like loving each other... I mean really loving each other. And other stuff, like consciousness, and aura... all kinds of stuff."

"Stephen?"

"Yeah." A smile came slowly to her face like a sunrise. "It would be really neat to go and listen to him again."

Dave was transfixed by the dark wainscot. There was a dent in the top of it near the door, where someone had once dropped something on it. It had been repainted several times. A collage of the people who might have lived in this room in the past flowed across his imagination.

From the open window he could hear the distant sound of a child's voice, the closing of a car door, a crow far away. Columbia went about its business on this ordinary September evening. There is only this moment, he thought. That's what Zen teaches us—Zen which sounds so simple, yet is so difficult to attain. He ran his finger along the dusty top of the wainscot, painted brown by some unknown hand. He saw the wood as it had looked when it was new—straight, clean and aromatic.

A branch of the oak tree touched the wall outside the room, scratching softly. ""What's that?" Allison asked.

"My spiritual guide. The tree," Dave said. He saw the spirit of the tree, preoccupied with the things only trees know.

Allison got out a lid of pot she found behind the stack of books and started rolling a joint.

"Hey, wait a minute," Dave said. "I'm high already. That isn't drug use—it's drug abuse."

She licked the joint closed sensually and held it up,

perfectly rolled. "Anything worth doing is worth overdoing." She lit it from the candle and took a long hit.

"In the candlelight your smile looks like sunrise," Dave said.

"I smile a lot, sorry," Allison said tightly through a lungful of smoke. "It just happens. Like the sun coming up."

After a while they took off their clothes and made love. When Dave woke, his head hurt and Allison was gone.

# Chapter 4

Jeff laid a silver ankh and chain on the wooden counter and pulled out a five dollar bill. The guy behind the counter put the money in a box and handed him back a worn one-dollar bill. "I thought the price was three fifty," Jeff said mildly.

"Tax," the guy said with a snotty grin. His girlfriend tilted her purple granny glasses down and snickered. "For the revolution, man." The guy adjusted his headband and eyed Jeff's slacks and corduroy sports jacket with contempt.

"You're not a revolution, man," Jeff said, already regretting his sarcasm. "You're just sex, drugs, and rock and roll."

The other two laughed. "That *is* the revolution, man. Where have you been?"

Jeff shook his head. He was waiting for the guy to offer to put the ankh and chain in a box for him. "You've been listening to TV reporters quoting every half-assed 'spokesman' and rock star."

"Bullshit!" the girl said. She put her sandaled feet up on the counter. "If you're not part of the solution, you're part of the problem. Do some righteous acid, man, get in touch with your head, get real."

"Any more clichés you need to quote?" The guy unknotted his headband and shook his hair out of his eyes in a gesture Jeff disliked instantly. I sound like my parents, Jeff thought. "You're not doing anything new."

The girl put her feet down and got up. "I'll tell you what's new. It's dropping 500 micrograms of orange windowpane and grooving to the lightshow at a Big Brother concert..."

"We're hitching to San Francisco next week," the guy interrupted her. "Golden Gate Park, the center of the universe, man."

The girl speared Jeff with a glare over the top of her glasses. "There's so much energy there, because people like you are all back here."

Jeff put the ankh and chain in his pocket. "Draft's going to get you."

The guy brayed, "Not me, man. That's for fascists like you. I've already got a cannabis conviction—felony charge—so I'm draft exempt." His girlfriend straightened up and put her arm around him protectively, "So bullshit, arresting people for something that grows naturally in the world. So bullshit."

Jeff turned, raised his fist in a salute, "Power to the people." The little bell on the door jangled behind him.

* * *

That evening, Jeff ushered Susan ahead of him into the trailer. She walked around the living room he'd just neatened up after forcing Mark and Bill out for the evening. She studied the jazz posters he'd hastily pinned to the wall.

"This is nice," she touched the coffee table he'd surreptitiously taken from his parents' family room.

Jeff poured Jim Beam and Pepsi over ice in the highball glasses he'd bought at Kmart that afternoon, mixing one of the highballs considerably stronger than the other.

"Pick out a record," he said, setting the full glasses on coasters. She flipped through the records and put on Herb Alpert's *Whipped Cream*. "Love that sound," Susan smiled.

He slid the stronger drink over to her and sipped his, making appreciative sounds. She took a drink, wrinkled her face, "Wow! That's strong."

"After you graduate, you'll be moving to New York?"

"It'll be exciting," she said a little too brightly. "Anyway, that's where the jobs are in fashion design."

"The Big Apple," Jeff said, raising a toast.

"And you?"

"Well...I don't know—maybe McDonnell-Douglas in St. Louis...I haven't really decided yet."

The record ended and she got up to turn it over. "What's this?" Susan said, picking up the ankh Jeff had laid on the table.

"A little gift. I was thinking of you, and so..."

"Thanks," she said, turning it over and over. It suddenly seemed small and tawdry to Jeff. "Free love," he said neutrally.

She laid it carefully on the table. "Actually it's the symbol for eternal life in ancient Egyptian mythology."

"Really?" Jeff said.

Susan took a microscopic sip of her drink. "The free love meaning is just hippie marketing."

"Oh... I thought... well..." Jeff set his drink down, put his arm around her, and kissed her. She didn't respond.

There was an awkward silence.

Jeff got up and took the arm off the record. He flipped clumsily through his albums and put on The Lovin' Spoonful.

Susan was up looking out the window. Jeff tried to hug her, but she pulled away. "I'm sorry, I..." he trailed off.

"I think I should go back to the dorm now. I'll call a cab."

He tried to turn her around to face him but she walked away from him. "I'm sorry, let's go out and eat," he struggled.

"Not tonight." She went to the door.

"Come on," Jeff said. It sounded like a whine even to him. "Sit down, finish your drink. Let's talk at least."

"No, Jeff."

He circled the room while the music asked if you'd ever had to make up your mind. He started to sit down, but the silver ankh was still lying in the middle of the coffee table.

Instead he picked up the two highball glasses and took them to the kitchen. He stood there looking at the glasses for a minute, then he drove her back to her dorm in silence.

* * *

Four thousand feet over Columbia in a clear blue sky, the Cessna's engine throttled back to an idle. Dave stepped out the open door into the prop blast, one foot on the step and one foot on the plane's wheel. Mark scrambled off the bare aluminum floor. He shot a glance at the ground below, pried Dave's hand off the strut, and watched him tumble away into empty air for a second before following him. For an instant it was silent, then as Mark accelerated toward the ground, the blast of air rose around him. Below him the drop zone was a tiny smear of orange on the green grass beside the row of parked cars. With his body parallel to the earth, arms and legs outstretched, he fell as slowly as possible, extending his time in free fall.

This high above the surface it didn't feel like falling, more like being suspended above the earth, balanced on an upward jet of air. He pivoted, using his hands as airfoils, saw Dave below him, and pulled his arms and legs in tight to fall faster. When he came level with Dave, he pushed his arms and legs back out to slow down. They were only twenty feet apart, but the blast of rushing air prevented any communication.

Mark glanced at the altimeter at the front of his harness. It was almost down to twenty-five hundred feet, time to open their chutes. Mark turned and tilted head down to propel himself away from Dave, then flattened back out. There was nothing around him in any direction except the clear blue sky and the flat green landscape below. Perfect freedom. He brought his hands in to his shoulders, hooked his right thumb into the ripcord handle, and extended both arms while pulling the ripcord. The chute opened smoothly and he was sitting in his nylon harness under a perfect circle of white and orange nylon, a half mile of empty air under his boots. It was silent. The cars parked on the grass by the drop zone looked like toys.

A hundred feet away, Dave sat in his harness admiring the scenery. He pulled his left toggle down a little to face Mark. "Jerk!" he called. Mark laughed. Mark pulled down the left toggle line on his riser, turning his chute left and moving downwind, closer to the target in the dying evening breeze. When he was only a hundred feet above the pea gravel circle he turned to face upwind for the landing. The ground rose up smoothly toward him. He touched down gently, flexing his knees, and strode away to keep the chute straight as it floated to the ground behind him. He was about three meters from the paper plate set dead center in the circle of pea gravel. His chute crumpled silently to the ground behind him.

"Nice jump," the pilot's wife said as she finished putting her folding chair and picnic basket in her van.

Dave came down fifteen feet to the other side of the target. "You owe me a beer for that stunt," he told Mark.

Mark stepped back to straighten the nylon lines and pull his canopy out, then walked toward it figure-eighting the nylon risers and canopy panels loosely around his arms. He carried it to his Chevy and laid it neatly in the trunk while the Cessna came in for a landing.

Wings rocking, the plane taxied off to its parking space at the end of the row of planes. Mark changed his jump-boots for tennis shoes and slid out of his jumpsuit. "Well, I'm going to go study."

Dave sat on the grass by his gear, helmet off, massaging his temples. He nodded and slowly rose to begin gathering up his parachute. "I don't feel so well."

"I know what you mean," Mark said, misunderstanding completely. "I still can't believe Tim's dead."

Mark closed the trunk of his Chevy and slid in behind the wheel. "See ya."

* * *

Dave drove back to Paquin Avenue, slowed to jounce over the rutted driveway, and parked his TR3 in his usual spot under the big oak tree. He carefully closed the screen door behind him and went up the narrow stairway holding on to the handrail. The dim light seemed hazy. His stomach felt queasy. He was sweating. He laid his head against the cool wall, soothing his pounding pulse. After a moment he eased himself up the last few steps and into his room. Outside the window, insects chirred and the oak leaves rustled in the afternoon wind. He lay down on the mattress and fell into a sleep clogged with frustrating dreams.

When he woke, the room was gray with dawn. He'd slept the night through. His head had stopped hurting. He sat up slowly, straightened his back, and focused his eyes on the wood floor a few feet in front of him. He took a long breath, in through his nose, out through his mouth, then another breath. He tried to think only of the air going into his lungs and back out. Random thoughts intruded—get gas for the car, review the last three chapters in international banking…he pushed them away, concentrating on making his mind the surface of a mirror. He adjusted to a more comfortable position and meditated for a time. He concentrated on breathing slowly, completely filling his lungs with each inhalation. His mind cleared. The dawn was silent except for the occasional scratch of the oak leaves on the window.

Empty the mind, live only in the present moment, go straight ahead without confusion or hesitation. He thought of a statement in a book he was reading—*I thought I had a long way to go to reach my destination, but when I turned around and looked behind me, I realized I had passed it long ago.*

By the time he had showered and dressed he felt great.

Mark strolled out of the library into the hot clear sunshine, stood for a moment on the steps, then turned left. Time for a beer at the Italian Village. He checked his watch. He'd spent exactly one hour studying, although some of the time had been spent daydreaming. A car separated itself from traffic and pulled into an empty parking space beside Mark. Larry Mitchell grinned up at him from the open window of his Mustang. "Let's go inside and get a beer, I'm buying." Larry was already out of the car and putting a coin in the meter.

Mark made a show of checking his watch. "I don't think so, not right now." Larry's ebullient energy could sometimes get a little abrasive, but Mark allowed himself to be propelled down Lowry Street.

"It's a big day, help me celebrate. I'm getting married," Larry announced.

Mark stopped and stared. "What? Now?"

"Next spring."

Mark didn't need to ask who Larry was marrying. Larry and Brenda had been dating since junior year in high school. Mark shifted his books and they shook hands. The I.V. was pleasantly empty. They slid into a booth while Grant poured a pitcher of Hamm's and set it in front of Mark, "You jumping next Sunday?"

"Yeah. You?"

Grant nodded.

Mark poured the glasses full and they toasted. "Well, Brenda is a great girl." He didn't say that he thought this was one of the dumbest ideas he'd ever heard. Get married to the same girl you've always dated. Straight out of college to work. Probably have a kid right away. House in the suburbs with a mortgage to match. The beer spread a glow of contentment in Mark, embellished by his sense of superiority over Larry, whose life was now over for all intents and purposes. Married at age twenty-one.

In the past Mark had often been a little intimidated by Larry, with his new Mustang (bought by his parents), his extensive wardrobe (bought by his parents), and his blonde and beautiful girlfriend (insisted on by his parents), and his sense of purpose. He was also a mechanical engineering major, making passable grades, studying hard but not appearing to be over-stressed.

Mark kept the smile on his face from becoming smug. "Congratulations Larry, I know this is what you want."

Larry gave him a quizzical look. "You don't?"

"Someday, but not soon."

"You still dating that girl from Columbia College?"

"Yeah." Mark studied his beer.

"Well, don't be afraid of commitment. The days pass, she won't wait for you forever..."

"We see each other all the time."

"Sure, sure," Larry drank a healthy mouthful of cheap beer, "but does she know you're serious, or does she think you're just dating. Get serious or get out."

Mark sighed, not quite a snort. This, from a guy who never got out of a relationship in his whole life.

"Hey, you know her?" Larry's voice dropped to a conspiratorial whisper. "She's giving you the eye."

Mark spotted Debbie standing just inside the door, waiting for him to recognize her. "Yeah, slightly." Mark lifted his hand and Debbie came over with a big smile. Larry got up so she would sit between them.

"Hi," Larry said with a predatory grin, "I'm Larry Mitchell."

"Been looking for you," she said to Mark while Larry went to the bar for a glass.

"Yeah, well, I've been studying." Mark pulled some change out of his pocket. "Go play some music, would you Debbie?"

Larry admired Debbie's tight blue jeans and white tee shirt, no bra, as she studied the selections in the jukebox. "Nice. Where'd you meet her?"

Mark snorted again. “Get serious or get out, right?”

But the sarcasm was lost on Larry, who was admiring Debbie as she came back to the booth humming along with the music, “‘...lazy diamond studded flunkies’...I really like that song.”

Mark stood up and gave her a hug. “Listen Debbie, I really have to leave, sorry. Drink a beer with Larry.”

# Chapter 5

By Friday afternoon of the first week of the semester, Mark knew his Thermodynamics class would be as bad as it had seemed on the first day. Bradley, a slicked-back-hair-Robert-McNamara type in a pressed shirt and tie, started the class with a quiz which Mark was certain he failed. Bradley told the class, "There'll be a quiz every other Friday—they'll be twenty-five percent of your grade, homework due every Wednesday, another twenty-five percent, exams are the rest of your grade." Then he turned to the board and began writing out one formula derivation after another at high speed while Mark struggled to copy it all down. Fifty minutes later, Mark stumbled out, humbled. "Focus on the homework and the quizzes," he muttered as he walked through the crowd of students to his next class. "Even if the midterm exam and the final are as bad as I expect they will be, I need to get a C in the course." By the time he got to his next class in McAlester Hall, the gloom of Thermodynamics had lifted and he noticed it was a bright day, clear and crisp, not quite cool, but not hot and humid—the first hint of autumn. Mark went into the old high-ceilinged classroom and slid up one of the casement windows to let cool air wash in.

Last class of the day, last class of the week, and it was his easy one. For the last two years Mark had been treating himself to one non-engineering course per semester because they were interesting, and also because they helped keep his grade point average up. Politics and Economics was his easy course for the fall semester. It was proving to be as interesting as he'd hoped, plus there were girls in it, unlike his engineering classes. Carol Bianchi, Dave's former not-quite-girlfriend, was one of them.

Professor Wollheim was comparing capitalism to socialism. Mark grinned. This was one of the beautiful Carol's hot buttons, so there should be an interesting discussion today. Mark glanced at his watch. Forty minutes of class, then to happy hour at the Heidelberg.

He had actually read the material, so he found his mind drifting on the cool breeze of the afternoon. Larry Mitchell, bulldozed by his parent's expectations into getting married. A life-changing choice. Mitchell at least had had a choice, unlike Tim or Keith, even if he'd made the wrong one. Mark shook his head and tried to concentrate, put the feeling of superiority out of his mind, but it crept back. I have my freedom, Larry never will. Of course, I'm sure he feels he's the one making the right decision, not me. True love, marriage right out of college, a job, a career, money, all that.

Wollheim paced, juggling his chalk in one hand like a crap shooter about to roll the dice. "...free markets," he was saying. "Complete freedom to buy good quality at a low price. Because competitive market forces keep the price low and the quality high." He wrote the word "freedom" on the board.

The class murmured agreement.

"Think so?" he grinned. "Or in free markets can big sellers manipulate small buyers, control supply, force small competitors out of business by artificially low prices, or take in excess profits by artificially high prices, let quality drop because they are the only supplier?" He wrote the word "coercion" on the board. "That's not freedom."

Mark, usually silent, found himself saying, "Unless small buyers band together to balance the power of the big seller."

Wollheim nodded. "Venceremos," Mark added conversationally. Out of the corner of his eye he noticed Carol nodding approval. There was scattered laughter. Wollheim smiled. "True, you may 'overcome,' but it usually depends on whether all the small buyers can stay unified long enough to effect change."

Wollheim paused and let the distant voice of a speaker in the park drift in through the window. "Every Friday afternoon I hear this," he nodded toward the park. "Are they unified enough to effect change?"

"They could be," Carol said. "If they formed a coalition with one voice."

"True, Miss Bianchi, but that will take a leader to convince them their shared interests are greater than their differences." Wollheim raised his chin at the park where students lolled on the grass listening to the speakers on the platform. "Disparate opinions are hard to form into a unified agenda. It may surprise you to know that I've read the Port Huron Statement and tend to agree with most of it. But I don't see the SDS leadership really getting behind it."

"They will though, there's power in numbers," somebody said from the back of the room.

"They? Who's they? I think you mean you. But you're right about there being power in numbers. Mussolini thought so." Wollheim sketched what looked to Mark like a bundle of sticks with an axe blade sticking out of it. Wollheim grinned, "One person's opinion, no dissent. The opposite of democracy and of free markets. Free markets, like democracy, are imperfect, inefficient, and can be manipulated, but, like democracy itself, they are the best thing we've come up with so far." He perched on the edge of the ancient wooden table at the front of the room, looking thoughtfully at the clock high on the wall. "Take the rest of the afternoon off, get over to the Heidelberg, or the Hofbrau, or the Ivanhoe, and exercise your freedom of choice in which beer you drink, as long as it's Hamm's. Chapter three on Monday."

There was an ebullient racket as students snapped notebooks closed and scrambled for the door, oblivious to Wollheim's irony. Mark hurried after Carol and caught up with her.

"Hi Carol, got time for a beer? Or a cup of coffee?"

She shrugged, "Maybe." They walked across the quad in the clear sunshine and stood on Ninth Street facing the Heidelberg. "But I think, not today. We've got to get the *Columbia Free Press* finished up tonight so it can go to the printer tomorrow."

"You're sure?" Mark said. He nodded at the Heidelberg across the street. "I'll buy you a beer and you can show me how Marxism is going to save the free world."

She smiled her brilliant smile. Mark recognized a couple of local SDS chapter members hurrying down the sidewalk toward them.

"I liked what you said today in class," she told Mark. "You should join us, maybe do some volunteer work with the *Columbia Free Press*."

Mark nodded as she was hastened away.

* * *

Friday afternoon the crowd was already thick, even though happy hour didn't start for forty more minutes. Early in the semester, exams still distant, the weather perfect. Mark pushed his way in and found Jeff by himself at their usual table by the window, staring gloomily at two empty beer glasses and humming along with the Grassroots on the jukebox. He glanced up at Mark, "And 'where were you when I needed you' to introduce me to that blonde you were just a talking to."

"Carol Bianchi," Mark slid into a chair. "Dave's former, not girlfriend, but more than a friend."

"Well, you should buy the next round," Jeff said. "I've had to sit here holding this table for ten minutes without anything to drink."

When Mark had brought the beers back and drank a comfortable quantity he mused, "That class Carol and I are in, Politics and Economics, I'm getting some good points to argue with Dave about. Where is he anyway?"

"Probably got a hot date. He's secretive, like you."

"Me?" Mark set his beer down.

"I never see you in here with Jennifer. You seem to like to keep her sort of secret; you don't bring her to happy hour, for example."

"Hey," Mark bridled. "She and I both deserve a little time off from each other. I deserve some freedom."

"Speaking of which, did you hear about Mitchell?"

"Yeah. Poor sucker."

"Brenda is a nice girl," Jeff protested.

Mark laughed, "Yeah, I've seen you eying her." He pulled a handful of change out of his pocket and slapped it on the table. "I'll buy if you'll fly." Jeff shouldered his way through the growing crowd. "And I've seen you eying Jennifer, too," Mark said to himself. Jeff returned with four full glasses. "I assume you want me to ask Jennifer to get you a blind date?" Jeff raised his eyebrows and looked around the room, his gaze pausing on a babe in a pink Pi Epsilon Phi tee shirt, surrounded by guys. Mark followed his gaze. "I don't think Jennifer knows any girls like that."

Jeff shook his head. "That's not what I'm looking for."

"That's what you're going to find at the Stephens mixers and out at the Black and Gold Saturday nights. They're all pretentious as hell."

Jeff finished a beer and waved the glass in Mark's face, "I'll tell you what's pretentious—Dave moving out of Tiger Village and into that rat-hole on Paquin, pretending to be some sort of Zen disciple, but still driving his little sports car."

Mark felt guilty and good, tried not to, but still felt superior to Jeff.

"Jeff, can I give you some advice?" Mark leaned in confidentially.

"No," Jeff said, his eyes on the crowd around them.

"You might want to try being less eager with your blind dates. Kind of pretend like you can take it or leave it, go out with a girl three or four times before you put the make on her, you know. You shouldn't seem too eager, makes you look desperate."

"You're the expert?" Jeff said defensively. He hid his mouth behind his glass. "You haven't dated anybody since you hooked up with Jennifer. I've been to a mixer every week and out at the Black and Gold on Saturday nights."

"That's what I was talking about. What's it got you?"

Jeff, embarrassed, changed the subject, "Did you see the jazz poll in the October *Playboy*? Getz wasn't even on the list, but the Fifth Dimension was. Speaking of jazz, I haven't seen Keith in a while. I heard he's playing guitar in some club these days."

"The Hofbrau, Wednesday nights, but not for long. He'll be playing M-16 pretty soon. He got his draft notice," Mark said.

"What! When?"

Mark shrugged, "Jennifer and I heard him play at the Hofbrau last Wednesday. I haven't seen him since."

Jeff and Mark sat in silence.

After a while Mark pushed his chair back. "I'm out of here."

He unchained his Suzuki motorcycle and rode down Ninth Street, the air rushing by like water in a cool mountain stream, clear and full of the promise of autumn. He'd had the bike since he was a Freshman, had planned to sell it every autumn for the last three years, but somehow when the days were like this, there was nothing better than riding the bike down country roads. Out of town, on a two-lane blacktop, he twisted the throttle up to seventy miles-per-hour, the countryside around him brilliant green grass and trees beginning to change color.

Then he turned back to the tiny trailer park where Keith lived; over the speed bump to the third trailer on the left, the smallest one. Keith's white Corvair was not in the driveway. Mark idled down the row of old trailers, front yards dotted with redneck litter. He made a circle through the place and got back on the highway.

The wind whipped by. Freedom. Less of that around that we all think. Keith had plans to graduate in Business, get a job with an accounting firm, make the big bucks, buy a Porsche, clothes, big apartment, first class airfare.

Guess all that's changed now.

* * *

Lying on the mattress in Dave's stuffy apartment, Allison toed the stack of books and magazines which slid out across the floor in a colorful fan. "What's this?" She picked up a *Playboy*. "Miss October had better watch her weight or that baby fat is going to be permanent."

"Look at the Jazz poll," Dave said. "Look where they put Monk, and Getz isn't even on the list."

Allison laughed. "I'm sure that was the first thing you turned to." She pulled up her Mexican peasant blouse and flashed Dave her tits. Dave wrestled her to the mattress and onto the floor across books and the tangled Indian blanket. "Ow!" Allison said, holding up a book titled *Capitalism and Freedom*. "Get this fascist crap out of my butt."

Dave let go of her and picked the book up. "Friedman's no fascist. He's a liberal in the true sense of the word, not like those blockheads in SDS. Speaking of which, you should have been in Peace Park this afternoon. Idiots lecturing idiots. Unilateral disarmament, macrobiotic vegetarianism, solar power, eliminate all money…if he'd come up with one more half-assed idea I would have puked right there. He doesn't have any idea how society works."

"And you do?"

"More than him."

Allison was lying on the bed, her blouse riding up to show her left nipple. "Gonna be a revolution..." she sang. Dave ignored her and flipped the book open. "Listen to this. Here's some of the stuff Friedman thinks the government should not do—draft people into the army, that will get a lot of applause, agricultural price supports—lots of farmers here in Missouri live off the subsidies..."

"My dad says soybean price supports are the only way he can stay in farming..." She looked at Dave but his attention was elsewhere. Her voice changed, "He's so weak these days he can barely climb up on his tractor."

"Price supports distort the market, cause artificially high prices. Low prices are the market's way of telling farmers to quit growing soybeans. The country needs fewer farmers." Dave continued to flip through the Friedman book.

"He loves that old farm. It's his life," Allison said quietly. She sat up and pulled her blouse straight.

Dave looked up. "What did you say?"

"Nothing."

Dave continued, "The SDS up in Chicago has a good agenda, Hayden and those guys, but these bean-heads here in town... they're just idiots. They say they want freedom, but freedom means taking more responsibility, not less. Responsibility for ourselves and for each other. The bean-heads in the park want big daddy government to take care of everything for them, and they want total freedom too. They are like five-year-olds, depending on their parents and hating them too."

"Childlike is good."

"Childish is not good," Dave tossed the book aside and turned on the window fan. "It's hot in here."

"Must be all this hot air." Allison stripped her blouse off, then raised up and slid out of her jeans. Dave stripped off his clothes too, but he wasn't quite finished lecturing. "Back in the park this afternoon I should have expressed my opinion, right then and there, but I missed my chance." She put her hard little hands on him. They kissed and fell silent except for the movement of their bodies. The last of the sunlight changed slowly from gold to red on the old wallpaper, and the air softened and cooled with the coming of evening. After making love, they dozed. Dave woke as the last light of the sun tinted Allison's dark brown hair with gold. She looked very young as she slept. He gently pulled the sheet around her.

* * *

Mark thought about dropping in on Dave, but instead went back to his trailer. He parked his Suzuki in the driveway and opened the hood of his car.

His roommate Bill stuck his head out the trailer door. "Need any help?"

Mark waved, "No, thanks. Just going to re-gap the points and plugs. This old 283 gets out of tune fast. I've got to pick up Jennifer in thirty minutes and this thing will barely start."

Friday night and Bill's home studying, thought Mark. But he's clear about what he's doing and where he's going too. He'll have a solid career with a reputable firm, doing good work. And he knows that's the best route to what he wants: a house in the suburbs, good-looking wife, two kids, two cars, a dog. He knows what he wants, but I don't. I have all the freedom in the world, and still I'm not happy. I would be happy if I could keep everything just as it is, nothing changing, my friends and family happy, healthy and living forever.

Mark stared at a small scratch in the shiny black distributor cap. It had been a sunny afternoon four years ago when his screwdriver had slipped and he'd made that scratch. September 1964. He'd just re-tuned his old Chevy and the three of them, he, Dave and Jeff, had driven to the Uptown Theater to see the Beatles movie *A Hard Day's Night*. Afterward, the music still filling their minds, they had cruised around Columbia recapping the movie. They were all eighteen years old, just graduated from Hickman High, just starting their freshman year at MU. He'd lived at home that year. He'd sat at his old desk and paged through his crisp new Physics 20 textbook absorbing the smell of the fresh pages, the perfect neatness of the formulae, the symmetrical beauty of the diagrams. On the bookcase behind him were the red and yellow and blue and green spines of the science fiction books he had read and reread since he was ten years old. He stared at his Physics book and dreamed of starships falling through the endless night of space, stars glittering like jewels on black velvet. He was on his way to becoming an engineer. Maybe one day he would be involved in the space program. He saw himself working in an ultra-modern office overlooking a Southern California beach, designing launch vehicles destined for the space station or the lunar surface. The delicious future with its unlimited potential. And for that moment, like this moment staring at the engine of his car, the future and the past coexisted, the familiar and the new, a savory mix of what was, what had been, and what could be.

Mark came back to the present, snapped the two retainers off with a screwdriver, took off the cap and rotor, disconnected wires, loosened or tightened screws, adjusted gaps. He started the engine, and it idled smoothly.

He stretched the kinks out of his back, smiled at the evening sky. I'm happy. I have everything I want. Later in life, I'll have more—more money, cars, things. I'll have been places and done things, but I won't feel any happier than right now, this minute.

* * *

As Jennifer came down the stairs of her dorm where Mark was waiting, guys' heads turned. She tilted her head down to let her long hair hide her embarrassment. She was wearing a short red minidress that was perfect for her slim tanned legs and long black hair. "You look great!" Mark told her. She shifted the paperback she was carrying and took his arm. "We're going to study tonight?" he asked. She smiled.

At the Hofbrau they ordered their usual bratwurst plates with a draft beer and a Coke. "I love Blake," Jennifer said. "I want you to hear this." She opened her book and read "The Crystal Cabinet."

"Sounds like a science fiction story, alternate worlds," Mark grinned. He took her hand. "Is there another Jennifer in an alternate world..." he tilted his head and read "*...translucent, lovely, shining, clear...*?"

"Perhaps," she said with a sly smile. "Would you love her?"

"I love you, here in this world."

She stopped eating. "I can't believe it. You said 'love' right out loud in public."

"I often tell you I love you..."

"...when we're having sex," she said.

"Well, yeah." Mark looked around. "Read me some of 'Auguries of Innocence,'" Mark said.

"Later," Jennifer said archly. Mark grinned. He left money on the table and they slid out quietly into the cold night. In the car, Mark tapped the heater a couple of times to get the fan started. Jennifer huddled in her coat. "Winter's coming," she said. "Yeah," Mark replied. Sadness flooded through him. He busied himself wiping condensation off the windshield as they drove down Providence Road. "Time flies by," he said. "Remember that demonstration the cops broke up last summer? I remember running down Maryland Avenue dodging tear gas."

"Revolution for the fun of it, right?" she said. "Like Abbie Hoffman."

"Maybe...but now, I'm taking this really great class called Politics and Economics. A girl in the class was pointing out that Hobbes..."

"Can you get the heater running?" Jennifer said.

Mark tapped and the fan grudgingly began to turn again. Mark wiped the windshield by hand. "Hobbes said social disorder is the worst of all possible situations, even worse than dictatorship, and I think he may be right." It had been Carol quoting Hobbes in Wollheim's class.

In the dash lights Mark could see Jennifer's attention was elsewhere. The heater fan stopped and Mark tapped it to life again. "By the way," he said, "what's your roommate like this semester?"

"Jeff wants me to get him another blind date?"

Mark parked at the trailer and they hurried inside. Bill was sitting on the couch in front of the little black and white TV. Empty blue and white Busch cans littered the room. Jeff wandered into the room dressed in slacks and a sweater.

"What band is playing at the Black and Gold?"

"Wolfgang and the Warlocks." The commercial ended and Bill reabsorbed himself in *Star Trek*. Mark got two beers from the refrigerator, handed one to Jennifer, and they took seats on the couch. Jeff, suddenly interested in a TV show he detested, opened a beer for himself and sat down on the couch beside Jennifer.

The *Enterprise* was surrounded by three Klingon ships. "Klingon-design," Jeff noted, feigning great interest. "But they are Romulan ships," Bill said. Jeff grinned, "Saves on the show's production costs when you can use the same models for both."

The Romulan commander turned out to be a woman. Kirk and Spock beamed over to her ship to negotiate, and she slapped Kirk in the brig. "Now she'll put the moves on Spock," Jeff whispered. He got three cans of Busch from the refrigerator and passed them around.

"How'd they get in this mess, anyway?" Mark asked. "The usual Kirk stupidity?"

"Romulan cloaking device," Jeff said. "Spock looks like he may make a deal with the Romulans."

At the next commercial Mark and Jennifer withdrew quietly into the darkness of Mark's microscopic bedroom. They took off their clothes and lay together, but Mark made no move to touch her. In the other room, *Star Trek* played on, very softly. Mark whispered. "I do love you."

"I love you too." She paused. "Is something wrong?"

He lay silent for a minute. "No."

* * *

The University library Friday night at nine. Mark forced his attention onto his Thermodynamics textbook. Around him the cavernous library was silent. He worked at his homework until ten o'clock, then drove the ten miles to his parent's farm. The house was already dark. He let himself in and went to bed in his old room, tossed and turned in the dark for a while, then clicked the light back on. He took down Heinlein's *Tunnel in the Sky* and reread chapter one.

The next morning, it was just his father and sister at the breakfast table with him. "Your mother is not feeling very well this morning," his father said. He took her some food on a tray.

After awhile Mark went with his father to the shed where they got the old tractor started, hooked up the trailer, and drove out across familiar fields to one of the new walnut tree plantations on a hillside overlooking one of the ponds. With long-handled shears they each walked down a row of ten-foot-tall trees, pruning and throwing the cut branches on the trailer.

"Nice trees," his father said. "Planted them ten years ago.

The first couple of years are slow going. There's lots of competition from the residual fescue in these fields, but once they get up to about six or eight feet tall they do fine."

After an hour they took a break, sitting on the back of the trailer. The day was mild and sunny. The oak and maple trees were brilliant with color.

Mark's father was quiet. A light breeze had come up and was rippling the surface of the pond. Red and yellow, brown and green leaves waved in the wind. The air was intoxicatingly clear and cool. Mark's father looked at the grass and the trees, the wind ripples on the pond, the crystal blue sky with a filigree of cirrus clouds to the north. "Your mother is not well," he said quietly. "She goes in for more tests next week, but it's just to confirm the diagnosis. She has cancer."

Cancer. Mark's mind retreated from the word. "What can be done?" he asked.

"The doctors will do all that can be done," his father said with a bit too much confidence. "You just need to keep to your studying." His father turned to him and removed his glasses, looking strangely defenseless without them. "And spend as much time with her as you can these next months."

At the house, Mark went into his mother's room and chatted with her for a while. She seemed tired but cheerful. He sat in the blue easy chair and they watched a rerun of *Have Gun—Will Travel*. She hadn't touched her breakfast. Beside the TV, the drapes were open a little. He could see her garden carefully prepared for next spring. Mark kept his mind empty as the show wound on. Eventually, Richard Boone pronounced the final benediction and the theme music played. Mark saw his mother was sleeping and slipped out of the room.

# Chapter 6

The plane lumbered over the grass, wings rocking, and paused in front of Grant, Mark, and Dave. They clambered in. It wheeled around, careful not to blow prop-wash over the other skydivers' chutes stretched out on the grass, maneuvered onto the runway, and took off. The day was cool and sunny and perfect.

At altitude over the drop zone, the pilot settled the plane into a glide. The three jumpers stepped out onto the strut and fell away in quick succession. In free fall Dave was grabbing air, slowing to let Mark catch up. Mark kept his legs and arms pulled in until he was even with Dave, then spread out and they maneuvered toward each other.

Isolated in the roar of the air, the brilliant sunshine, the world spread out below him, Mark's mind was fully absorbed and entirely relaxed. He and Dave drifted past each other just out of reach, then slowly drifted toward one another. Mark reached out; his hand brushed Dave's jumpsuit but couldn't grip. His reach caused him to tumble and fall faster as he angled away. He stabilized, laughing, and saw Dave too far away to reach in the time that remained. He angled his body to track upwind of the drop zone and watched the ground spreading out hypnotically as he fell. He was absolutely free. His altimeter said twenty-eight hundred feet, then twenty-six. He hooked his thumb in his ripcord ring, but waited another second. Twenty-four hundred. He pulled and his chute rippled open, the harness yanked him upward in a great swoop, and he was sitting in clear air two thousand feet above the ground.

"Why'd you go so low?" a voice above him said conversationally. Mark looked up and saw a shadow pass over the orange and white panels of his parachute. Dave floated out into his range of vision. Mark spread his hands. "Just enjoying the ride."

"Better watch it." Dave turned and used his toggle lines to maneuver toward the touchdown point.

Grant touched down, then Dave, both within ten feet of the center target. Mark touched down thirty feet away and sat on the ground for a moment, then gathered up his chute and took it over to the packing area.

He staked the top of his parachute down, straightened the spaghetti of white nylon risers, then smoothed the alternating orange and white leaves of the canopy one by one, going through the motions by rote, while he mind drifted.

His mother had cancer. No one had said anything, but Mark was certain it was terminal. The atmosphere in the house had changed.

Mark noticed a small tear in the nylon of one panel and taped four inches of rip-stop tape over it. Then he slid the shroud over the chute and laced the rope of risers into the big rubber loops set into the casing. He folded the chute in three folds in the green nylon case, compressed the pilot chute with his knee, and pulled both flaps of the case shut. He knelt on the closed case to hold the spring in the pilot chute compressed while he threaded the four stainless steel pins of the ripcord through the four cones that held the case closed. He pushed the ripcord handle into its pocket on the shoulder strap of the case, checked that the quick release Capewells on the shoulder straps were snapped closed, and set the packed chute on the grass by his helmet. He stretched out on the grass, head on his chute, eyes closed, and let the mild day clear his mind of gloom.

Overhead the plane inched across the sky. He opened his eyes, found the dot of black in the clear blue sky. A speck appeared beside it, then another and another, the distant engine noise went silent as the pilot turned the plane away from the jumpers and into a steep downward spiral.

"You going over to the Berg tonight?" Dave asked. "Rod wants to talk about the meet in Florida."

"Maybe," Mark said. He shaded his eyes at the sky. A few seconds later a white and orange chute bloomed, then a second one, then Rod's black and red para-commander. Rod had founded the skydiving club, had the most advanced chute, and had taught them all skydiving. Despite being a former army sergeant, he was a likeable guy. He was pushing them to join him at the annual inter-collegiate skydiving competition in Florida. It would be the first time the University of Missouri had ever entered.

"I don't think I'm going to the Berg tonight to hear Rod tell us why we need to enter the competition."

"Thought you didn't need to study anymore," Mark said a little petulantly.

Dave put the top down on the little Triumph and put his gear in the space behind the seats.

"But, let me know what Rod says, okay?" Dave got in his car and started it up.

Mark picked up his gear and loaded it into the trunk of his car, "When's the competition?"

"December. First week of Christmas break, some little town in Florida near Clearwater."

The plane came idling up the runway and onto the grass shoulder. Overhead the three chutes drifted toward the pea gravel circle in silence. Rod swung the slotted red and black chute around, settling fast. Mark could see he had the toggles pulled way out, opening slots, letting the chute fall faster. Then he let up, the chute slowed, angled, and Rod came in to a gentle stand up landing and walked away.

"Rod," Mark called. "Put me down to go with you guys in December to the jump meet. But I can't make it to your meeting tonight."

"Good," Rod said, gathering up his chute. The two orange and white chutes drifted serenely toward the target, the jumpers keeping feet together, ready to touchdown. The first one touched the edge of the gravel circle and rolled smoothly, then the second. They stood up and began gathering in their chutes. Mark got in his car and drove to campus, his mind elsewhere.

* * *

In one of the dark phone booths in the lobby of the library, Mark phoned Jennifer and muttered some untruths at her, cancelling their date for the night. He hated the hurt tone in her voice. He wanted only to get the conversation over with, to hang up, to not speak, to not explain. "I'll call you tomorrow."

He trudged up two flights of stairs to a row of study carrels under bleak fluorescent lights high overhead. Talk was meaningless, and so was sympathy. There were no words that would change anything. But if he concentrated, kept his mind always occupied, then he would be okay. He clicked on the desk lamp. It made a pool of light on the imitation wood Formica. He sat down and stared at the orange cover of his Thermodynamics book. Down the row of desks someone rustled papers.

I wish there were gods, Mark thought. Something to pray to. Or some mantra, some method of mind that could stop things from changing. Some way I could put everything back to the way it had been just a few months ago. And keep it that way forever. "Give us this day our daily lives," he muttered with great sarcasm. He opened the Thermo book—entropy always increases, nothing can remain the same, order always deteriorates slowly to disorder. The hours pass, people change, nothing can be kept the same, no matter what we do or how hard we pray, he thought. I want things never to change, yet always be fresh and new, like the summer wind rippling the leaves of the trees on Dad's farm. Always changing, but always the same.

Down the row of desks someone coughed. Mark slid the orange Thermodynamics book an inch toward him, opened it to chapter three, and began reading. Forcing his mind line by line into the words. He read two pages but comprehended nothing, so reread the same two pages. Then he turned to the problems at the end of the chapter. Number six, the pressure times the volume equals the Reynolds number times the temperature, for all processes, reversible or irreversible.

But life is not reversible, nor is death. He forced his mind into the problem, worked and reworked it until he had it right, then went to work on the next one and the next. He checked his watch periodically and when two hours had passed, he went to the trailer and went to bed.

* * *

The next day after class, Mark got on his Suzuki at the Engineering building and started down Sixth Street. The cool air and the leaves beginning to turn brown were surreal, a movie flowing past him with the sound turned off. The clarity he'd felt skydiving was gone. The blankness he'd felt working on problems from his textbook was gone. Now he felt only exhaustion.

Traffic had slowed to a stop on Sixth Street. With a flash of irritation, Mark wheeled the bike over the curb, across the sidewalk, and into Peace Park intending to cut through to Ninth Street. Past the shrubs at the other side of the park he could see red lights flashing. He cut off the engine of the bike and sat watching the ragtag crowd of students chanting and waving signs in the middle of Elm Street. In front of them was a row of campus cops augmented by city police. The loudspeaker on top of a patrol car was blaring something unintelligible. Several hotheads at the front of the crowd were chanting, "Stop the war now!" Mark saw Carol Bianchi trying to make herself heard with a bullhorn, but the crowd was more interested in sparking a confrontation with the blue-clad squad of police. Mark saw one of the cops talking on the radio in a squad car.

"March to the state capitol! Insist on a referendum!" Carol's voice was becoming strident as the tumult escalated. "Don't block the street. Don't get arrested. It doesn't help things," she shouted, but the crowd in the street continued to heckle the cops, anticipation of confrontation thick in the air.

Two more squad cars pulled up and four cops piled out to join the row along the sidewalk. The crowd shuffled to a stop. Then from the back of the crowd of protestors, Mark heard a couple of pimply-faced longhairs start shouting, "FTA! FTA!" and the crowd took up the chant. A scrawny long-haired punk gave the cops the finger and shouted, "Fascist pigs!" Four blue uniforms snagged him, wrestled him to the ground. A hail of stones and empty beers cans rained down, the cops charged into the crowd swinging nightsticks. Mark ran back to his bike, got it started, and ripped across Peace Park between the azalea bushes and across a mulched flower bed. He reached Ninth Street, hopped the curb, and got into traffic before risking a look back. A gray cloud of tear gas was rising from the park and students were running.

Entertainment, he thought. Street theater. Despite what I told Dave and everybody last spring about my commitment to women's rights and ending the war, at heart it was just entertainment. Abbie Hoffman's "Revolution for the hell of it."

Traffic inched forward. A guy in Haggar slacks and buttoned-down shirt was coming down the row of cars pushing a clipboard in the windows. He looked contemptuously at Mark on his motorcycle, but said, "Sign the referendum for visitation rights in the dorms?" Mark grinned. "Sure." He noticed Carol coming his way accompanied by two serious-faced guys in preppy dress.

"What you said makes sense," Mark told her when they came even with him.

"Didn't have much effect." She said, still walking. "Tomorrow's papers will talk about a student riot." She stopped and came back to him. "Nobody will have the slightest idea what it was all about, including those who were there."

Traffic started moving. "What is it about?" Mark asked. He put the bike in gear and inched forward.

"About change, constructive change," she said over her shoulder. "You should join us."

* * *

Two blocks away on Broadway, Jeff spotted Jennifer walking with a friend in front of Barth's Menswear. He elbowed through the dispersing crowd and caught up with them. "Thought I saw you in the crowd. Hello," Jeff said.

"Hello, Jeff," Jennifer's smile drained away. "Stephanie, this is Jeff." Jeff and Stephanie shook hands. The crowd flowed past, chattering about the protest and the cops. The three of them stood against the glass windows awkwardly, searching for something to say. Stephanie moved slowly along the display window, trying to get Jennifer to come along. Jennifer studied the manikins in tweed blazers and wool caps.

"Is Mark okay?" Jennifer said.

"Yeah, he's fine." Then Jeff caught her meaning. "Well, he's keeping to himself a lot recently. He's studying all the time, I think." He didn't notice he was leaning toward her, but she did and took a step away.

She nodded. "Well, do you think I should phone him?"

Jeff looked at his reflection in the glass and at her reflection beside his. "Well, yes." The faint scent of tear gas came through the air, bringing a new burst of jokes and laughter from the crowd. Jennifer brightened. "Okay, I will. Well, we need to get back to campus." She put her hand on Jeff's arm. "Thanks. Now that you've met Stephanie, maybe the four of us can go out sometime."

Jeff nodded. "I'd like that."

Jennifer waved but Stephanie did not as they walked up Ninth Street toward Columbia College.

* * *

The police had University Avenue blocked, so Mark turned down Hitt and onto Paquin. He parked his bike in the gravel lot beside Dave's TR3. As he came up the last flight of stairs he could hear Steve Griffin's voice "...domino theory."

Steve was a townie too, tall, and dark haired, conservative in view, who had elected to stay in ROTC after it stopped being mandatory. He could usually be relied on to spark Dave's indignation with right wing remarks. Mark grinned. This should be interesting. Mark stepped through the open door and a stocky girl with a great halo of dark brown hair handed him a joint. Steve and Dave were sitting on the floor in candlelight, surrounded by empty Busch cans and full ashtrays. Mark stepped over a Stan Getz record album covered in pot and found some floor space near the bookshelf. There were three perfectly shaped joints on the record jacket. The girl put the arm back at the beginning of the record began rolling another joint. Beside her was a copy of *Stanyan Street*. A beer was pushed into his hand.

"Where's Jennifer?" Dave said in a passable imitation of Jeff's voice. He grinned, looking better than he had earlier and tilted his head at the girl. "Meet Allison."

Allison nodded to Mark, licked one joint closed and started

rolling another. Steve handed Mark a joint, he took a hit, then passed it to Dave. The candle on the end block of the makeshift bookcase flickered and steadied. So Dave's gone from bright and ambitious Carol to this trailer bimbo. Mark took a long pull from his can of Busch and tried to keep from staring at Allison's boobs, nipples dark against her white tee shirt. Mark took a hit on a joint that came his way and leaned back on a pillow, letting his eyes rest on a new Monterey Jazz Festival poster tacked to the slanted ceiling. Relaxed.

"Tet lost us the war, Steve," Dave said in lecture mode. "It was all over the news." He must be feeling better, Mark thought.

"Bullshit," Steve interjected, "it was all over the news, and that's what lost us public support. The news portrayed it as a defeat—VC on the American Embassy compound—all that hysteria. But the fact is that the North Vietnamese had planned Tet to be a countrywide uprising against the government and the Americans, but nothing happened. It failed. It's back to business as usual."

"Which isn't saying much," Dave said. "Eventually we'll have our own little Dien Bien Phu, just like the French did." Dave was in the place of honor next to the window fan and the record player. "Maybe we already have—the battle of Khe Sanh." Allison sat beside him, knee to knee. She passed him a bottle of Lambrusco.

"Bullshit," Steve repeated. He took a hit on a joint and passed it. "We won the battle of Khe Sanh. Massive air strikes called Operation Pegasus, then the Air Cav came in to relieve the Marines. There was no resemblance to Dien Bien Phu. The French had no air support, no relief forces, a tiny infantry force with no artillery. There's no parallel between Dien Bien Phu and Khe Sanh."

Mark felt a peaceful kind of melancholy. This familiar feeling—sitting with friends, drinking beer, smoking dope, talking—this is what's important, this is what we'll remember, not riots in the park. And all this will be gone soon. We can't make it last forever.

"I'm thinking about registering for classes," Allison said out of the blue. They turned her way. Embarrassed at this change of subject, Dave took a slug from the Lambrusco bottle and passed it on. "What program?" His skeptical look was not sympathetic. Allison's face had a slightly defiant look that Mark thought made her very beautiful. "Journalism or maybe Creative Writing," she said in a defensive tone. "I've got over thirty hours of credits at Moberly Junior College." She took a generous pull from the wine bottle.

"Moberly," Dave said, carefully neutral. "What's your GPA?"

"Three point four."

Mark and Steve laughed. "Hell of a lot better than my grade point," Mark said. Maybe she isn't trailer trash after all, he thought.

"Grades don't matter," Dave said piously. He took a deep drag on a joint.

"Yes they do," Steve said. "If you want to get a job after college."

"You won't have to worry," Dave said softly. "How long's the Navy got you for?" Steve had stayed in Naval ROTC all four years of college even though it was no longer mandatory.

"Three years," Steve said quietly.

Dave took a hit from the joint and leaned back into the shadow. "When do you report?"

"Fifteenth of February," Steve said. He took another gargantuan hit from the joint and passed it to Allison. "It's a citizen's duty, and I'd just as soon get on with it," he said around a lungful of smoke. "Maybe while I'm doing my time we'll reach some kind of détente at the Paris peace talks."

"Know where you'll be stationed yet?" Dave said slowly

to the floor in front of him. The record had stopped and a new kind of silence had come into the room.

"Oakland Navy Base until I get my ship assignment. Probably be there all summer. You guys should come out for a visit." Allison put a Coltrane record on and let his sax smooth the smoky air in the room.

Steve finished his beer. "When I was in officer's basic at Camp Lejeune last summer the old timers would talk. They'd been to Vietnam, some had been in Korea. They'd talk about it a little, not bragging, just talking. Vietnam is our generation's war, whether we like it or not."

"Our war," Dave said quietly. "First war that will be won or lost on TV, by popularity vote. Revolution isn't about political systems, or even rich and poor, it's about media, about publicity, about style." He looked at Allison. "The riots in Detroit and Watts, the Black Panthers and the Weathermen, the peace marchers, the SDS, SNCC, the communist demonstrators in Tokyo, the student riots in France, even the war in Vietnam, it's all just entertainment."

Steve got slowly to his feet. "Guess I'd better be going." He seemed embarrassed. "Anyway. I'll do my time, regardless of what TV says. Citizenship has a price and each of us is either willing to pay it or not."

Mark looked up, "Heinlein, *Starship Troopers*," he pronounced slowly. Then he grinned at Steve. "And Heinlein was right."

While Coltrane's saxophone stroked the night, Allison opened the apartment door wider to let more cool evening air in. Steve shook out a Marlboro and lit it. In some trick of candlelight, Steve and Dave and Allison's faces all seemed both familiar and unfamiliar to Mark. They seemed both old and filled with wisdom, and young and naïve. The MFA calendar on the wall said September, 1968.

This is just a small room on the third floor of an old house on a side street in a small town in the Midwest, Mark thought. But it's where friendship lives, where we are at this moment in time.

But nothing lasts forever. Mark said his goodbyes, made his way down the dim stairwell and out into the cold night air. He got on his motorcycle, shivering, and rode through the cold toward the trailer.

We'll go our separate ways, the years will pass, times will change, we will change. Irreversible processes.

# Chapter 7

For a week Mark did nothing but go to class, eat, sleep, and go to the library. He'd sit staring at his open textbooks for hours at a time, but the words and the numbers might as well have been written in Sanscrit.

His Thermo book was open to page one hundred sixty-six. As an example of the Carnot cycle, consider the four steps: isothermal compression, adiabatic compression, followed by isothermal expansion and adiabatic expansion. Perfectly reversible, ideal, and so non-existent. He flipped to the questions at the end of the chapter. What happens to the entropy produced in a steady-flow steady state-system? He stared at the words but could no more understand them than the patterns of scratches in the Formica desktop. He really had no interest in the differential calculations used to define and describe thermodynamic processes. His Machine Design course was much better. Better professors, better textbook, clearer processes. But he was stuck with Bradley for Thermo.

A guy sneezed; Mark glanced down the row of study carrels to the students hunched over their books in the glow of the desk lamps, monks at their meditations. Mark sat, hour after agonizing hour, trying to force the concepts on the page into his head, however precariously, long enough to pass the next exam. That's all; just get through the week, then through the next week. After a while, Mark closed his books and walked out into a day beginning to clear under a cold wind from the north.

"You been hiding?" Dave was leaning against the stone handrail of the library steps, hunched under the hood of his parka.

"You look like shit," Mark said. "What are you doing here? I thought you didn't study anymore."

"Needed to look up some references related to Hobbes' *Leviathan*," he shivered, "which you should read sometime."

"Let's go get a cup of coffee," Mark said. Images of the warm Heidelberg sprang to mind.

"I'm going over to my parent's house." Dave looked around. "Why don't you come over too? Join us for supper tonight?"

"You look like you don't feel so well."

"I don't," Dave said. They stepped closer to the stone wall of the library, out of the wind. Dave shook a Winston out of a crumpled pack and offered Mark one. They both lit up. "I thought you quit."

"I did."

Mark said, "You going skydiving this afternoon?"

Dave shook his head, "No. Dad wants to watch the Cardinals and Oakland this afternoon, and since I'm 'feeling poorly' as my grandmother used to say, I think I'll lie on the couch at their house and pretend to watch. Want to come over? We're having a late lunch first." He checked his watch. "They're going to be serving in about thirty minutes."

Mark shook his head, "You know me well enough to know I couldn't care less about sports…need to study…Thermo is killing me."

Dave took a drag on his cigarette. "Yeah. Well, if you change your mind, come on over."

Mark looked up at the gray stone of the library. "You know, I think I will change my mind. I need a break."

Dave shivered, "See you at the house."

* * *

Jeff came out of his room at the trailer after the phone had rung five times. A girl said "Hello" in a very faint voice.

"Jennifer?"

"Yes," her voice strengthened a little. "Is Mark there?"

"No he's not. He's spending most of his time at the library these days."

There was silence on the line for a time. "Well, tell him to call me when he gets back, okay?"

"Sure." Jeff wrapped some cord around his index finger and unwrapped it. "You know, I see you guys, and sometimes you don't seem very happy, you know?" Jeff said. "Mark's a nice guy, I've known him since high school, but sometimes, in fact a lot lately, he doesn't seem real happy, you know?"

Jeff stood in the silent trailer, the phone to his ear, listening to silence.

"Do you think it's because of me?" Jennifer said finally.

Jeff drew a long breath. "No."

More silence. Then, "What should I do?"

Jeff stared at the silent trailer park outside the window. "That's hard to say." He wrapped the cord tight around his finger, then let it go. "You could…well…I guess the best thing is to just give it time."

"Will you talk to him for me?"

"I don't think I could persuade him…"

"Well, just tell him I called," she said in a rising voice that indicated she was ready to hang up. "Tell him I worry about him."

Jeff said slowly, "I'll tell him," and they said their goodbyes.

* * *

Mark parked his Chevy behind Dave's black TR3. Dave's father's pickup truck and his mother's '62 Chevy were in their usual places. The flowerbeds along the front of the house had been mulched for the winter. Mark stood by his car, feeling a relaxed sense of time he hadn't known since he was ten years old, and summer vacation would stretch away, limitless. Dave's father opened the front door, "Hello young feller, come on in."

The house had the same pleasant scent it had had since Mark first got to know Dave in high school. Dave was sitting on the couch, parts of the Sunday *Post-Dispatch* spread around him. "Hey Mark."

Dave's mother stuck her head in. "Well hello stranger. We haven't seen you in a while."

Mark didn't think he was hungry but ate three pieces of fried chicken, a big helping of mashed potatoes and gravy, and some home-canned green beans. There was over-sweet iced tea in big plastic glasses with yellow flowers painted on the side. Mrs. Gardner talked about who had been at church and who had not been at church. After lunch Mark and Dave followed Dave's father into the family room and they took their usual places. Mr. Gardner put the footrest of his Barcalounger up to the middle position. "Going to be a good game," he postulated. "Cards versus Oakland."

Mark and Dave grinned dutifully.

From the kitchen Dave's mother called, "Dave, could you run up to the hardware store real quick and get another spring for this screen door? This one's stretched all out of kilter."

"Tomorrow," Dave said. "It's Sunday. Hardware store's closed."

Mark remembered the day he'd helped Dave and his father paint this room. They'd ridden in Dave's father's old Dodge pickup, the three of them squeezed into the front seat, up to Orscheln's hardware to buy the paint, brushes and paint trays. It was the spring he and Dave had been juniors in high school—a hundred years ago, and yet just yesterday. Mark stayed for nearly an hour pretending to watch the game, sitting in the same place on the couch where he had always sat. Mrs. Gardner had the back door open to let some of the cooking smell out. Late afternoon light stretched across the lawn. The comfortable warmth, the friendly chit-chat, the familiar worn furniture. Mark declined a can of Falstaff. He let the soft chant of the baseball announcer pull him into a dream state.

But eventually he said, "Well, I should go. Thanks for lunch, or was it dinner?"

"Come back and visit again soon," Mrs. Gardner told him.

* * *

Mark intended to go back to the library, but instead drove to the airport. Mrs. Karsch, the pilot's wife, was in her folding chair beside their van, clipboard on her lap. "You want to go?" She studied her manifest. "Last lift today, better hurry."

Mark hurriedly put on his jump boots, slipped his chute on, and put on his helmet as he climbed into the idling plane.

The plane rose through the late afternoon sunshine. Mark stared at the back of Rod's chute and thought of nothing. When the glide began, Rod and Grant pushed out into clear air. Mark followed them out tumbling forward head over heels, then stabilized face up, floating on a blast of air. The sky was clear blue. He kept his eyes off his altimeter, just falling, his mind as clear as the air above him. Falling backward through the cleansing blast of air, suspended between heaven and earth. He rolled over, noticed his altimeter already said twenty-two hundred feet, and hurriedly pulled his ripcord. He drifted down and landed. Rod tromped over to him. "What the hell are you doing?" Rod snapped, sounding like the Army Airborne sergeant he had been. "That low opening stuff. I thought you were smarter than that."

"Just misread my altimeter I guess." Mark avoided his eye, slowly gathering up his chute until Rod walked away. The Karsch's van pulled up beside him. Mr. Karsch leaned out the passenger window. "Put the plane away for me, will you Mark? We've got to go. We're late already." He tossed Mark the keys and they sped away. Mark finished repacking his chute and laid it in the trunk with his boots and helmet. Then he taxied the plane to its tie-down spot and knotted the ropes. As he walked back to his car he took a detour into the open hangar where sparrows were chattering in the rafters overhead. The hangar had a pleasant smell of fuel and aluminum, sunshine and summer air. He saw himself, fifteen years old, taking flying lessons in the old Cessna 140 parked at the back of the hangar. His father had driven him to the airport one Sunday afternoon and offered to pay for flying lessons. Once a week for the rest of the summer, the instructor would take him up into the bumpy summer air, cooling as they rose, to practice turns, glides, climbs, and stall recovery.

Since then, whenever Mark heard the distant drone of a Cessna high overhead, he'd pause and scan the sky until he spotted the tiny dot against the blue. And he'd feel again how the summer of his fifteenth year had felt.

A year later, the September he turned sixteen, he passed the exam and the checkride and got his private pilot's license. But with the ingratitude of youth, he was much more interested in driving the family car with his newly acquired driver's license than he was in flying.

Mark stood still, absorbing the nostalgic scent of aluminum, the soft sound of a cricket. He touched the smooth aluminum skin of a Cessna 140 and visualized it flying somewhere up in a summer sky, disappearing into endless blue.

"Seen Dave?" somebody nearby said and Mark jumped at the voice.

Allison was standing by the hangar door.

"He's at his parent's house. You scared me."

"Sorry." She stood looking at the planes. "What are you doing in here?"

He looked at her for a moment. "Stopping time."

"Dave's not real good about telling people his plans, is he?" asked Allison.

"He never was."

She touched the faded blue paint of a plane. "He's never even invited me out here to watch you guys skydive." Mark took her arm and they walked out into the mild evening. The sun was just above the horizon. As they passed the Cessna 180 he'd just parked, Mark had a thought.

"Hop in," Mark said. "We'll see two sunsets instead of one." He quickly untied the plane.

"You're crazy," she said with an uncertain laugh, but a big smile.

"Don't worry," Mark said. "I've had a pilot's license since I was sixteen. I fly this plane for the skydivers when the regular pilot isn't here." Mark climbed in the pilot's seat and flipped the in-flight door up, exposing a bare aluminum interior. She clambered in and he swung the in-flight door down. "You'll have to just kneel on the floor, it's rigged for skydiving. And there's no seatbelt for you." He grinned, pushed in the mixture control, adjusted the choke, and flipped both magneto switches on, then he turned the key and the engine cranked up with its familiar clunk and rattle. Mark let it idle for a minute, watching the oil pressure coming up, then he taxied to the nearest runway and took off. Allison kneeled beside him, peering at the orange-gray horizon as they climbed up to three thousand feet. Mark flew straight south over Columbia.

The sun backed up into the sky as the plane climbed, changing color from red to orange to yellow. Mark pulled the throttle back to an idle and settled the plane in an easy glide. The sun sank through yellow to red and kissed the horizon, then he pushed the throttle back in and climbed back to twenty-five hundred feet and they watched the sun rise, brightening. Allison laughed and clapped her hands.

"Seen enough?"

"One more time," she shouted.

He let the plane glide down to fifteen hundred feet, then climbed back to two thousand feet and again the sun on the horizon rose slightly and grew brighter.

Allison laughed and clapped. "I love it!"

I can stop time, Mark thought. But only for a moment. Then entropy begins to increase again. "Time to go home. Back to reality," he said. He pulled the throttle back to idle, rolled the plane hard into a tight spiraling descent down to five hundred feet, then pulled up with a swoop and held it nose high, near-stall as they came over lights at the end of the runway. He set fifteen degrees of flaps and let the plane glide, losing speed. He pulled back on the wheel as speed diminished and then they were rolling down the runway. He let the plane roll straight for its tie-down spot at the end of the row, pushed the left wheel brake to spin the plane gently around, gave a touch of power, and the plane was exactly at its spot. Brakes on, he let the engine idle for a few seconds, then pulled the mixture control out, clicked off both magnetos, and caged the gyro.

"That was neat!" Allison said too loud in the silence. "Really really neat." The cooling engine clicked like a metronome. Mark helped Allison out and into an evening turned cool. He showed her how to knot the soft cotton tie-down ropes to the eye bolts on the underside of each wing. He checked the lines to make sure they weren't too tight or too loose. "How about a burger?" she said.

"Sounds good, Allie."

"Allison. Call me Allison."

Sunday night at Glenn's Café they had their choice of booths. Allison picked a window seat. "I'd rather people call me Allison," she explained. "Only my dad calls me Allie, and I'd rather..." The waitress brought them water in plastic glasses. "What can I get you folks?"

They ordered burgers and Cokes. "You miss your dad?"

"Yes." Her tone was so sad.

"But you don't miss Moberly, right?" Mark prompted.

"No, I don't miss it, but I don't hate it. I miss being away from my parents." Allison tilted her head and her tangle of thick hair fell forward, hiding her eyes. "I drive up to Moberly every couple of weeks." She looked up with brimming eyes. "I don't visit as often as I should. My father is sick. Each time I visit he is a little weaker. It's selfish, I know, but it hurts me to see him, sinking, so I stay away, trying to remember him as he was."

Mark nodded. Their burgers and Cokes came.

"Talk about something else, okay?" She dried her eyes with a crumpled paper napkin. "My dad says, no matter how big or small our problems, we always seem to worry about the same amount. We all worry too much." She sniffed. "But it's hard not to worry." Mark touched her hand and she pulled it away. "Talk about something else."

"You and Dave look pretty good together, pretty happy."

She smiled, "Dave's a great guy, fun to be with, and we do get along real well, but he's kind of secretive, you know? He talks about you and Jennifer a lot. He envies you two."

"Really. Well, I think..." Allison reached over and put her finger on his lips. "I shouldn't have told you. Don't say anything to him." She slid to the edge of the booth, suddenly seeming to be in a hurry. "Ready to go?"

Mark followed her out to his car. "Dave said he wasn't feeling too well today. Spent the afternoon at his parent's house." He let her off at the old house on Paquin.

"Thanks for the sunsets," she said with a wave and her big smile.

He hadn't told her about his own mother's illness. And he wouldn't. Not Allison, not Dave or Jeff, and certainly not

Jennifer. I want things to be fun with her, just like they always were. I don't want that to change. Besides, nobody can help, not really.

# Chapter 8

Mark rode the Suzuki down the winding two-lane blacktop to his parents' farm. At seventy miles per hour, the air was so clear and thrilling that he laughed out loud. He twisted the throttle on the bike, shot ahead on the straightaway, slowed for the curves, a familiar pattern he'd known ever since he'd had a driver's license. But as he came to the farm he slowed. The euphoria faded, the bright day was gone. He pulled into the driveway and parked in the carport.

His father and his mother, dressed in work clothes, were just coming out the door. "Hello Mark, you're just in time to help," his father said a little over-heartily. Mark's mother was smiling. She had on the worn yellow outdoors hat she always wore.

Mark changed clothes and met them in the sunny field where his father had planted rows of seedling trees three years ago. The trees were now six feet tall, ready for pruning. His mother was pale and unsteady on her feet. But she was smiling, and she worked slowly but steadily, smoothing the mulch around the trees, trimming the smaller limbs. A transistor radio in the tractor trailer was tuned to KFRU, and his parents would smile at each other and name this tune or that from the big band music being played. "I remember the Saturday night crowds at the old Pla-Mor ballroom in Kansas City," his father said with a chuckle, and Mark's mother laughed a tiny laugh, the first one he had heard from her in months. "You wanted to do the foxtrot to every tune," she said, "no matter what kind of music it was."

"Foxtrot is a good dance."

"Even though we weren't very good at it."

The slow, easy, non-verbal work was soothing in the sunshine. Mark's mind relaxed as his muscles took over. After an hour they returned to the house and had chicken salad sandwiches and iced tea for lunch.

Afterwards, Mark did the dishes while his father helped his mother to her room. Then he went to his old room and lay down for a nap. In a restless doze Mark saw himself as a kid again, right here in this room, surrounded by his science fiction books, his head full of distant worlds that somehow blended neatly with the fields and woods of the farm. He often wandered the property and spent hours exploring the edge of the pond, pretending to explore alien planets.

But now, the familiar was becoming the unfamiliar. His room, the fields would still be here, but after his mother was gone, it would not be the same. Mark tried to empty his mind, but could not. After a while he got up and pulled *The Starmen* by Leigh Brackett off the shelf. He stared at the cover, remembering how he used to be filled with anticipation and the thrill of imagination, even though he'd read it a dozen times. He opened the book and tried to immerse himself, but it was not the same. He closed the book and left the silent house. He walked slowly down the sloping field toward the small pond where he and his sister had gone swimming on summer days. A meadowlark called. Among the weeds he noticed the dusty green blades of an iris. He remembered the summer his mother had planted the bulbs at the corner of the pond while his father finished building a rickety wooden diving pier. He stared at the still muddy water, an occasional water bug dancing across its surface. Only seven feet deep, he could let himself slide down from the warm water at the top to the cool water at the bottom. When his bare feet touched the cold mud he'd push up and be back in hot sunlight.

The pier was gone now and the trees had grown up around the little pond. He tried to clear his mind and let the peace of nature enter, but it would not. After a few moments he walked slowly back up the field and around the big open shed where his father kept the tractor. Barn swallows swooped in and out of the rafters with cheerful chatter. That's when he noticed his father sitting in a lawn chair by the tractor, staring straight ahead. He didn't move for a full minute, and Mark withdrew silently.

In the house he tiptoed into his mother's bedroom, where the little black and white TV was whispering to itself. His mother, worn and thin, was sleeping at an awkward angle on her bed. He gathered up his books and fled to the University library, where he sought out the most distant desk he could find and sat in the silent gloom staring at his books.

* * *

Dave's headache woke him. Outside the window in the stark light of the streetlamp, the oak tree branches shook occasionally. Dave eased himself up and leaned his head against the window frame. The old brown paint smelled like steel, dust and fresh-cut grapefruit. A branch scratched the wall of the house, a language he could not quite understand. He glanced at his wrist, but he didn't have his watch on. When his stomach settled he got gingerly to his feet and staggered to the bathroom to splash cool water on his face. He was careful not to make any sudden movements that would start his head pounding again.

Back in his room, he lay down on the mattress and closed his eyes. His dream resumed. A cold wind blew snow-ghosts over the glittering drifts and among the bare trees. Dave shivered. The long chords of his dream became the pulse in his temple. There seemed to be a dull haze in the dark room. He tried to lie perfectly still so that he would not throw up and his pulse would not pound.

Dave breathed softly in the hazy dimness. It was silent except for the faint scraping of the oak branches on the other side of the wall. The cold felt good to him. He became aware of a deeper sound, perhaps distant thunder, or perhaps a voice. Was there someone just outside the door?

The sound resolved itself into footsteps coming up the stairs.

"Dave?" Allison called softly. "Are you sleeping?" She came into the room with a cold breath of air from the hall. He levered himself up to a sitting position. "Hi," he croaked.

"Are you alright?" She sat down beside him on the mattress.

Outside, thunder rumbled and the oak tree thrashed. "Is it raining?" he asked.

"Any minute." She put her arm around him. "You look pale, and your head is hot." She put a motherly hand on his forehead and he felt embarrassed for the sweat that was there. She went down the hall to the bathroom and came back with a damp towel and pressed it against his forehead.

"That feels good. Yeah, maybe I'm catching cold or something. I don't feel well," he said. "I don't know..."

She reached into her Indian bead bag and pulled out a bottle. "I picked up some Riunite from Nowell's. They didn't even check my ID. But maybe some tea first."

Thunder crashed and echoed as the scent of rain came into the room. Allison pushed the window down a little as rain began to fleck the glass. He pulled the blanket around him and leaned against the wall watching Allison make the tea. She lit the candle and they sat in the yellow light, listening to the rain and drinking their tea like of couple of kids on a camping trip.

He put down his cup and pulled Allison to him. "Thanks for coming over." She kissed him. "Sorry to wake you."

"I wasn't really sleeping."

They lay together but did not make love. After a time they

dozed and when they woke the rain had stopped.

"What time is it?" Allison said in a sleepy voice.

"I don't know. It doesn't matter."

"You know," Allison said, "I'm really glad I moved to Columbia. I wonder sometimes if I'll look back on these days as the happiest days of my life."

"Don't." He pulled the blanket closer. "Cold."

"Hey…don't take the whole thing." Allison pulled the blanket back but slid up to him, her body warm under the blanket.

"These are good days, but…" Dave said. "There will always be more to come. The trick is to be satisfied with the day, every day." He chuckled. "Lots of people looking for ecstasy, thrills, kicks, but I think the best we can do, over the long run, is to be satisfied." He gestured at the pile of paperback books. "We can learn to be."

Allison's warm hands roamed over Dave's body under the blanket. "Yeah, I like being satisfied." He gently disengaged her. "But, I have trouble seeing myself working eight to five, all day long, every day. Only two weeks a year off." He raised his eyebrows. "I like having more control of my time. Anyway…" He put his teacup on top of the stack of books and screwed the cap off the Riunite bottle. "Sometimes…well…" He took a drink, then another drink, and slowly put the cap back on. "I'm not sure I want to go to work, ever. I've done a bunch of reading these last few months: Zen, Tao, Kerouac, Miller, Burroughs, all those guys. And I want to do more. And I like discussing it with my friends, sitting around this room."

Allison took the bottle from him and took a swig. "And with me, or do you think I'm too dumb?"

A glib answer came to his lips, but he paused. "You're not dumb, Allison. My friends and I talk about all sorts of things, but we're still just students, we haven't travelled the world, not yet. We've read a lot of books, that's all." He glanced at her Rod McKuen books. "You don't need to feel intimidated. Read what you like, listen to the music you like." Dave suddenly realized something he hadn't known before. "It's always interesting to hear someone talking passionately about something they enjoy, truly enjoy. That's what makes conversation interesting, not talking about things just because they are in style." He grinned. "I'm realizing this as I speak." He kissed her. "I really don't want to go to work. Grad school is where I belong."

Allison sat up holding the blanket to her chest. "Well I don't have any interest at all in working nine to five. And you can tell anybody you want." She grinned.

Dave took a swig from the wine bottle and passed it to Allison. "But you don't have the draft hanging over your head. I don't want to go to work, but I don't want go into the Army either."

She fell silent, fingering the wine bottle.

"What's the matter?" Dave asked.

She shook her head.

"Well I feel much better," he said. He felt fine, in fact. He took a drink of the sweet wine. The rain had stopped and the tree was black and white in the streetlight. He felt weak but relaxed, dazed in that strange after-the-hangover kind of way. A car hissed by on the rain-wet street.

Dave shivered, suddenly cold, and slid down next to Allison under the blanket. He pulled her to him and they kissed and made love. And in the deep short sleep that followed, Dave saw the glittering snow on a windy winter day. Ice crystals skittered and whirlwinds flickered across the perfect white. He woke suddenly.

Allison was staring at the candle as it guttered. "You grunt and moan in your sleep."

"I was dreaming," said Dave.

"You never answered my question. About me."

Dave thought of Carol fleetingly and without regret. The room darkened as the candle went out. Allison got out a new candle and lit it. She was naked, the curves of her body beautiful. She slipped back under the blanket.

"I'm trying to practice the Zen precept of living in the moment," Dave said. "But you already know how to do that, Allison. You do it naturally. That's part of what I like about you. You've got a very pure soul. Do I think you're dumb? No, not at all. I love talking with you. But right now what I want is to make love to you, drink the rest of this wine, smoke some of that lid of pot I've got stashed behind the bookshelf over there. Listen to Getz and Coltrane, and Monk and Gillespie, Brubeck, and Davis. I want to read Watts and Suzuki and Lao Tzu, Hesse and Mann and Henry Miller, you know?" He paused. "And Friedman and Samuelson and Keynes and Adam Smith, and books on physics and cosmology. I need lots of lifetimes."

"I want to travel." Allison said tentatively. "I heard someone talking about Taos the other day. I haven't thought about New Mexico since I was a kid. I've never been there. But all the things you guys talk about, all the places you want to go, that's what I want too. I guess I never knew it until I met you... guys." Dave noticed the pause.

"Sunset in the mountains behind Taos," he said. "Dawn over the temple roofs of Katmandu, San Francisco, the Pacific islands, backcountry Japan, the outback of Australia, or the beach in Bali. Cross Russia by train, through the Siberian steppes, to the walled cities of Irkutsk and Samarkand. Across the Urals to Prague, down to the Greek islands, Paris and London and New York."

"Yeah," she said. They fell silent, dreaming. "But I guess all that takes money. Where's that stash?"

"Look behind *Tropic of Capricorn*."

She got it out and expertly rolled a joint. When she ran it

in and out of her mouth to seal it, Dave could feel his desire growing. She lit the joint and handed it to Dave with her big, chipped-tooth smile. "Wasn't it Lao Tzu who said dope will get you through times of no money better than money will get you through times of no dope?"

* * *

Mark marched across the quadrangle, the list of weekly quiz grades burning in his mind—another F. Asshole Bradley and Thermodynamics. He got in his car and drove around for a while until his anger subsided. He found himself on Old Highway 63 and turned into the seedy little trailer park where Keith's trailer was. Keith's white Corvair was not in the driveway; there were no signs of life.

* * *

Jeff emerged from his room at the trailer reeking of Jade East. He and Mark got in Mark's car to pick up their dates at Columbia College. Mark rolled his window down. "I can't breathe with all that perfume you've got on." Jeff ignored him.

They picked up Jennifer and her roommate Stephanie. In the car, Mark unexpectedly announced that they had to go back to the trailer to watch *Star Trek*. Jennifer gave him a look, but kept quiet. Jeff and Stephanie said nothing. When they got to the trailer, the show was already underway. Bill was stretched out in his usual place on the floor in front of the TV. They seated themselves in a row on the couch.

After a few minutes Mark groused, "Worst of all possible worlds—kids and lawyers. That's Melvin Belli playing the ghostly alien. Green glow and balloon coat. What a buffoon. And all these kids..."

"Not so loud," Bill said, inching forward toward the screen.

"I don't know," Jeff said, "I like kids."

"Me too," Stephanie agreed. She was looking very nice in

a blue minidress and her honey-red hair pulled back in a pony tail. *Star Trek* resumed. "Kirk's anxiety attack looks more like someone running for the can with diarrhea," Mark chortled.

"Hold down the talking, will you?" Bill, who was lying on the floor, had inched forward until he was only three feet from the screen.

After a few minutes more Jeff said, "Let's leave Triacus and go out to the Black and Gold. Wolfgang and the Warlocks are playing."

Stephanie was on her feet. "Yeah, let's go." Jennifer put her hand on Mark's arm. "That sounds like fun." Mark kept his eyes on the TV, but after a minute said, "Okay, okay, let's go. I'll drive." They piled out into the night and Mark drove furiously to the bar, which was packed. The band was working their way through something that might have been "Temptation Eyes."

Jeff pulled Stephanie out to the dance floor, leaving Mark and Jennifer standing awkwardly along the wall. A table opened up and Mark stepped in front of two other couples and plunked down in a chair. He smiled at the dance floor, ignoring the dirty looks and snotty remarks. Mark went to the bar and got a pitcher and four glasses. He poured them full and drank half of his. Then he grabbed Jennifer and pulled her out onto the dance floor where he thrashed and wheeled, jostling others, a complete embarrassment. When the song ended, Jennifer turned for their table with relief, but Mark caught her wrist and kept her on the dance floor. The music started again and Mark hopped and thrashed some more. After a minute, Jennifer had had enough and made her way back to their table, followed by a truculent Mark. He drained his glass and refilled it. To distance themselves from this discord, Jeff and Stephanie stayed on the dance floor. Jennifer told Mark, "If I've done something wrong, I'm sorry."

He shook his head darkly. "It's not you." He let the remark

sit unexplained while he stolidly drank beer and avoided her eye.

After a while the band went on break and Stephanie and Jeff came back to the table.

"You're a good dancer Jeff," Stephanie told him. Jennifer nodded.

"You'll laugh when I tell you where I learned to dance." He filled everyone's glasses. "PE class. Phys Ed was a required class freshman year and I hated intramural sports, volleyball and all that, so to escape that I signed up for dance. It was mostly waltz and polka, but there was some current stuff too." Jennifer and Stephanie smiled. Mark stared at the crowd, stone-faced.

"Looks like the McGovern campaign is already collapsing," Jeff said. "Three more weeks to the election and the Republicans are already assuming they've won. It's a shame."

Mark stirred from his funk. "Well, nobody wants the war, but the Great Society is not working either. People will vote for Nixon just to get things changed."

Stephanie brightened. "I like Nixon's campaign slogan, 'Bringing Us Together.' It's time to stop the fighting, not just the war but all this rioting, it's terrible. I never saw anything like it. It's on TV every night."

"It is terrible," Jeff said, nodding. "I hate to see this country pulling itself apart."

"The networks need excitement," Mark said dourly. "And the rabble-rousers need publicity."

"That's so negative, Mark," Jennifer interrupted, fed up with the whole evening's events. "Don't be so pompous."

"Why not?" Mark snapped. "Lot of pompous people around: Professor Asshole Bradley, for example, my Thermo instructor."

"Watch your language," Jeff said.

The band started up and the conversation stopped. Jeff looked inquiringly at Jennifer, who glanced at Mark pretending an interest in the band. She took Jeff's hand and they went out to the dance floor. Stephanie, perched on the edge of her chair, turned a quarter turn away from Mark, pretending to watch the dancers.

When the song ended and Jeff and Jennifer returned, Mark finished his beer. "I'm ready to leave any time."

They drove back to the dorm in silence. Mark and Jeff saw the girls inside, then drove back to the trailer. Halfway there, Jeff shook his head. "Jesus, Mark, what the hell's the matter with you?"

When they got to the trailer Mark went to his room and pretended to sleep.

## Chapter 9

Friday evening at the trailer Mark had intended to study Thermodynamics, but instead sat slumped on the couch, staring at Channel 13. The Archies were guest starring on *The Dean Martin Show*. Martin acted tipsy while the laugh track pulsed.

Mark heard Jeff drive up and the Volkswagen door clump shut. He slumped further. Jeff came in and bustled about putting his books in his room, his coat in the closet, hanging up Mark's coat which was slung over the back of a kitchen chair. "Cold outside," said Jeff as he sat down on the couch and stared at the TV. Mark could tell by the increasing tempo of deep breaths and leg crossing that Jeff would soon be lecturing him.

"Bubblegum," Jeff said as The Archies finished "Sugar, Sugar" to tumultuous canned applause. Mark maintained his silence.

"Car radio said John Sebastian left the Lovin' Spoonful," Jeff said helpfully. Mark let this comment ride, but Jeff pressed ahead, determined to hold a conversation. "And Jimmy Page is forming a new Yardbirds group. Called Led something, I forget..."

Mark went to the refrigerator and got a can of Busch he didn't want. "Want a beer?"

"Sure."

They sat on the couch drinking their beers. Mark put his tab top in an ashtray, Jeff carried his to the kitchen and threw it in the trash. The next guest on the show was a juggling act. "Got to be something better than this on," Jeff said. He turned the TV to Channel 8 to *Gomer Pyle USMC*. Mark sighed a great sigh. "Shut that thing off."

They sat there in silence for a moment.

"You should call Jennifer," Jeff said in a small voice. "She's probably worried about you."

"Yeah, I should," Mark said.

"Girl like that..." Jeff held his can of beer close to his mouth, reducing the impact of his words. "Too good to lose for no reason."

Mark felt like blurting out several reasons, but controlled himself.

Jeff continued, "She's going to find somebody else. A week has gone by."

"Hey," Mark blurted, "what are you? My social secretary? It's none of your business. And besides who are you to talk, you don't..." He stopped himself, took a deep breath. "Ah forget it." He pulled on his jacket and went out into the cold night.

* * *

There were a few people at the Heidelberg, but nobody Mark knew. He sipped a draft beer he didn't really want, then played three games of pinball on the old Speedway machine back near the hallway to the restrooms.

He cruised down Ninth Street, turned on Paquin, and let the car idle down the street past Dave's house to the stop sign at the corner. Mark sat there for a full minute, before he resolutely turned toward the highway, determined to go to the farm. But instead he found himself turning down Highway 63 and driving to the old trailer park to Keith's trailer.

Keith's trailer was dark. Mark left the car running, headlights on, and tried to peer in the window by the door. He could see three textbooks and an MU notebook on the table under the window, but nothing else. He tried the door but it was locked. Two trailers down the row a shade was drawn back and someone peered out.

At the trailer Mark was dismayed to see Jeff's Volkswagen still there. Jeff looked like he was about to go out. "Sorry about that," Mark said without preamble. "My mother's ill and I'm not prepared for mid-terms." He shrugged and stared around the room. "I get irritable."

"Forget it," Jeff said. "Come with me to my parents for dinner. A couple of my brothers are in town. Afterward we can go get a couple of beers at the Black and Gold." He pulled on his tweed jacket with the leather elbow patches.

A way to make amends. "Sure." Mark changed into a clean shirt and put on his corduroy sports jacket.

In the milieu of his big noisy family, Jeff reverted to the helpful, deferential middle brother. Mark was amused to hear Evan, the oldest son, using the same nagging tone Jeff used on him. Evan was only thirty years old and already condescending to his parents. Jeff's parents carried on a continuous bickering dialogue with each other that Mark resolved never to let himself descend to.

Everyone sat down to dinner in the formal dining room that was apparently never used, since Jeff's parents couldn't find the silverware. Evan had ostentatiously seated his mother and father first, forcing everyone else to squeeze by them to their chairs. Jeff was up and down, back and forth to the kitchen. Mark overate as he assumed he was expected to do. Eventually the meal ended and they migrated en masse to the living room to watch TV.

Mercifully, Jeff pulled Mark aside. "Ready to go?"

* * *

The Black and Gold was a ramshackle bar of many little rooms, a converted house on Old Highway 63 South. The back wall of the family room had been knocked out and the screened-in porch enclosed to form the dance floor. On the way, Jeff had counseled Mark. "Jennifer is your girlfriend, this is just therapy. Dance with a couple of girls tonight, call Jennifer tomorrow."

"Yes, Dad."

Their timing was perfect. They walked in just as the band was coming back from break. Jeff made a bee line for a table near the dance floor where four girls were sitting. Mark trailed after him, feeling much refreshed by autumn, the bar, the band and the girls. He and Jeff were seniors, this was their time, and this town was their turf. The four girls looked up as Jeff and Mark approached. Mark locked eyes with one as he had been counseled. All the girls had perfect hair and heavy makeup. Jeff greeted the table in general. Mark's choice was a brunette wearing a blue jacket with a Tri Delt pledge pin. "Like to dance?" he asked.

When she stood up, Mark noticed she was a little on the chunky side. The band swung into "Wild Thing" and they thrashed around pretending to have fun. Out of the corner of his eye he noticed Jeff was a pretty good dancer. There were only three other couples on the floor, enough people that they felt like they were part of the crowd.

After struggling through the tune, the guitarist raised his guitar and crashed a chord while the drummer rolled a flourish to signal the end of the song, but the keyboard player didn't notice and continued playing after they'd stopped. All the dancers stopped. The keyboardist covered his error by a long impromptu solo full of sophomoric psychedelic noodling. Eventually he wound down. Mark saw Jeff escort his date to her table and go to the bar.

Mark stood there. "How about another dance?"

"Sure." They chatted while they were waiting. Mark learned her name was Connie, she was from White Plains, New York, a freshman majoring in Sociology.

The next dance was a slow number. Mark liked the way her chunky body felt as they swayed, and he liked her perfume which was not Chantilly. "Can I call you sometime?"

"Sure. Just call the Tri Delt house and ask for me." Mark wasn't quite sure what he should do next. "Want to join me and my friend at the bar? I'll buy you a beer."

"No, I should go back to my table, but thanks." She squeezed his hand.

"The band's going to think you're a music critic with that scowl on your face," Mark told Jeff.

"Did you get her name?"

"Yes. Connie. She's a freshman from White Plains, New York."

Jeff poured both their beer glasses full. "I may call her some time."

"What happened with your date?" grilled Mark.

Jeff shrugged dismissively.

"Sure, call Connie tomorrow if you want," Mark said. " I'm not going to." Jeff took some paper napkins and fastidiously cleaned off the table before propping his leather elbow patches on the table.

"Not tomorrow. There's a strict code to these things. You can't call too soon, makes you look desperate, but you can't wait too long either, because then she can't accept since it would make her look desperate. Two days is just right." Jeff moved into lecture mode. "She's a Tri Delt, needs to be seen dating fraternity guys, usually Kappa Alpha. But, she's also a freshman from out of state, so she probably hasn't made any long-term commitments to the morons at the KA house yet. She wouldn't be here tonight with a bunch of girls if she had, so she's available."

"I see you have Greek mating habits carefully analyzed." Mark poured more beer in his glass but didn't drink it.

The four Tri Delts were making their way to the door. "Ignore them," Jeff counseled, but Mark noted he was poised to wave if they acknowledged him. They didn't.

"Where'd you learn to dance anyway?"

Jeff laughed. "Freshman year PE class. It was either dance, or intramural sports, which I hate."

"I can't envision you prancing around Rothwell Gym with a bunch of other dweebs, doing the polka."

Jeff laughed again. "It was mostly women, which was nice. Plus I did learn some stuff, which is more than most guys. You for instance."

Mark checked his watch. "I need to get going. And yes, I will call Jennifer. I acted badly the other night. I need to apologize."

Jeff slapped him on the back. "Good for you." On the drive back to the trailer Mark told Jeff, "You may envy me because I'm dating Jennifer, but she has her faults."

"Everyone does, but she's cultured, you know?" Jeff said. "She loves literature, she's pretty and well-mannered. Elegant."

Mark started to make a flippant remark, but instead changed the subject. "I envy you and Dave, graduating in January. Moving on to the next phase. Got a job lined up yet?"

"I'm interviewing. Think the draft board will give Dave a deferment to study Philosophy in grad school?"

"No."

"After I graduate and get settled in my job, I'm going to get married."

"You sure? Why not enjoy the high life for a while first. Women, apartment, new car, lots of cash."

Jeff laughed. "While you're still taking that Thermo course for the fifth or sixth time."

At the trailer, Mark found it was already too late to call

Jennifer since the college switchboard would not put through calls after ten p.m. He felt relieved and guilty, so got in his car and drove to the farm.

* * *

The house was dark except for the single light behind drapes in the bedroom. Mark crept into the house, into his room, and into bed. He willed himself to sleep, but it would not come. Do all relationships, all marriages, end like my parents' soon will? One dies, one is left behind? Maybe it's better to live only for the moment.

Next morning he put himself in cheerful mode, helped his father with breakfast, visited with his mother, chatted with his sister. Although it was Saturday, he went to the library and worked on Thermo for two hours. Then he made his way to the Memorial Union. Downstairs, in the last phone booth in the row, he pulled the folding door closed, and sat down on the wooden plank seat. A dim light came on. He stared at the ancient black wall phone, the circle of numbers, the yellow paper circle in the middle. He dropped a dime in the slot and dialed.

"You're in your room," he said, surprised when Jennifer answered.

"I'm working on a paper that's due."

He steeled himself and rushed through a clumsy apology. She accepted with good grace.

Pushing his luck, he said, "How about a break? It's Saturday afternoon, let's go see a movie."

After a pause she said, "*Wild Strawberries* is playing at the North Theater. I love Bergman's films."

"I'll pick you up at two."

* * *

Before Mark picked up Jennifer he decided to check his

grades. The Engineering building was silent, the corridors empty. Beside Professor Bradley's door a single sheet of paper was posted. On it were two neatly typed columns, student numbers and mid-term exam grades. Mark's eyes darted down the left column to 106608, his student number. To the right of it, was the number 58—an F. So now he'd flunked the mid-term exam and most of the weekly quizzes.

He took a deep breath and went to Professor Martin's office, ran his eyes down the list, and found an 88 beside his number—a B. A grin spread over Mark's face. Mark hurried out the front door of the building, but turned immediately around and went back inside to recheck his ME 311 grade. It was a B. He put his pencil under his number to make sure he was on the right line—it was a B, sure enough. He glanced up and down the list and saw all the grades were As and Bs.

He strolled back outside and stood in the wind on the front steps, mentally calculating his grade point average.

"What are you mumbling about, daydreamer?" It was Rich Behr, the same gangling six-footer, he'd been in high school, except now he wore his hair shoulder length and sported embroidered jeans and a worn field jacket. The MU notebook under his arm was covered with doodles and graffiti. Mark zipped up his jacket. "Hey Rich, just checking my midterm grades," Mark explained for no reason. "How are your grades?"

Rich shrugged, "I don't even check them."

Same old Rich, so smart he didn't even doubt he'd get straight As. He took off smudged wire-rims and polished them with his thumb.

"Got any pot for sale?" Mark asked.

"Sure." Rich stepped up on the stone steps out of the wind. "Got some great psilocybin too, just in from San Francisco. Five dollars per tab."

"I'll take four," Mark said expansively. His grade on the ME 311 midterm called for a celebration. And his grade on the Thermo mid-term called for consolation. Either way, dope was good.

Rich's fingers drummed his notebook in little bongo-drum bursts. "Meet me at the Shack at six this evening." He turned to go.

"I'll take a lid of grass too," Mark said to hold Rich for another moment. "Mind if I ask..."

"Why I quit Caltech and came back here?"

"Well, yeah. Sorry. It's a bullshit question."

Rich raised his eyebrows. "Actually it's a good question. I asked it myself." He rubbed his dirty glasses again and slipped them back on. "When I went off to Caltech, it was with a lot of expectations from everybody, including myself. Caltech's a fabulous school, some really great minds there. But I was spending ten hours a day, every day, in class, in the labs, or studying."

"So what happened?"

"I realized one day that there is more to life than studying. One afternoon I was walking down the long walkway that runs almost the length of campus. This wall was covered with a hibiscus vine, the flowers were beautiful. Then I realized I'd walked by it for three years and never noticed it. I looked around at the clear Southern California sky, the white stuccoed walls, the red tile roofs, and I just kept walking, past my class, off campus, three blocks to Colorado Boulevard and caught the bus down to LA. Spent a week on the Sunset Strip—it's all flower children now—music, dope, sunshine, good people. Money is not important. Went to some clubs, heard Morrison, McGuinn, PG&E. Lots of good dope." Rich came back to the present.

"How'd your parents take it?"

Rich Behr shrugged. "Not very well. They're better now."

"You look pretty happy though. I see you with that same chick..."

"Kristen. Yeah. Things are good. You've only got one life, don't waste it." Rich's face scrunched up. He tucked his notebook under his arm. "We're not in school to learn a trade, at least I'm not—not any more. See you at the Shack at six."

His stoop-shouldered form sauntered away.

* * *

Mark noticed the autumn wind, blue sky and the noisy torrents of brown leaves skittering and scraping down the sidewalk as he and Jennifer walked back to Columbia College from the North Theater.

"I love this time of year," he said expansively, "and I love you." His heart thrilled to hear himself say it right out loud.

"I'm glad," Jennifer said. "You don't say it very often."

"The hard-core artsy types probably think Wild Strawberries is too sentimental, except for maybe the professor's dream sequence at the beginning." Mark hugged her awkwardly as they walked. "The end is what I like best. The dream sequence where the professor sees his parents sitting fishing in that idyllic setting."

"You're a romantic," Jennifer said.

"Probably so."

At the little coffee shop in the lower level of the building across from Jennifer's dorm, they got hot chocolate in paper cups.

"Proust's Madeleines," Mark said. "Your perfume, Chantilly, is my Madeleine." He took her hand. "You seem subdued."

"My mind's on my paper." She toyed with her paper cup. "And the future. You'll go into the Army next summer?"

"There's no way around it."

"Then what?"

"I don't think that far ahead," Mark said.

"I meant...us," her voice dropped.

He took a deep breath. "I want you to wait for me, while I'm in the Army. Will you do that?"

She looked around the crowded coffee shop, out the window at orange and yellow and red leaves blown into intricate patterns around a maple tree. She looked back at Mark and, after a full minute said, "Yes I'll wait."

He grinned, ducked his head, took both her hands in his, warm from the cup of chocolate. "I love you," he told her again. "Always remember that."

"I was just thinking…" Jennifer said.

"About?""

"We don't spend time with your friends."

"You told me once I spent too much time with them."

"You do. By yourself." The scent of Chantilly came to him as she leaned forward to make her point. "But not us, together."

Mark studied the brown dregs of chocolate in his cup. "Like you, I have a lot on my mind." He started to tell her about his mother's illness but couldn't do it. "I'm flunking one of my courses, Thermo."

She touched his hand on the Formica tabletop, took it in hers. "I'm sorry. I know you work hard at it." She looked into his eyes. He loved her dark brown eyes. "You're so good at literature, Mark. I've always wondered why you decided to go into engineering."

"I love machines. I always have. I want to design beautiful machines someday." He shook his head and picked up his cup, forgetting it was empty. "But also, and maybe this is the truest reason, because I wanted to spend my University years studying something I knew less about than something I knew more about." He snorted, "University shouldn't be a trade school. Sounds kind of stupid, I guess, me taking Engineering courses, and making such bad grades."

Jennifer stood, "I hate to do it, but I have to go work on

my paper." She pulled on her blue coat and buttoned the big wooden buttons through their rope loops.

"Work on it for a few hours, then let's go visit Dave," Mark said.

She hesitated, then nodded.

* * *

Mark got the dope from Rich, then picked up Jennifer at her dorm and drove to Paquin. The door to Dave's apartment was ajar. Mark stuck his hand in holding the pot he'd just bought from Rich. "We come in peace. Direct from the Shack where Rich Behr was dispensing wisdom and dope."

"Always welcome," Dave said. Allison and Jennifer were introduced and Allison set to work rolling joints with production line efficiency. They smoked the pot, listened to Dave Brubeck, talked about whether Rinzai or Soto was the purer form of Zen. "I know Amida is not. Too much icon worshipping, magical incantation stuff," Dave said. "It's too much like those old power-centric middle eastern religions."

Allison laughed her melodious laugh. "You sound like a professor."

"I'm thinking about becoming one," said Dave.

They smoked joint after joint and talked about religion. "All religions are bullshit," Dave opined.

"Buddhism's the best," Allison offered.

"Buddhism's not a religion, it's a philosophy, a way of life—no gods, no afterlife, no heaven, no hell…"

"…no holy book…" Jennifer chimed in.

"…and no holy men to interpret it." Mark added.

"…and no churches to enforce the rules," Allison said.

"Looks like we have consensus," Dave said, and they all burst out laughing.

"The pompous professor," Allison said, which got them all laughing again.

Rain came, speckling the window in quick hungry bursts, and for a few moments the oak tree threshed and thunder boomed softly in the distance. Then the rain settled into a smooth stream of sound. Mark and Jennifer lay together on the blanket, Dave and Allison on the mattress. The candle flickered. Jennifer whispered in Mark's ear, "I need to be going."

He touched her hair. "Let's go back to my place."

"No, Mark, not tonight." They crept out.

On the drive back to her dorm, Jennifer said thoughtfully, "Allison and Dave. She lives *for* the moment, he lives *in* the moment." The windshield wipers were like a metronome measuring time.

At the dorm she told him, "You don't need to walk me to the door," and she was out and running through the rain to the door of her dorm.

# Chapter 10

"You're pensive tonight," Stephanie said. She and Jennifer were at their desks on either side of their room. Jennifer's steady sighing, her pencil tapping, and her jittery leg had finally brought Stephanie to say something.

"I am?" Jennifer said, defensive.

"Something bothering you?" They both pivoted in their chairs at the same time, which brought a smile to both their faces. "Synchronized desk chairs, new intramural sport," Stephanie said. She paused. "I assume you're worrying if Mark is going to call. He does seem kind of…intermittent."

"Intermittent. Yeah."

"How long have you been dating?"

"Since last spring." Jennifer got up and stood at the window looking at the curved driveway. "I think we were happier back then." It was eleven and cars were appearing, bringing girls back to the dorm before curfew. "It seemed easier back then. We had no expectations of the future. Each date felt new and fun. If he didn't call for a few days, I never worried about it. But now, he seems distant and we have expectations of each other. I'm not sure I'm the person he's looking for."

"You didn't seem real happy yesterday evening."

"Funny thing is, it was my fault, kind of," Jennifer said. She kept her eyes on the cars coming and going. "I finally told Mark I wanted to meet some of his friends. I always felt like we'd go out, but we never really talked with anybody."

"Except Jeff, right?"

Jennifer turned to Stephanie, smiling in the glow of her desk lamp.

"You gave me quite a sales pitch to go out with him. He's okay, but, you know." Stephanie shrugged.

"Well, we went over to this friend of Mark's last night, a guy named Dave. His girlfriend was there, a hippie girl. I could tell Mark was attracted to her. And he's always talking about hippie stuff—being free, changing himself and the world, all that stuff. He wants me to take psychedelics with him, but I can't do that. I think he sees me as just this boring, middle class girl from Florida. Middle class through and through."

"Through and through." Stephanie's laugh was good natured. "You really are just a middle class girl. And so am I."

Jennifer smiled, finally.

"If Mark asks you to spend Thanksgiving with him at his parents, that will be a sign he's serious," Stephanie said.

And if he doesn't? Jennifer wondered.

* * *

Mark bounded up the stairs of the old house on Paquin. A samba was playing on somebody's stereo. An apartment door was open on the second floor. "Hey Allison. I didn't know you rented an apartment here."

She laughed her big laugh. "Neither did Dave until a week after I met him. Think he wondered how I got home so fast? Listen to this." She pointed at the little record player. "Samba, Joachim Gilbert."

"Just like in the movie *A Man and a Woman*."

"I love that movie," Allison said cheerfully. "Two years ago when it came out I went to see it four times. I didn't think guys liked that sentimental stuff."

Mark shook his head. "Or maybe I just liked the Ford GT-40 Jean-Louis Trintignant drives."

"Watcha doing here anyway?" she asked.

"Just came over to see Dave."

She shrugged. "I haven't seen him all day. Got any psilocybin I can buy from you?"

"I've got a couple of hits left," Mark said reluctantly.

"I'd buy a couple."

"Well, I don't know…"

Allison took out a joint, lit it, and passed it to him. "This'll help you think." She sat down cross-legged on the floor and Mark followed suit. He picked up a paperback, *Monday Night Class*, then another from the jumble by the bed. *Astral Projection*, the *I Ching*, *Journey to the East*.

"Doing a lot of reading?"

"For the first time in my life," Allison said. She stacked the books while Mark tried to keep his eyes off her big boobs in the white cotton blouse. "I like reading and I like smoking dope too. The dope really enhances the imagery in the books. Back in Moberly smoking dope was just to get high, to kill the boredom. But down here, with you guys, it's more like psychic exploration. I also want to explore the real world. The whole wide world. I'm thinking about going to Taos, Mark. I was talking to this guy who just got back. There's this great commune there, up on a mountaintop. Sacred Mountain Tribe…" She stopped, embarrassed at her monologue.

"Dave would miss you. We'd all miss you," Mark said carefully.

She smiled that chipped tooth smile Mark had come to love. "Dave would get over it. He's pretty independent. Opinionated too," she said. She toked the joint and passed it back. "Sometimes I think Dave thinks I'm kind of shallow. He's smarter than me, I know that. He's the cool intellectual and I'm just some farm girl from Moberly living the hippie life." She looked at Mark and he could tell she wanted to say something more to him, but she didn't. "How about selling me a couple of hits of that dope?" she repeated.

Mark unrolled the tinfoil and gave her two. She handed him ten dollars. "We could do a hit right now," she offered. Mark wavered then got to his feet. "No, I've got homework I've got to get done. Can't." He fled before he could change his mind.

By the time Mark drove back to the trailer his head had mostly cleared. The TV was on, but nobody was in the living room. Chet Huntley was describing a US Army incursion in the A Shau valley. "...but the body count comparisons, ten to one, are cause for cautious optimism..." Then there was an interview with General Westmoreland at Clark Air Force Base.

A thick cloud of English Leather scent seeped into the living room and Jeff emerged from his room, dressed in a black turtle-necked sweater and a tan corduroy sports jacket with elbow patches.

"You look like something out of *Playboy*," Mark said. He got out a can of tuna, opened it, and sat at the kitchen table eating out of the can listening to David Brinkley reporting that high levels of mercury had been found in tuna.

"See ya." Jeff checked his reflection in the glass door panel and then went out. Mark turned the TV off, which brought Bill out of his room.

"Man he plays the TV loud," Bill said. He got another can of tuna out of the cabinet, opened it, and sat down with Mark.

"Jeff is a nice guy who thinks he needs to 'get out of his shell,'" Mark said. "I hope he and Steph stay together, I really do. But I don't think it's very likely if Jeff treats her the way he treats all his dates."

"He seems like he'd be real courteous, real gentlemanly," Bill said.

"He is at first. I know. I've double dated with him lots of times. He'll take some girl out a couple of times, the usual preliminaries—dinner, beers, movie. Very courteous, almost formal, maybe a little too formal. Then on about the fourth date he'll maneuver her into somebody's apartment and dive on her, expecting to have sex right away. The date ends badly, and that's the last time that girl will go out with him. Then Jeff asks me to ask Jennifer to get him another blind date, and the cycle will start again."

Bill retired to his room to study and Mark grudgingly took out his Thermodynamics book and opened it.

* * *

It was Friday afternoon, and Professor Wollheim was late for his Politics and Economics class. Mark was in his favorite seat, by the window overlooking the oak trees between McAlester Hall and Elm Street. Through the leafy filter came the chant "No More War."

Watching the weekly Friday afternoon protest in Peace Park outside, Mark could see movement in the crowd. The air was still and cold under an overcast sky that leaked the occasional tiny snowflake. The clanking steam radiator, the chalk and old furniture smell of the classroom, the last class of the day, of the week. Mark felt relaxed, comfortable. Not like that stinking Thermo class—calculate the heat loss in a 2T Carnot cycle, or the enthalpy of evaporation, using either the Maxwell equations or a derivation of the Otto cycle equations. Is the specific heat of a substance obeying the PV=RT law necessarily constant?

Mark never had enough time to really understand the stuff, just memorize enough to get through the next exam and keep going. His anxiety was swept away by a gust of cold air and the scent of snow.

Wollheim finally came in forty minutes late, looking preoccupied and took his place at the front of the classroom. He studied the class for a few moments, then handed around a list of topics for the next paper. Wind rattled the old casement windows.

"Your next paper is not due until after Thanksgiving." He picked up a piece of chalk and shook it in his left hand as though he were going to shoot craps. "If there are no questions on the list of topics I just passed out. Let's talk about order. The perception of order. Is order prettier, more attractive than disorder? Conventional wisdom would have us believe it is. But is it not only our perception? In the nineteenth century people everywhere were bent on conquering nature, imposing man's will on the biosphere. Now we are learning to preserve the natural world, recognizing that we are an integral part of it." He speared the class with a look over the top of his wire-rims. "We recognize a larger order, where before we saw disorder and attempted to order it. If we had continued our efforts we would have produced a larger disorder."

He stepped to the window. The last of the brown leaves were being blown into corners by the cold wind pushing ahead of storm clouds.

"A friend of mine over in the Engineering Department runs the new IBM 360 the dean is so proud of. He talks about the studies now underway on mathematical analysis of natural phenomena, weather, ocean currents, cell growth in plants using computing power to find the natural order that underlies what appears to be disorder." Wollheim juggled the chalk. "Also, using mathematics to study disorder, so that we understand chaos. Using orderly rigorous mathematical algorithms to generate patterns of disorder. I wish we could predict the future." Wollheim had forgotten the class, was talking to himself. "'There is no security in life, nowhere.' The most powerful man in the world wrote that twenty centuries ago. Marcus Aurelius—the only security is inside yourself, in the knowledge of having done the right thing." He put the chalk down in the blackboard tray. He stood there beside the blackboard not seeing it. Wind rattled glass; a radiator clicked an ascending rhythm. Wollheim sat down in the wooden chair beside the lectern and stared at the floor.

Carol said, "Revolution doesn't improve security. Locke said the worst thing that can happen is a breakdown of law and order. Worse than tyranny."

To impress Carol that he'd read *The Communist Manifesto*, Mark paraphrased: "The tyranny of the system, whether you call it the bourgeoisie or the military-industrial complex; that's what all the radicals want to destroy, the existing social structure…"

The slightest smile came to Wollheim's face. Carol continued as though she was the professor, "...the totalitarian universe of technological rationality as Marcuse puts it? 'The system' is this invisible oppressive *them*: an autocratic university administration. I used to think that was childish blaming. Somebody with more power is always to blame. Ask Professor Allen in the History Department or Professor Wurfel in Political Science."

Wollheim gave her a shrewd look. "So right." Then he got to his feet and launched into a rambling discourse on polyarchy, his mind clearly elsewhere.

When the class ended, Mark grabbed his books and elbowed past people to catch up with Carol.

"What was that all about?" he asked. "Do you have time for a cup of coffee?"

Wind fluttered papers on the bulletin board. "Let's get out of this wind," she said and started off without seeing if he was coming. Mark scuttled after her to the Heidelberg where they settled into a booth by the window and ordered coffee. Carol held up their textbook, *Politics and Markets*. "Lindblom is just an analyst ranking different political systems. Marcuse gets to the heart of the matter. But his protégé, Angela Davis, is just media-seeking. She's using Marcuse to excuse Black Panther extremism. In *One-Dimensional Man*, Marcuse argues that technological society as a whole is dehumanizing. That's what I was trying to get across to Wollheim. In a dissatisfied electorate, you have to make change happen fast to avoid letting extremism take root. He didn't get my drift. He's still captured by the idea that our focus needs to be on making different market systems coexist side by side."

Carol drank her coffee quickly, then flipped open her *Politics and Markets* book. "Right here on page one hundred five; he's got all these systems listed. Wollheim's just saying the proportion of them can change according to society's needs. It'll never happen. Marx thought the state would wither away under Communism, but in the Soviet states there's been the opposite effect, a growing repression and a gigantic expansion of the so-called intelligentsia, the people actually running the state. What? Is something funny?" She stopped talking.

"No," Mark said, "I'm interested in what you're saying, but what I really wanted to ask you was what's bothering Wollheim. He's obviously distracted."

Carol gave Mark a quizzical look. "The University administration denied him his annual raise. He's on some kind of probation. Next issue of the *Free Press* we're going to do an article about the brain drain..."

"Why's he on probation?" asked Mark.

"Same as Allen and Wurfel. For not supporting the war. But it's really more than that. The University sees him as some sort of neo-Marxist."

"He's not at the demonstrations," Mark said. "They can't condemn him for what's in his head."

"The demonstrations are not the issue unless they get TV coverage. Or the mayor of Columbia starts complaining to the dean." Carol smiled a tight smile, sipped her coffee and put the cup down on the wooden tabletop very gently. "For ninety percent of the people at these demonstrations, the cause is meaningless. It's just something fun to do for entertainment." She stared out the window.

"What did you say the *Free Press* was doing an article on?" asked Mark.

"The so-called brain drain," Carol said. "Good professors leaving MU, or being asked to leave, because they don't support the war, or they are too outspoken about this or that issue.

"Whether it's at the national level or in the University, autocracy is bad, and revolution is worse." She pushed her cup aside. "My parents travelled a lot when I was young. I've been to Eastern Europe, and South America, and Central Africa. All those 'worker's paradises' are just dictatorships. And revolution just replaces one dictator with another. They call themselves socialists when they're trying to get money from the World Bank. My father used to work for the World Bank. I'm sure Wollheim is under a lot of pressure from his department chair to conform. But we need to keep an open dialogue in the classroom and talk about real issues, not gloss over them and hide in the textbook." She held up a worn paperback titled *Soviet Marxism*. "The issue is not who owns the means of production, it's who controls them. That's Marcuse's analysis of Soviet Marxism, which you should read by the way."

Jeff picked that moment to appear. "Hi guys." He stood there waiting to be invited to sit down. Carol stood. "I've got to be going."

"Carol and I are in Wollheim's Politics and Economics class, it's really…"

"I've heard it's a good class," Jeff told Carol. "Are you going over to the protest in the park?"

"A waste of time," Carol said flatly. Jeff looked puzzled.

"Carol's becoming a bit disenchanted," said Mark.

"I can speak for myself," she said, softening it with a smile. "Those air-heads in the park don't have any idea how to make constructive change. Or even what the issues are. It's time for a different approach. The *Columbia Free Press* is going to publish a list of changes the University needs to make, things like military research transparency, balanced academics, eliminate limits on political activity for students, security police authority limits, a list of ten items. It's called the *One Voice Manifesto*. We'll organize a campus referendum. If we can get enough signatures, students and citizens, I can get a hearing with the Board of Regents."

"You're with the *Free Press*?" Jeff looked awed.

"Yeah, Editor. I started it with a couple of other people."

"That's fantastic," Mark inserted, trying to get back into the conversation and back into Carol's good graces. "*Columbia Free Press* is one of the best things to happen to Columbia."

She smiled a dazzling smile. "So you guys would sign the referendum right?"

"Of course," Jeff said quickly. Carol finished gathered up her things.

"The elections are today," Jeff said. "Nixon's already way ahead. I assume you'll vote Democrat, for McGovern?"

"Maybe," Carol surprised Mark. "He's got some of the correct platform, but his campaign is so disorganized. And the riots in Chicago. Lot of people will vote for Nixon just for his perceived stability. We'll know tomorrow." Jeff admired her as she went to the door.

"Boy is she good-looking."

"Thought you and Steph were going strong."

"We are." Jeff opened Mark's textbook then closed it. "So," Jeff sipped his coffee, "... Carol is with the *Free Press*."

"As strong-willed as she is, I'd say she *is* the *Free Press*," Mark replied.

## Chapter 11

Dave lay on the mattress in his room trying to keep his mind on *Descartes' Meditation*. But when he heard the back door slam and recognized Allison's footsteps on the stairs, he laid the book aside. He heard her door open and close, then silence. He had lay down to ease his throbbing head, but now his pulse was pounding again. He kept his eyes on the slanted ceiling for a moment, then gingerly got to his feet and opened the big Beyer aspirin jar he'd bought. He heard Allison's solid footsteps coming up the stairs and gulped down two aspirin.

"Hey, watcha doing?" she said, leaning in his doorway.

"Reading the *Descartes*." He grinned. "Trying to be rational. Resting up before I make one last trip to the library before it closes for the holiday. But that won't take long. Afterwards I was thinking we could smoke some dope."

"Can't." She gave him a hug. "I'm driving up to Moberly today. Going to spend Thanksgiving with my folks."

Dave held onto her, buried his face in her hair, felt her full body, strong arms around him. He pulled back after a moment and saw her face more serious than usual.

"Anything wrong?"

Allison shrugged.

"Well," he said slowly, "I feel like we haven't seen much of each other this last week."

"Yeah."

"There's nothing wrong?"

"With me, no." She moved past him to the window, then

sat down in her usual place by the bookshelf and thumbed through the paperbacks. "I feel fine, but..." She studied the cover of *Magister Ludi*. "But..." He could see her change direction in midsentence. "There's something wrong with you, Dave. Those headaches."

"Maybe, maybe not." Dave didn't like talking about it, but couldn't think of a way to avoid it.

"If you're sick, you should see a doctor," Allison said in a flat tone, just short of blaming. "Instead you hide it." She slid the window closed an inch. "And sometimes you hide from me too."

"Not intentionally. And I feel great around you. No headaches. You staying in Moberly until Sunday?"

"Yeah. I need to spend more time with my folks."

"I'll miss you," he said. They both thought about that statement for a moment. She straightened up the paperbacks on the bookshelf, slid the end bricks in until the row was straight and tight. "I'll be back Sunday afternoon." She got up and went to the door. "See a doctor, Dave." She put her face up to his, her eyes determined. "You can't deal with pain by ignoring it. Not for very long." She gave him a hug. "See you after Thanksgiving." She went out into the corridor, then came back. "I'll miss you too." This time her smile was there. He listened to her footsteps on the stairs, the creak of the old door, and the bang of the screen.

* * *

Mark let the flow of students carry him along the campus walkway under a cloudy sky, intoxicated with cold autumn air. Elegant equations from his Materials Design class flowed across his mind. His two morning classes had not been as bad as usual. Even the evil Bradley in Thermodynamics seemed more relaxed. He wrote out formulas on the blackboard with a little less ferocity. Mark kept his head down, copying everything that was written on the board, understanding none of it. When class ended he was first out the door.

On the second floor of the library, Mark selected a desk near a window with a view of Lowry Street. Brown leaves swirled into piles along the weathered stone of Yardley Hall. The anticipation of Thanksgiving holiday glowed inside him.

He worked through a chapter of  Materials Design. The perfect diagrams were like sacred figures, as beautiful as the impressions of Monet or Pissarro, practically leaping off the page with imagination. But then his mind drifted to a favorite science fiction book he'd read years ago in which the starship *Leonora Christine*, out of control and endlessly gaining speed, watched time dilate and the universe collapse and be reborn—all matter, energy, and time itself contract and explode in another big bang, and a new universe is born and time starts again.

He forced his attention back on the book, read the assigned chapter, and worked two problems. From time to time he glanced at the brown leaves swirling over the sidewalk. Clouds were thickening into what might become rain or possibly snow. After an hour and a half of study, he could stand it no longer. He closed his books, went outside, and wandered down the street, letting the cold wind clear his mind.

A shout from across the street startled him. Dave was standing in front of the Heidelberg pointing at the door. Mark altered course and they went in together.

It was crowded, the students boisterous with the advent of the Thanksgiving holiday, but they managed to get their usual booth.

"Wandering down the street you looked lost in thought," Dave said over his glass of Hamm's. "Mooning over Jennifer, I suppose."

"Hardly." Mark took a sip. The beer that usually tasted so good seemed flat and insipid. "I'm sometimes happy to have time away from her. People need space. I don't know how married people live with each other day and night, day in day out."

"Sounds like your leash is getting a little too tight. Got your eye on some other girl?"

"No. She's the one for me."

"Could be. In any case you're not the date-around type," said Dave.

"...like Mitchell..." they said in unison. "And that idiot is getting married," Dave snorted. "You're serially monogamous Mark, always were, always will be."

"Thanks for the analysis, Dr. Freud."

They touched glasses. "Here's to the holidays. By tomorrow night it'll be our town again, us townies."

"Is Allison staying in Columbia?"

"She left for Moberly today."

"You two look..."

"I'm leaving too," Dave said carefully. "Going to St. Louis for Thanksgiving. My uncle's having a family reunion over the holiday."

"Back in town Sunday, though, right? Got to go skydiving, practice up for the meet."

Dave tilted his beer. "I don't think so."

The jukebox started "Time Has Come Today." And just then Mark spotted Jeff making his way through the crowd. Behind him he could see the top of Stephanie's strawberry-blond hair. Jeff shoved four full glasses onto the table and dragged up chairs for himself and Stephanie.

"Band tonight at the I.V.," Jeff said. "Steph and I are going. You guys grab your dates and let's go." Steph nudged him. "Well, I meant...we're going."

Mark shook his head, studied the brown leaves blowing along the sidewalk.

"How did midterms go?" Jeff asked guilelessly.

Dave shrugged. "No sweat."

Mark raised his glass. "Grades are not a topic for mixed company. Actually I was thinking about where Keith is these days, not my bad grades." Mark took a long drink of beer.

"He's been gone a month. Probably skipped across the border to Canada," Dave opined.

Jeff avoided his usual ogling of the girls in deference to Stephanie. "Keith is not going to give up his plan for getting a job with a big company, making tons of money, living the high life. You've heard him talk. He's not going to give that up to dodge the draft."

"Plenty of big companies in Canada," Mark said mildly.

"Speaking of making a regrettable decision, I saw Rich Behr the other day," Jeff said. "Dropped out of Caltech to come back here and live the hippie life."

"He won't regret it," Mark said. "He's doing what he always wanted to do. Taking courses in theoretical mathematics, living the hippie life. He tuned in, turned on, and dropped out. He told me he never really had wanted that other life that was so carefully planned for him. He made a change. We just talk about it."

Dave avoided Mark's eye. Jeff shook his head. The music ended and the conversations around them lulled and became bleak in the fading light.

"I need to go run an errand," Mark said and stepped out into the wind.

Mark walked briskly up Ninth Street to Lowry and went into the Memorial Student Union. Planned lives, endless love, marriage. Last spring had been good with Jennifer. And while she was in Florida for the summer he had missed her but was glad to have the time to himself. And when she'd come back, things had felt right again. He thought he could see hid future filled with her, but he wanted to settle into that future slowly, not rush into something just because society expected it.

He went to the last phone booth in the row and called the Columbia College number. The operator put him through to the phone in her room, but it rang and rang with no answer. He went back to the Heidelberg and rejoined the others.

"Staying in town over the holiday?" he said to Stephanie.

Jeff put his arm around her, which she didn't seem to enjoy much. "Just until tomorrow," Jeff said proudly. "My brothers are in town so my family is having Thanksgiving dinner tonight instead of tomorrow. Steph's joining us."

Mark nodded, sipped weak coffee and wished he hadn't strayed into the Heidelberg. He slurped up a little more of the too-hot coffee and rummaged in his pockets for money. "Well, I'm studying over the holiday," he said, trying to keep an even tone in his voice, but managing to sound only self-righteous and pitiful. "I tried to call Jennifer but I guess she's out." He looked at Stephanie.

Jeff and Stephanie exchanged looks. Stephanie sighed and looked Mark in the eye, addressing him as though speaking to a retarded child, "She left for Florida yesterday, Mark."

"Yeah, well..." Mark zipped his jacket up. "I'll call her at her parents' house in Florida."

He stalked down Ninth Street toward downtown. It was time to find out where Keith had gone. Rumor had it there was an underground railroad operating in Columbia with people that could help draft dodgers get across the border into Canada.

The enclave of old houses on Paquin had been a student ghetto from times immemorial. It was now also the center of the counterculture in Columbia, and the target of regular police raids. At random, Mark chose a house on Paquin and picked his way between a battered Volkswagen, two Honda motorcycles, and a bicycle littering the front yard. He didn't notice the white Buick LeSabre parked at the curb. He went up the sagging wooden steps, dodging the wind chimes, and knocked on the door. A rangy guy with long hair tied in a bandana opened the door four inches and eyed him over granny glasses. "Yes?"

"I'm looking for a friend of mine, Keith, he's sort of disappeared about a month ago…"

"Nobody here by that name."

A girl in a tie-dyed muumuu craned over the guy's shoulder. "What are you? Some kind of narc?"

"No. I'm just trying to find my friend. Make sure he's alright."

The door opened wider, and there was Carol Bianchi. "The *Free Press* doesn't have an advertising section. You can't place ads for missing persons. Oh, hello. It's Mark isn't it? From Wollheim's class."

"Yeah." Mark smiled. "That's me." He shifted his weight from foot to foot. "I just thought somebody might know…"

"This is the *Columbia Free Press* office," Carol said. "Everything we know about guys dodging the draft is in the September issue. Get him a copy, will you Ian." The guy rummaged around in a pile of old issues and thrust one into Mark's hand.

"Can I talk to the reporter?"

"Not here," the officious guy interjected.

"And we're in the middle of layout for the December issue," Carol said. She flashed Mark her dazzling smile and retreated to a back room. The sullen girl in the dirty muumuu closed the door in his face.

The article on the draft didn't tell him much. But spread across the center two pages was something titled the *One Voice Manifesto*. He stepped out of the wind and read it. The writing was beautiful, clear, urgent, thoughtful, but not strident. It cited a dozen historical, political, and economic sources, from Hobbes' *Leviathan* through John Locke's *Second Treatise on Government*, to Thomas Paine's *Common Sense* and the SDS's

*Port Huron Statement*. There were excerpts from the Missouri State Code and Constitution with appropriate paragraphs noted for proposed changes, and a page from the University student government charter with proposed changes.

Oblivious of the wind, Mark read the document from beginning to end, then went back through it again. It was the best political tract he had ever read.

## Chapter 12

Thanksgiving vacation began. With Jennifer back in Florida with her parents, Mark planned to spend a couple of nights at the farm. Wednesday night he enjoyed a pleasant dinner with his parents and sister and immediately afterward went to his old room and tried to read.

The next morning was foggy and overcast, but not cold. Mark ate eggs and bacon with his family, not talking much. Afterwards his father changed into his work clothes and went out to work in the garden. The fog had changed to a light drizzle. In the kitchen his mother started preparing a traditional turkey dinner. Mark stood on the big Persian carpet in the living room, a cup of tea in his hand, looking out the window at his father's purposeful digging, trimming and raking. His father seemed a small figure among the planter boxes, asparagus beds, and apple trees. Mark watched him rake up a wheelbarrow full of litter and trundle it off, his black rubber boots shiny, drizzle darkening the shoulders of his denim jacket. Behind him, his mother had the radio tuned to KFRU's big band music.

My parents are invisible anchors to my life, Mark said to himself. This house and garden have shaped me in unknowable ways. They've been happy, but I know so little about them. My father retired, they bought this farm, made themselves part of the community and the land. He watched his father roll a wheelbarrow full of mulch up to one of the rows of iris and carefully begin spreading it. The drizzle continued. I appreciate all this—this house, this farm, the way they have treated me.

I always will. His mind slid back over the years they had lived there. He remembered himself in high school, taking all this for granted, looking ahead to a happy future endlessly stretching out before them all. When I am old, I will retire here and live out my days. The figure of his father shoveling mulch, in faded denim and black rubber boots became him.

* * *

He left his textbooks stacked on the corner of his desk and took down a book he'd been given for his tenth birthday, *Islands in the Sky,* an Arthur C. Clarke. He began rereading the familiar story.

The next morning Mark was wakened by the scent of fresh-baked coffee cake. He joined his parents and sister at the table for a leisurely breakfast, and for a time they recaptured the happy days when the future lay bright and safe before the four of them.

The drizzle stopped at noon, the clouds cleared and the temperature climbed into the low fifties.

"Going to work outside today?" Mark asked his father.

"Not today." Mark's mother was sitting on the couch wrapped in a blanket. "Your mother and I plan to watch the Macy's Thanksgiving Day parade."

In better days they would have been outside, working among the trees, pruning and burning the cut brush. Mark had helped his parents trim and burn an area near the pond nine or ten years ago, and the irises his mother had planted there were now overgrown with brush. There was no sign of their work.

Steve called to see if Mark would borrow his father's chainsaw and come over to cut up some tree limbs that had fallen in their back yard.

Mark went to the shed, got the chainsaw, tightened the chain, and filled it with fuel and oil. A pair of worn leather gloves lay on the worktable in the shape of his father's hands. Mark put his own hand beside one. It was the shape of his hand too.

* * *

Mark drove to Steve Griffin's parents' house on Parkridge Drive. He had football on the radio. Mark knew nothing of football and had no interest in it, but the autumn college-town ritual was pleasant. Traffic was very light over the holiday weekend. He rolled down Business Loop 70 past Lee's Tires and Del Cornell Lincoln Mercury, listening to an ad on the radio for State Farm Insurance.

The Griffin's house was on a hillside, lots of glass looking out over autumn woods. Steve's room was on the walk-in lower level. The French doors stood open to a cool afternoon. Mark and Steve set to work cutting up the fallen limbs, stacking the brush at the curb to be hauled off, and cutting the branches to fireplace length. Steve had the MU football game on the radio. The sun was warm, and the afternoon still except for the screech of the chainsaw.

Afterward in the family room they listened to the end of the game. The ritualized phrases and cadencing of the announcer, the crowd sounds, and the local ads created a distinct atmosphere of Autumn in Columbia to Mark. The cool weather, then the coziness of winter and Christmas was ahead.

There was quiet laughter from upstairs.

"My dad," Steve said sheepishly. "He's reading Jerome K. Jerome's *Three Men in a Boat* for the tenth time. Remind you of anybody?"

Mark grinned, walked over to Steve's bookshelf, and pulled down a familiar book in a yellow dust jacket. He flipped it open and read, "'...reading *Three Men in a Boat* which he must know by heart by now.' Heinlein, *Have Spacesuit*. I must have read that book a dozen times in high school." Mark pulled down another volume. "*Tunnel in the Sky*, that's one of my favorites."

"I'm surprised you didn't invite Jennifer to spend Thanksgiving with you and your parents."

"Well, my mother's not well. It seemed like a bad time."

Steve stubbed out his Marlboro. "Sure you're not just leading Jennifer on?"

Mark shook his head. "I'm not. We're right for each other." He grinned at Steve. "It's your fault. I met her that night we double dated with you and Emily, remember?"

"Oh yeah."

"You and Emily…?"

"I've always been clear with her. We'll see each other, have a great time, but only until I graduate. Then I'm gone."

"And she was okay with that?"

Steve took a deep breath. "Not really. We stayed together a few months after I told her that, but it was no good. We should have broken up right then, right there. It's no good trying to be together when you know it's going to end."

Outside the French doors the light was turning gold as afternoon shaded toward evening. Steve and Mark sat in the comfortable lounge chairs, saying nothing, knowing that as soon as they spoke, the afternoon would be gone.

Back at the farm, Mark walked down to the shed and put the chainsaw back on the worktable where his father's gloves still lay.

* * *

There was no traffic. Not even at seven o'clock on a Friday night.

Mark cruised slowly down Old Highway 63. The bank sign said the temperature was forty degrees under a clear sky. On impulse he turned onto Stadium and drove through the deserted campus. Nobody walking, no cars, the dorm windows were dark.

At Village Inn Pizza, there was only one car besides Steve Griffin's white 1959 Chevy. The night was clear and cold. Overhead the stars were chips of glass in a jet-black sky. Inside it smelled like beer and pizza. "Let's Spend the Night Together" ended and the jukebox fell silent. Steve was sitting at a booth near the fireplace watching the gas flames.

"Hi Steve." Mark slid into the booth and poured himself a glass of beer from the pitcher. "It was nice driving over here. No traffic. The town belongs to us townies again," said Mark.

"Yeah, but no women around either." Steve lit a Marlboro.

They sat sideways in the wooden booth, legs stretched out toward the fireplace. Their pepperoni pizza came and they ordered another pitcher of Busch.

"After my Navy time is over, I'm signing up with one of the geophysics firms that contract to the oil exploration companies. Work on an exploration crew, out in the jungle."

"Man in the wilderness..."

"Except that you've got these great gadgets to play with. Sit inside an air-conditioned van and study the seismic profiles coming in from the geosensors. That's paradise," Steve said.

"I thought paradise was women and cold beer?"

"That's when the company helicopter flies you out to the fleshpots of Thailand for R&R. You get the best of both worlds."

"What about settling down? Like Jeff's always talking about. A house in the suburbs. Two kids and a dog, or two dogs and a kid. Drive a station wagon. All that."

"Eventually. But not 'til I'm past thirty. Then it'll be time to trade the 'Vette in for a Ford and buy a house in Houston and start working at Gulf Oil's home office."

"Think you'd ever come back to Columbia?" asked Mark.

"Probably not. Except to visit my parents once in a while." Steve shook a Marlboro out with a studied gesture and signaled for another pitcher.

"You were smart to stay in ROTC. No draft pressure."

"Do your time now or do your time later." Steve shrugged. At least this way I've got some control over my assignment, and I'm an officer."

"But at heart you'll always be a Columbia kid, right?" Mark said.

Steve grinned, his Marlboro held at a cocky angle in the corner of his mouth, his face golden in the firelight. "I like Columbia too, but when I was in NROTC camp last July at the Marine Corps base at Quantico, I realized there's a big world out there, and I want to see some of it."

"Me too. But not in the military," Mark said. "You worried? About Vietnam?"

Steve cocked his head, something Mark had not seen him do before. It looked like he was listening for something, his conscience maybe, thought Mark.

"No. That's what training's all about. Doing the right thing under pressure."

Mark smiled to bring him back, "Hemingway, 'grace under pressure,' something we all want."

The waiter interrupted, "We're closing the kitchen early tonight, you guys want anything more?" He had a pained look on his face.

"Nothing more." The waiter sauntered off, relieved.

"He's a clod," Steve said. "St. Louis born and bred. You can tell by the accent. He'll graduate from Arts and Science here, go to work for Anheuser-Busch, buy a house in Webster Groves, marry a fat girl and raise stupid kids. He doesn't know it yet, but these years right here, as a student in Columbia, are the best years of his life."

"Why so bitter about these St. Louis geeks?" asked Mark.

"I just get tired of them thinking St. Louis is so cosmopolitan and Columbia is the sticks. Columbia's better. Always was, always will be."

"None of us will admit it, but there is a certain innocence, a certain purity, that comes from growing up in a small town," Mark said.

"Like Moberly, Allison's hometown?" Steve laughed.

"Well...Allison does have that purity I'm talking about," Mark countered.

"Jennifer, too," Steve said. "You shouldn't take her for granted.

"The night I met her, our double date, we went out to some club on Business 70, acid-rock band, light show, dark as a cave in there."

"I remember."

They both stared at the pale flame of the fireplace. "Mind if I ask why you broke up with Emily?"

"We diverged. She wanted to talk about Elizabethan poetry and Impressionist art and I wanted to talk about Robert Heinlein and geophysics. She wanted to talk about commitment and I didn't."

"Yeah, well..." Mark didn't like the sound of the word commitment. "Heinlein. From the late forties until the late fifties Heinlein wrote one book a year, some of the best young adult books ever written." Mark laughed, "I remember hurrying through my lunch in the cafeteria back in high school so I could go upstairs to the library and read ten minutes of a Heinlein book before my next class. I can't remember the classes at all, but I remember the books."

"In his final one, *Have Spacesuit—Will Travel*, I can see his transition toward his major work."

"...*Starship Troopers*, in 1959," Steve said. "Great book, his usual themes—coming of age and citizenship in a democracy."

"He was a great teacher," Mark said. "All that exuberant wisdom."

Steve grinned, Marlboro at an angle. "Exuberant?"

"Yeah," Mark said. "He said we should always act

honorably, work hard, educate ourselves, explore…"

"Which was what brought us to his books in the first place."

"…and in *Troopers* he was expressing his concern that the social contract between citizen and government was being ignored by most Americans these days."

"That's why we have a draft."

"Then came *Stranger in a Strange Land*, which was an endorsement of the counterculture."

"Lots of people read it that way, including the reviewers, but it wasn't. Not really. It was an exploration of learning, language, sociology and politics."

"And then *Glory Road*," Mark said. He downed the last of his beer. "What a change! An alternate-world fantasy, and it worked beautifully. He is an amazing writer."

Steve checked his watch. "Got to get going."

"My round. I'll wait for the check. See ya."

Steve pulled his jacket on and made his way to the door. Columbia kids, Mark thought. But not for much longer.

# Chapter 13

Sunday morning Mark sat drinking coffee and reading *Analog Science Fiction* magazine until ten o'clock, then drove to the airport.

He packed his chute fast and got onto the first flight with Rod, Jim and Grant. They had agreed to spend the day practicing for the competition in Florida. At three thousand feet, all three jumpers would pile out of the plane in quick succession, opening their chutes immediately and try to come down sequentially right on the same target. The day was cool, but clear and Mark felt good. In the cocoon of noise as the plane spiraled up into the clear day, Mark's mind was clear of everything except the moment.

At altitude, Mark eased out onto the strut with Grant and Rod, then they all let go and went out into the air. As soon as he got stable, he located the other two and the pea gravel target. Grant's chute was already deploying. Mark pulled the ripcord and the 7TU chute rippled open. He pulled the right toggle down hard to get aligned so that the wind would drift him down to the target. The top of Grant's chute was only forty feet away, a white half-sphere, unreal in the clear air with the trees and houses looking like toys below. This is when I feel best, he thought. Nothing on my mind except the moment. Dave would call it mindfulness. Mark reached a toe out to touch the target and came down in a roll, then was on his feet, whipping his chute into his arms. He laid his chute out near where Rod had laid out his Paracommander and was expertly packing it. Mark jerked his chute straight, flipped hurriedly through the twenty-four leaves of filmy nylon, and jerked the sleeve down over the canopy. He knelt beside the risers and started slapping handfuls of white nylon cord into the rubber retainer loops.

"Getting kind of sloppy with your packing aren't you?" Rod said drily.

"I'm careful enough," Mark said, focusing on his task. He heard the distinctive mutter of Dave's TR3. Mark pulled his helmet back on. "Get your gear on, Dave, we need to practice. It's only two weeks until the competition."

"I'm not going," Dave said. He cut the engine off but sat in his car. Mark heard the plane idling behind him. "Why not?" Mark asked.

"They're waiting, better get going," Dave said. "It would take too long to explain."

"I'll drop by your place tonight," Mark said. "You can explain it over a beer."

"Not tonight." Dave dropped the car into gear and drove off.

Mark slung on his chute and helmet and got in the plane. On the ascent Rod put his face close to Mark and Grant and shouted, "We'll drive down to Zephyrhills Friday. Maybe we can get in a practice jump Saturday morning." Rod shouted into Mark ear as the plane spiraled up to altitude, "As soon as the meet ends Sunday at noon, we start driving back."

Mark got in four jumps that day.

* * *

Monday Mark parked his car on Elm Street. "...I'll think of summer days again and dream of you..." He cut the radio off and stepped out into the cold wind. He hadn't tried to contact Jennifer and she hadn't tried to contact him since before Thanksgiving. Much of the time he spent with his books in the library he mooned over Jennifer, vacillating endlessly over whether to call her or not. He fell farther and farther behind in his Thermodynamics course. Even his English Literature course, which was fun and easy, could not keep his mind off her. He dreamed of having the time to sit with Jennifer reading Elizabethan verse on snowy mornings. He put that vision out of his mind and rehearsed Thermo formulas as he walked. Bradley held a quiz every Monday.

"What are you muttering about?" A big guy with crew cut red hair blocked the sidewalk. Then he grinned and Mark recognized Terry Starke.

"I'll be damned!" Mark said. They shook hands. "I haven't seen you in months."

"How are you doing?" Terry said.

Mark cocked his armful of books. "Struggling."

Terry was one of those guys who always seemed to know what he was doing, where he was going. In high school, when Mark had no clue as to what he would study at the University, Terry was already telling him about the advantages of a career in engineering. Mark remembered Terry striding purposefully down the halls in high school, his orange leather zippered notebook case under his arm. During their first years at the University they had had a number of classes together before Terry went into Civil Engineering and Mark to Mechanical. Terry always seemed prepared in class, his grades solid.

They stood saying nothing. Mark noticed Terry wasn't carrying any books.

"It's been what," Mark said, "a year or more?" Mark remembered sitting with Terry on a snowy day at the Memorial Union drinking coffee and debating whether to work for Boeing or Lockheed. "You graduating in January or June?"

Terry looked up at the canopy of bare tree limbs shaking in the cold wind. The sky was gray, threatening snow. "I left school last spring."

Mark was stunned. "What are you…?"

"Free lance draftsman. Good money, and lots of opportunity," Terry said heartily. "I feel pretty good about leaving all the meaningless memorization behind." His expression said otherwise.

Mark glanced at his watch. Only a couple of minutes until his Thermodynamics quiz. "Let's get together sometime soon," Mark said. "But right now I need to go."

"Sure," Terry said. "Stay in touch." He nodded and went on his way.

The Thermo quiz was a disaster. After class, Mark stood on the steps of the Engineering building scowling at the bare trees across the quad, then he marched off to get a cup of coffee.

The Memorial Union snack bar had been remodeled into a bright 1960's coffee shop, but Mark preferred it's earlier incarnation as the dark, paneled Bengal Lair. Once a week for one semester when Mark was ten years old, he would wait in the Bengal Lair for his father's evening management refresher class to end, by sitting in the Bengal Lair, drinking a Coke and trying to read his science fiction magazine by the dim table lamp. He would play Martin Denny's "Quiet Village" on the jukebox over and over until the manager told him to quit it. He'd liked the xylophone and the fake jungle animal cries.

Mark spotted Dave and Jeff at a table near the window, watching the stream of students hurrying through Memorial Union archway in the cold wind.

"Terry Starke dropped out of school." Mark put his books on the shelf at the window and dragged a plastic chair up.

A moody silence greeted this announcement.

"And speaking of quitting," Mark went on, "why are you quitting skydiving? Or was that just a momentary aberration."

"I'm done with it," Dave said. His dark look seemed angry.

"So you can spend more time with Allison?" Jeff smirked.

Dave gave him a withering look. "Avoiding Jennifer?" Dave asked Mark pointedly.

"She's avoiding me. Allison?"

"I'm avoiding her."

They both turned to Jeff. "Susan?"

"I saw the movie *Fail Safe* last night," Jeff said.

"That answers that," Dave said.

"Makes you think about nuclear war," Jeff pointed at the ceiling. "Looking Glass is up there twenty-four hours a day ready to fire those Atlases as soon as we see Soviet Bear bombers flying low over the arctic icepack, dodging the DEW line radar."

"I would welcome nuclear war if it would get me out of my Thermo course," Mark said.

"On the news last night President Johnson announced he was unilaterally stopping the bombing of North Vietnam," Jeff said cheerfully, "and that Ho Chi Minh could participate in the Paris Peace Talks. Looks like progress."

Dave snorted. "The news also quoted President Thieu saying it was a unilateral U.S. decision that he did not agree with."

"Why aren't you going to the jump meet in Florida?" Mark asked pointblank.

"Time to go in a different direction," Dave said.

"You guys want to go to the Black and Gold Friday night?" Jeff interrupted. "Good band, which usually means lots of women."

"And I may be finished with Allison too," Dave continued. Jeff and Mark stared at him. Mark pushed his chair back. "I'm going to hit the books for a while."

* * *

Three weeks went by. Mark did not go to the farm or to the Heidelberg, nor did he call Jennifer. Thermo was a lost cause, but his Machine Design course was fascinating and his English Lit course was wonderful, especially because, unlike his Engineering courses, there were more girls than guys in it. He kind of liked the girls' attention on him when he answered a question.

But mostly, he missed Jennifer. After Lit class Friday, buoyed by the discussion, he strolled down the stairs in the Arts and Science Building and out into the cold wind, smiling. I'll phone Jennifer tonight, he thought. In front of the Business School, in the middle of the sidewalk, he stopped and turned his face to the overcast sky. "I don't want to be in love," he said out loud. A couple of beefy guys in Ag school jackets pushed by him. "Who you talking to, butthead?"

I love Jennifer, Mark thought. I don't want to but I do. I like spending time with her, but I don't want things to change, commitments to deepen. We're both too young to lock ourselves into something permanent.

A car horn bleated. It was Dave in his black TR3 with the top down. Mark climbed in and they spurted away from the curb. "It's winter, you know," Mark said, hunching down in the seat. He tinkered with the controls of the miniscule heater, but nothing happened.

"Style over comfort," Dave said expansively. He drove to Stephens College and cruised around the campus a few times, but the few women walking between buildings ignored them.

"Your midterms over?" You don't seem to be sunk in your usual Thermo gloom."

"I just finished English Lit," Mark said. "Good course—Blake, Burns, Marvell, Milton..."

Dave snorted, "Milton '...of man's first transgression...' Jesus, that guy goes on and on. You need to be reading the San Francisco writers, Corso, Ginsburg, Robinson Jeffers."

"And Rod McKuen?"

"That was Allison's book."

Mark started to make a joke, but didn't.

Dave dropped Mark at his car. "The Pi Phi's are holding an open party out at the Black and Gold tonight," Dave said. "The Warlocks are playing. Wanna go?"

"No. I'm going to phone Jennifer." " He tried to keep from sounding apologetic.

"Married life." Dave revved the engine once for emphasis and drove off.

* * *

It was ten after three and no sign of Professor Wollheim. The class was fidgeting. People were waiting for someone to make the first move. Finally a big guy in a Kappa Alpha sweatshirt snapped his notebook closed and walked briskly out. In a moment the room was empty. Mark sat listening to the creaking of the steam radiators for a few minutes, then sauntered out. Carol had not been in class today.

Mark got on his Suzuki and started for Columbia College, rationalizing that if he just showed up at her class, she would have to talk to him. But at Paquin Street he stopped at the old house where the *Columbia Free Press* had its office. The front door was locked, but he could hear people inside.

"Can I help you?" A guy with long braided hair and granny glasses eyed him from a door opened a crack.

"Carol here?"

"She's busy."

Carol's face appeared over the guy's shoulder.

"You weren't in class today…" Mark started.

"I can't talk now," she said sharply. "Wollheim just quit under pressure from the University administration. I've got to rewrite the whole front page and get it to the printer by six this evening." She disappeared.

"Professor Wollheim quit?"

"Goddam fascist University forced him out," the guy in braids and granny glasses snarled. "Mark Rudd has got it right. Take over the University and burn it down."

Mark laughed in his face. "Right on, man."

Still looking for reasons not to go see Jennifer, Mark idled his bike down Tenth Street and stopped in front of a head shop called Alternate Reality. A guy was coming out as Mark tried to go in and they stepped into each other's way. "Sorry," the guy said. His hair was cut conservatively short but he was wearing hand-embroidered jeans, Dingo boots, and a denim jacket with a peace patch on the shoulder.

"Do you work here?" Mark said.

"Part-time."

"Listen, I've been trying to locate a friend of mine named Keith. He got his draft notice and disappeared about a month ago, nobody's heard anything, we're getting kind of worried." Mark paused expectantly.

The guy studied his face.

"There are narcs everywhere, man," the guy said. "So even if I knew where your friend was, I wouldn't tell some guy off the street."

Mark stood where he was, shivering in the wind. "Cold out here."

"I will tell you this—we haven't...I haven't...heard of anybody called Keith, not in the last few months, okay?" He started off. Mark caught his arm.

"Thanks, man. That helps."

Mark got back on his motorcycle and rode to Columbia College feeling considerably better. Maybe Keith hasn't made any irrevocable choices. He parked the bike and stood in front of Renfield Hall. Jennifer's two o'clock class should just be ending. Women were already coming out the door, and in a moment he spotted her. Before he lost his nerve, he walked over to her.

"Hi Jennifer, can we talk for a minute?" She didn't seem very surprised or very happy to see him. "I'm sorry for the way..."

"I don't want to continue like this, Mark." She stopped and concentrated on the distance. "I don't feel like I'm part of your life. We enjoy each other's company, I think, but when I hear you talking about skydiving or Dave and his girlfriend, or cars, all that other stuff, that's when you seem happy. Do you understand?"

"You make me happy, Jennifer." Mark felt anger rising up in him, and knew it wouldn't help him the situation. "Can we get together tonight? Talk about us?"

"Not tonight, Mark. And not tomorrow. Not for a while, okay?" She turned and walked away.

* * *

Mark, Rod and Grant drove all day Friday, out of Midwestern winter and into Gulf Coast Florida sunshine. After a night at the cheapest motel they could find, they were at the airport early, but the manifests were crowded so they were only able to schedule one jump before the meet began at noon. Mark lay in the grass in the sunshine, his head on his packed chute, his mind empty. The first afternoon's competition went well. By evening they'd made two jumps and placed second in their division, high enough to compete in the finals on Sunday. They ate at a drive-through, sat around the motel room drinking beer, and went to bed early.

Sunday morning was clear and calm. Luck rather than skill put them ahead of Georgia State. The University of North Carolina made some mistakes, so Missouri was effortlessly in fourth place. Another round of jumps put them in third. Only one round of jumps left. If they beat Oklahoma they would finish in second place under the University of Florida, which already had first place locked.

Mark was the third man out, falling forward at an angle and tumbling over even as he pulled the ripcord. And in that instant he knew he was in trouble. He should have gotten stable first, but he'd been in a hurry. The chute billowed up around him and he saw his boots rotating through the nylon cords. He was falling under a collapsed chute he would have no hope of untangling before he hit. From three thousand feet the ground was only twenty seconds away. Mark reached up and flipped open the two Capewell covers, hooked his thumbs in the wire rings, and pulled hard. He separated from the risers and fell free. The ground was terrifyingly close. He rolled on his back and pulled the reserve chute ripcord with his right hand. The little twenty-four foot diameter reserve chute snapped open with a gunshot crack, snapping his head down hard. He swung high to his left once and then his boots hit the ground and he was rolling in sand and grass.

He sat up. Nothing felt broken or sprained. People were running toward him, shouting questions. He pulled his helmet off and watched the orange and white tangle of his main chute flutter down into pine trees fifty yards away.

Rod and Grant were there helping him gather up his reserve chute. "I'm alright. I'm alright," he told them. He unsnapped his harness and shrugged out of it. They gathered up his chute and his gear while he walked back to the van, opened the side doors, and tossed his helmet in. "I'm alive," he said to no one.

After they'd gotten all their gear stowed in the van, they opened cans of Busch and stood there drinking them in the gathering dusk. The officials told them they had placed third, even with no score for Mark's out-of-target landing.

"We didn't win, but we did good," Rod said, climbing behind the wheel of the van. "There's a skydiving team at the University of Missouri." The pride in his voice was clear.

"You would have really put us on the map if you'd drilled in, Mark." They rolled up the highway in the Gulf Coast sunset. "Good reactions on that malfunction. No hesitation. And besides, any landing you live through is a good one."

## Chapter 14

Mark woke in his room at the farm and for a moment felt peaceful and rested. He could hear his parents moving around. Mark got up and dressed and went to the kitchen for coffee. The house was decorated for Christmas. A small pine tree his father had cut was decorated with familiar ornaments. Outside, a tangle of old lights, many of the bulbs hand-painted green and red, had been strung around the handrail of the deck. There were presents under the tree.

His mother looked thin and weak, but smiled. After getting his coffee, Mark quickly retired to his room and opened his ME 311 textbook to the section on stress rupture of metals. "A steel bolt is loaded in tension to ten thousand psi and rigidly attached at both ends. After three years of service at eight hundred degrees F, what is the stress in the bolt?" He flipped back to page three forty-nine and reread the section on high-temperature creep in steels. But his mind was elsewhere.

Mark swiveled his chair and sat looking at the snow-covered hayfield in the dawn light. The coffee was soothing. His parents had travelled the world when he and his sister were kids, but they'd always talked and dreamed of retiring to a farm in the Midwest. And ten years ago they had made their dream come true; buying this farm, building this house, retiring to this small town. In these few short years they had made their place in the community, spent time with the land they loved, his father planting trees and his mother tending flowers and her garden. Then his mother's illness had begun with the cancer diagnosis, followed by the treatment, the remission, the resurgence and new treatments.

Mark turned back to his book and focused his mind on chapter nine, sample problem 9-7: "For a material with the stress-strain curve shown, calculate the ratio of yield strength to tensile strength as a direct function of the strain hardening exponent." Mark worked stolidly through the problem.

From the other room he could hear an old Leontyne Price record of Christmas songs, the Schubert "Ave Maria," then "O Holy Night," then the Bach "Ave Maria." He struggled with the sample problems until he had worked half of them.

He again found himself staring at the frozen fields outside. We don't realize how precious our ordinary days are until they begin to end. If only things could be made to stay the same and never change. But we aren't always given that choice.

The day went by pleasantly enough. That evening was Christmas Eve, so they all got into his father's Chevy and drove around the snowy streets of Columbia looking at Christmas lights on people's houses. Then they went to a Christmas Eve service at First Christian Church which was heavily attended. Mark tried to put his heart into the prayers, but it felt meaningless.

At home his parents lit a fire in the fireplace and sat in the glow of the Christmas tree while Mark retired to his room, pulled *Fate is the Hunter* off his bookshelf, and concentrated on the story until he was tired enough to sleep.

Christmas morning they drank coffee and ate coffee cake and opened gifts. His father stoked the fire in the fireplace. The day was mild and windless under a high overcast. No cars passed on the road.

Mark felt a little embarrassed at the gifts he had bought them—nothing of any significance. He received three pairs of sweat socks, a pair of slacks from Penney's, and two science fiction books he'd asked for.

He went to his room and read the new books for a while. Then he and his father walked on the crunchy snow down the slope of fields to where an elm tree had blown down. His father had brought his little red Homelite chainsaw and they cut and stacked limbs. They spoke little and when they did, they talked of the activities at hand, the safe and comfortable. Mark walked back to the shed and brought the tractor and trailer. They loaded the cut wood in it, hauled it to the woodpile behind the shed, and stacked it neatly. "This will make good firewood," his father said. When the work was done Mark's father stood looking out over the silent fields. Mark gave him his silence and returned to the house.

After a lunch of sliced ham sandwiches, Mark napped for a while, then put his old clothes back on and took his Suzuki out slipping and sliding across the snowy fields, spinning his back tire in the slushy mud, going up over terraces and down along the mowed hayfields to the old pond. He cut the engine off and sat on the bike. The pond was edged with ice, the center a black circle. The silence was broken only by three birds flitting through the bare limbs of a persimmon tree. And then they were gone. The sky was a featureless gray.

He thought of the seconds he had spent in the air over Florida when death had been very close. He'd not told his parents. Why was I not profoundly changed by that? Death passed me by in a flash, he thought, but death hovers like a dark presence in my mother's room. The real death, silent and inexorable.

My mother and father dreamed of living here, deep in the country. They realized that dream, but it has lasted only a handful of years. There is no life after death, Mark thought, no happy reunion in some afterlife. But her spirit will remain here, in my mind, and when I look at this little pond I may remember her happiness. The sky, the wind in the trees, winter snow and summer rain will come as they always have.

* * *

Dave idled his TR3 down Paquin. Allison's white Plymouth was not parked behind the house. With a sigh of relief and of resignation, he began moving out of his apartment.

In two hours he had moved his books and records, his two sheets and two towels, a few plates, cups and glasses, and the little record player to his parents' basement. He horsed the old mattress down the narrow stairs, Allison's clean scent in his nostrils as it pressed against his face. He tipped it into the dumpster and dashed back inside, got the last two boxes and wedged them into the passenger seat of his car, then clumped up the dark stairs for the last time. With everything cleared out, the posters off the wall, and the books gone, the room seemed tiny. He sat down on the floor by the window like he had a hundred times before. The bare branches of the oak tree flexed in the winter wind and the swaying movement across the gray sky caused his stomach to heave.

The room was suddenly too warm.

Dave opened the window a crack to let cool air in while he waited for his equilibrium to return. He saw the room as it had been. The brick and board bookcase cluttered with paperbacks. The Fillmore and Avalon and Monterey Jazz posters Allison had tacked onto the sloping ceiling. Brubeck and Getz and Monk and Davis and Gillespie and Coltrane playing on the record player. Everyone's faces as they had looked in candlelight. Mark and Jennifer, Jeff, Steve Griffin, Keith before he disappeared. And Allison.

He recalled the Indian summer nights when cool air had flowed in the window like honey along with the sound of crickets and Allison shivering as she rolled out from under the Indian blanket they'd bought at the used furniture shop.

There is no tomorrow and no yesterday, they exist only in our minds, there is only this instant, he told himself. Dave slid the window closed and eased himself to his feet. The oak tree stood as it had the day he moved in. The Bodhisattva found enlightenment under a tree, perhaps I found a little too, he thought. Then he closed the window, switched off the light, and left the room, closing the door softly behind him.

* * *

At the farm, mornings and afternoons, Mark sat at his desk in ferocious concentration. One hour on each course, then on to the next. Anything to occupy his mind. He found he was learning a little of it too. But it was not satisfying.

From time to time he would ride his Suzuki through the frozen fields just to feel the cold wind on his face. He wrote letters to Jennifer, but there was little to say. The words were always the same. They spoke on the phone twice.

But when he had exhausted his mind with his books, and riding his motorcycle in the cold had cauterized his body, when he returned to the warmth of the familiar house, thoughts would intrude, the ones he labored to ignore. Mark's father had confided to Mark that the doctors had told him, "She has only a few months left. There's nothing more we can do."

From the moment Mark heard those words, a fist of tension had been wrapped around his heart. The unspoken hope that his mother might still recover had irrevocably been taken from him.

* * *

On an overcast afternoon with snow flurries threatening, Mark couldn't stay in his room any longer. He got in his Chevy and drove aimlessly around Columbia until he found himself on Paquin Street. Allison's white Plymouth was parked in the lot behind the house.

An angel's wing of snow had recently been swept off the step by someone opening the old black screen door. As he trudged up the stairs he could hear the faint sound of a record playing—guitar and voice and violin. "...white bird, in a golden cage, in the rain..."

The door to Allison's apartment was ajar; she was crying. Mark stood motionless in the dim hallway listening to her sobbing. Then he knocked softly and pushed the door open. "Allison? It's Mark." She was lying on the print bedspread brought from her parents' house, crying and crying.

"...white bird must fly, or she will die..."

Mark picked the arm up off the record and turned the player off. "Can I help?" he said softly. He wanted to touch her, but didn't. She rolled away from him to face the wall. "That song is so melancholy," he said for lack of anything better. "You shouldn't listen to it."

There were several cardboard boxes stacked in the middle of the room. One was partly full of her clothes.

After a while she composed herself, got up and dried her tears, and set about heating water for tea. Mark sat down by the window. It had begun to snow.

Allison brought the tea and they sat on the floor facing each other. The early dusk laid a veil of snow over the streetlight.

"Dave's moving to St. Louis," Allison said. "He just told me today. He'll graduate in three weeks and then he's gone. I guess he interviewed for a job in St. Louis and they accepted him." Allison said. "He's very secretive. And selfish." She kept her cup close to her mouth. "I don't like that. I like to be right up front about things. Even unpleasant things."

The tea was good, Earl Grey, not the cinnamon accent of Constant Comment. "Sometimes I do the same thing," Mark said. "I don't say anything right away because I want to keep things as good as they can be for as long as possible. As soon as you say the bad news, it changes everything."

Allison's mouth crinkled as she began to silently cry. "Dave's leaving. My father is sick. I don't want to stay here and I don't want to go home."

The snow fell in gentle arcs across the streetlight. He visualized his parents' living room, the Christmas tree. His throat closed and he felt a tear run down his face. Put that out of mind. Focus only on this moment, this breath, and the next after that. When he had control again he found Allison lying on the bed on her side facing the wall, her hands under her face. He lay down beside her, put his arm around her. After a time her breathing became regular. They both drifted into the refuge of sleep.

In the middle of the night they got out of their clothes and under the comforter and made love without saying a word, then slept again. In the white glow from the window, Allison's expression was relaxed. Her hair was spread around her like a halo.

When Mark woke again the clock said one thirty. The snow had stopped and the streetlight painted the room with a harsher light. He kissed Allison gently and she came slowly awake. "I'm going to go," he whispered. "I need to get back to the farm. My mother is dying." He pulled his clothes on.

"I'm sorry," Allison said. "I didn't know she was so sick."

Mark had to change the subject. "You're definitely leaving?" He nodded at the boxes. "Not going to take classes after all?"

"Too many things have happened. I need to go somewhere, take time to think. I'm driving to Taos." She got up, wrapping the comforter around her, and kissed him. "Thank you," she whispered. Then she handed him his jacket. "Goodbye Mark."

He made his way down the stairs, scraped snow off his car, and drove carefully to the farm through snowy streets unmarked by any cars.

* * *

Two days later Mark was driving down University Avenue on a sparkling winter day, his mind on his Strength of Materials course, when he saw a flash of yellow in the traffic ahead. A yellow '57 Plymouth turned on Wilson Street and Mark followed. But the Plymouth turned into a driveway and a woman in a green coat got out and went into a house.

Tim's car had been that color. Freshman year they'd been cruising around, enjoying the bright spring day, when they spotted an engineless go-kart with a hand-lettered "For Sale" sign on it.

"Let's see what the guy's asking for it." Tim grinned. He still wore braces.

A young redneck in Wrangler jeans and no shirt came to the door. "Fifty bucks." They stood in a circle around it like spectators at a traffic accident. "She handles good. But I blew the engine—a piece of Jap crap."

"This motor mount's bent," Tim said. They squatted down to examine it.

"Easy to bend it back. Won't cause no problem," the kid said indifferently.

"Take twenty-five bucks?" Mark said.

"Nah," he turned to go back inside.

"Alright, here's thirty," Mark said.

They hoisted it into the trunk of Tim's Plymouth, drove to Mark's parents' farm, and set the go-kart under the carport. "Lot of good wear left on these slicks," Tim said, touching a wide rear tire with the toe of his loafer.

"I think the engine off my parents' garden tractor engine would fit." Mark nodded at the garden tractor parked nearby.

"They won't mind?"

"They won't even know. They're in Kansas City for the weekend," Mark said. "We'll put the engine back on the garden tractor Sunday before they get back."

Mark got his toolbox and a radio from the family room. "Let's have some tunes." He tuned it to KXOK. In a few minutes Tim had the belt drive disconnected and was disconnecting the throttle linkage. Mark put a socket wrench on the engine mounting bolts. They lifted the engine off the garden tractor while the radio played Jan and Dean's "Surf City."

"Slotted holes on the kart. We can adjust the mounting location, that's good," Tim said. He started bolting the engine in. "Got some shims for these bolts? They're too long."

"This lever engages the drive pulley," Mark said. "I guess that's the only gear you've got, full bore or nothing."

"Only way to live," Tim said with a laugh. But when The Shirelles' "Soldier Boy" came on the radio his expression darkened. "Don't like to hear that one." They both bent to their tasks.

In a few more minutes they were connecting the fuel line and adjusting the throttle cable. "My boyfriend's back and you're gonna be in trouble, hey la de da..." Mark sang. "Do you think that song's stupid? The Angels."

"I like Ronnie and the Daytonas," Tim said. "Bought their album the other day."

"Little GTO," Mark said. He bolted the throttle cable to the bracket on top of the engine.

Tim was lying on the concrete tightening up the steering linkage. He got up and checked that the fuel line valve was open.

"Try the clutch."

"It works. Probably a little too tight."

"It'll work itself out." They put the tools away.

"Hop in, Tim," Mark said. He pulled the starter cable a couple of times but nothing happened. "Guess it might help if I turned the switch on." Mark said. He clicked the switch to run and the engine started.

Tim made a couple of circuits of the driveway, then pulled over and climbed out and Mark did the same. It was almost dark by then, so they parked the go-kart. Mark got a couple of Pepsis and they sat on the mismatched old furniture in front of the Admiral TV and watched Patrick McGoohan in *Secret Agent*.

Afterward, they stood over the go-kart like drivers in the pits the night before Le Mans. The smell of gasoline, steel and tires blended subtly with the scent of new grass and the sound of the frogs on the pond down the hill. They talked about how great it would be too go to Europe and follow the Grand Prix circuit for a summer—the exotic machines, the drivers and sponsors, the champagne, the women.

"Well, I'd better get going," Tim said. "Want to run the kart tomorrow?"

"Yeah, in the morning. Then we need to put the engine back on the garden tractor before my parents get back."

Tim grinned and waved from the open window of his Plymouth as he sped off into the brilliant winter afternoon sunshine.

## Chapter 15

"Would you guys shut up!" Bill had crowded up to the TV until he was nearly touching it. "I can't hear."

"Who'd want to," Jennifer said. "'The Lights of Zetar.' What bullshit. Scotty's in love, fawning over miss romaine lettuce like some kid in a high school play." Jennifer got up and poured the last of her Busch down the kitchen sink, then made her way slowly back to the couch and sat down with a sigh. Mark tried to think of an excuse for taking her back to the dorm early but could think of nothing that wouldn't cause an explosion. He got up and got a Busch from the solid phalanx of blue and white beer cans on the bottom shelf of the refrigerator. Sav-Mor had Busch on sale for $2.40 a six-pack and Mark and Bill had splurged, planning on a pleasant evening at home with lots of beer and *Star Trek*. Jennifer's attitude had taken all that away from them.

"You could have offered me one," Jennifer whispered loudly when he sat back down. Bill studiously focused on the alien energy cloud that was killing people on space station *Memory Alpha*.

Mark got up and brought Jennifer a beer, which she set on the side table unopened.

"If you don't want one why did you ask for one? When you poured the last one out I assumed…"

"You assume a lot, Mark. But you never ask. All you think about is you. Never me."

"I'm thinking about you now, wondering what the problem

is. It's a cold night, I thought we could have a nice evening at home."

She raised her eyebrows without taking her eyes off the TV. "You call this home?" The *Enterprise* faded to a Pepto-Bismol commercial.

"I'm going outside," Jennifer announced. "I need some fresh air." She pulled on her coat and stomped out into the dark.

Bill rolled over on the floor. "Having a good time are we?"

"Yeah. I can't figure out why she's been so irritable the last few weeks. Real emotional. But it comes and goes. Last week we had a great time. Tonight, she's some kind of alien life form that I would like to beam out of here." He shrugged. "I'd better go chase her down."

"She might not want that."

"She probably doesn't. But it will be worse if I ignore her. You're smart to date around. Never go steady."

There were no streetlights in the trailer park, no moon out in the cold clear sky. "At least there's no wind," Mark muttered and started off down the sidewalk. He caught up with Jennifer at the corner. He walked beside her for a while. Her meandering pace was infuriating but he kept his peace. "Would you like to talk?" he said eventually.

They walked further and passed what Mark had always thought of as the redneck section of Woodstock—pickup trucks littered with tools and 7-11 coffee cups, kids' toys abandoned in yards, rusty Plymouths with engines removed.

"Is it something I'm doing that's bothering you?"

She said nothing.

I hate this, he thought. Does being in touch with your feelings mean it's okay to act like some spoiled brat, sulking and making yourself look pitiful.

"No," she said finally.

They walked another block. Well, Mark thought, that

doesn't give me a whole lot to go on.

"Is it school, or your parents?"

She stopped. A cold wind blew between the trailers and the parked cars.

"Look, Mark, why don't you go back inside. This isn't helping, having you grill me over why I feel the way I do."

She was making little neck motions that meant her ears were cold, nestling first one then the other into her collar.

"Why don't we go back inside where it's warm?" Mark suggested. "We could talk..."

"Not with Bill there."

"We could go somewhere, go get a cup of coffee somewhere."

"You go back. Go on back inside. You like that drivel. Watch your TV show, make jokes with Bill. You don't need me." She started across the street.

Jesus. Why do I put up with this? Mark thought. He crossed to her.

"I told you to go on back," she said. "I know you're cold out here. This is...I just want to think for a while. I'll be back inside in a minute."

This is bullshit, he thought. Usually she's the one who has to get in out of the cold immediately. Sometimes she overdoes that Florida-native image she likes so well.

He started back to the trailer, then froze. Is she pregnant? No, the pills will prevent that. He looked up at crystalline stars in a black sky. Not since after Thanksgiving. When she started taking birth control pills. That's it—the pills are causing these mood swings. Now what? I want to have sex with her, I don't want her pregnant, but I don't want her so moody.

He stood there shivering, staring at the constellations; Orion was clear and bright. He picked out the Big and Little Dippers and the North Star. His mind drifted to the old science fiction books he kept in his room at the farm. *Secret of the*

*Martian Moons*. He remembered asking his parents to buy it for him when he was ten years old. They'd been browsing through a little bookstore in Prairie Village on a trip to visit his grandparents in Kansas City.

When he'd found that book on the shelf, the bright cover picture had fired his imagination. The mysterious enemies in baggy spacesuits about to attack a guy taking cargo out of the hatch of a shuttle craft on Deimos. The book he always kept beside it on his bookcase was *Trouble on Titan*, the front cover showing a rocket sled passing through a ravine, an explosion nearby, hurrying back to the dome city on Titan where the hero's father was working to keep the ruthenium mines operational. On the back cover a photo of Alan E. Nourse in a plaid shirt, smoking a pipe, sitting at his typewriter.

I want both of those things, Mark thought. I want to go into space, see Mars and walk on the lunar surface. And I want the farmhouse, the smell of coffee in the morning. I want to look out the window at the bright leaves of autumn in the familiar sweep of lawn and sit in a book-lined study, reading, with all the time in the world.

He felt warmth beside him. Jennifer took his arm. "Let's go inside. It's cold out here." They sat close together in silence as *Star Trek* ended, then disappeared into the bedroom and lay together but did not make love. He felt a tear roll down her cheek, then another one. "I'm sorry," she said in a trembling voice.

He soothed her and she dozed for a while. At ten thirty he woke her gently. "Time to get you back to the dorm."

Looking wan and exhausted, Jennifer huddled shivering in the cold car. Mark tapped and tapped on the heater but it refused to come on. He parked and turned off the engine.

"Can we still see each other?"

"Of course," Mark said. He walked her to the door. She felt warm on his arm. Inside she didn't wave, but hurried up the stairs.

He drove down Providence Road to the highway, still thinking of his old science fiction books on the shelf in his room. At Wilkes Boulevard he made a U-turn and drove back to the trailer.

* * *

Thursday morning Mark woke to the sound of the door closing. Bill was leaving for his early class. Mark had the trailer to himself. He made a cup of Constant Comment and sat at the dining table watching the clouds spitting snow. Tuesday and Thursday were his easy days—no Thermo, no Machine Design, just his English Literature class and his Materials Science course which was all lecture, easy and interesting. The difficult classes were Mondays, Wednesdays, and Fridays and Mark reminded himself he had homework due in two of them. He would do it tonight. But for now, he put all thoughts out of his mind and settled into his Lit book, the scent of tea in the air and the snowy day outside. After a moment he went into his bedroom and took down the small wooden box that held the remains of a baggie of pot, a packet of EZ Widers, and a piece of tinfoil. Inside the wrinkled foil were two small white tablets, the last of the psilocybin Rich had sold him. If Jennifer won't join me, I'll take the trip alone. He swallowed one.

He opened the textbook to page nine forty-one and the words flowed images through his mind like liquid fire. He began to mumble aloud "...standing in god's holy fire, as in the gold mosaic of a wall..." He finished the poem and sat staring at the blowing snow outside, the words neatly printed on the page, the clock ticking on the wall, and felt completely a part of the universe, extending out to infinity, then back in time to the original big bang. He brought himself back to the present by sipping his tea. Some thoughts were too big. He simultaneously felt like he was floating above the chair and sinking into it. He looked at the clock on the kitchen wall, reminding himself he needed to leave for class in an hour.

His eye followed the delicate lines the intermittent snowflakes traced across the gray sky. They came from nowhere and moved in beautiful arcs across the sky and the dark frozen lawn. He could see the dark ground slowly becoming white with the accumulating snow. It was incredibly beautiful. He felt his oneness with natural processes. He got up, carefully aware of the infinite detail in everything in the kitchen, the cheap Formica and chrome tubing chairs and dining table. The worn beige carpet and dark blue couch seemed well-made articles of great value. He clicked on Bill's record player, put the Lovin' Spoonful album back in its jacket, and started *Rubber Soul*. The easy rhythmic chords of "Michelle" fit the pattern of snow blowing across the sky perfectly. Mark was careful to keep all negative thoughts out of his mind, and it was easy now. He was in synch with the cosmos. Everything was an infinitely complex whole fitted together to work mysteriously but beautifully—the snow swirling past, the paneling of the trailer, the cup of tea in front of him, the music playing softly, the book, the Formica tabletop, and the words flowing up from Yeats' "Byzantium."

When it was time to go he turned the record player off, pulled on his coat, and went out to start his car and let it warm up. The cold air made him shiver, but as much with joy as with cold. He set his Lit book and MU notebook on the black and white vinyl seat cover and ran his hand over the textures, feeling their variety and sturdiness. He felt he could see inside the parts of the car, the seats, the dashboard, the engine idling. It was incredibly beautiful. He loved the materialness of it all. He savored the thought of being part of teams designing and manufacturing these machines, perhaps on snowy days like this. An entire life story passed through his mind, an alternate universe of years came and went in a moment as he sat in the cold car. He saw himself working, the successes and challenges, the gleaming final products; it wasn't clear if they were cars or spaceships or machines of other kinds. The office camaraderie, the clean technical books and tools and computers, the drawings with elegance as great as the greatest works of art. His comfortable home, living room with Mondrian and Gauguin reproductions on the walls, sitting with his wife by the fireplace on a snowy day like this one. They were deeply in love. Mark looked into her brown eyes, eyes just like Jennifer's, but her features were different, different but the same, endlessly changing but changing back into the same beautiful features.

* * *

Mark drove to campus carefully, even though his reflexes felt fine and he was incredibly aware of everything around him. This wasn't like drinking at all. There was little traffic. He parked and walked down a slushy sidewalk to the Arts and Sciences Building. The mat inside the door was soaked from wet shoes tracking across it. Mark pulled his eyes away from it and focused on the yellow-painted concrete block stairwell. He went up to the third floor and took his usual seat near the window. He was early, only three other students were there. He put his books down and hung his coat on the coat rack. The view was even better from the classroom on the third floor—snow blowing gently across the pale yellow bricks of the next building. A girl came in wearing a red sweater and blue jeans. She hung up her coat and sat down at the desk just in front of Mark. Her hair was braided into a yellow-gold ponytail, shiny and incredibly beautiful.

Mark drifted through the class, listening but saying nothing. He came away feeling like he had sampled the wisdom of the ages.

* * *

The following Saturday Mark and Jennifer sat at the window table in the Heidelberg watching students trudge by through the slush, heads down, into the wind.

"Is this the Necronomicon?" Jennifer touched the orange cover of Mark's Thermodynamics textbook lying between them on the table.

"Yes," Mark warmed his hands on his coffee cup. "And this is the new me," he touched the book. "This semester I have my course of study all laid out. I'll work my way through this stuff, pass the course, and get on with life."

He had persuaded her to join him that afternoon on her break between classes, a peace offering, a gesture toward forgetting last weekend's unhappiness. He glanced at the wintery sky. "Of course once spring gets here and the outdoors start calling me, well, we'll see." She remained withdrawn. "But, having said that, I like winter. It makes being inside feel cozy and pleasant."

Jeff strolled up. "I thought I saw you two. I heard from Griffin yesterday," he said. "He's at Oakland Navy Base." Jeff ordered coffee. "I remember him furtively carrying his uniform in a gym bag, changing clothes in the locker room just before his ROTC class. I guess the longhairs gave him a lot of hassle."

"But he stuck to it," Mark said, "finished the course, got his commission. He never had any doubt about where he was going." A flash of autumn colors, the afternoon at Steve's parents' house cutting up firewood on a perfect autumn day, MU Tiger football on the radio. Steve's father in the house laughing over a book he was reading upstairs. Steve's face, gold in the firelight at Village Inn Pizza, and how his expression had changed talking about the war in Vietnam. But, as Heinlein had taught them, "Eventually you have to look into your mind and decide what's right and what's wrong, and then do it. Nobody can decide it for you."

"Remember all those stories he kept telling us about his summer training at camp Lejeune," Jeff continued. "You could tell he liked the idea of being in the Navy."

"I think he liked the idea of doing the right thing, the honorable thing. He's clear about where he's going and where that puts him in the political spectrum."

"Yeah, a little too clear and too far right for my taste," Jeff said morosely. "He gets a few beers in him and he comes on too right wing for this time and place."

Jennifer looked at her watch.

"Do we need to go?" Mark said.

"I can walk. My class starts in thirty minutes, but if you two are going to talk politics…"

"I'm sorry," Jeff said quickly. "We can talk about something else."

Jennifer stood up and got her coat. "No, I've got to go." She waved and hurried out into the wind.

"Sorry," Jeff told Mark. "She's got a Saturday class?"

"Literature workshop. The professor critiques student writing. They read your stuff out loud and Jennifer doesn't think hers is any good. That on top of the real problem."

"You?" Jeff joked.

"Partly yeah. But mostly it's the birth control pills she's taking. Her brother helped her get them last Thanksgiving in Florida. The sex is good, but man oh man, it puts her emotions on a roller coaster ride."

Jeff smirked. "You lucky dog. No rubbers."

Mark snorted. "Yeah, but she's moody as hell. Good thing she left, actually, she's been looking for an opportunity to give you some grief about the way you treated Stephanie."

Jeff bristled. "I didn't do anything to Steph. We went out a few times, had some fun. It's over. She was fine with that. I think."

Mark held up a hand. "I know, you're right. But Jennifer feels bad because she went to great lengths to get Steph to go out with you, then after a few dates you call it off. Them being roommates makes things a little delicate, you know."

"Hey man, I graduated, moved to St. Louis."

"Forget it. Tell me about Griffin," said Mark.

"Nothing to tell, just got a card inviting us to visit him before he shipped out next August."

"Let's go," Mark said, "as soon as the semester ends. Oh yeah, you graduated and moved to St. Louis. And you're working full time." Mark set his coffee cup down. "Speaking of which, why do I see you back here in Columbia a lot of weekends, just hanging around campus? Like now." Mark toasted Jeff with his coffee cup. "You've got a good job with McDonnell. In a few years and you'll get married, buy a house in Webster Groves, and have two kids, two dogs, two cars, two wives."

Jeff forced a smile. "Yeah." The Heidelberg was warm with the pleasant smell of coffee and breakfast food. Outside the wind buffeted bare trees.

"You don't seem very happy about it. Got doubts?" Mark questioned.

"Yeah."

"You shouldn't. You made a good choice, got you out of the draft and into a solid career. A lot of guys who majored in Political Science can't find jobs. I heard them talking last semester in Wollheim's class. And look at Professor Wollheim himself. Out on the street with no tenure. I saw Carol the other day. She told me about it." Mark raised an eyebrow at Jeff. "Yes, the beautiful Carol. She's still around. She graduated and went into grad school. Economics."

Jeff changed the subject, but Mark noticed he seemed to brighten a little. "I do want a wife, a house, two kids, and a dog. I want to have a reasonable income, live in the suburbs, be a respected member of the community, have a family, the way my parents lived."

"Marry Carol?" asked Mark.

"She's got her own agenda."

"I thought that socialist democratic stuff was your agenda too."

"It is. In fact I'm going to be coming back here weekends, helping her with it. She's organizing a march on the state capitol. This spring."

Mark laughed out loud. "You sneaky dog. You've been coming down here to see Carol. How long has this been going on?"

"Don't give me that bullshit. I'm not 'seeing' Carol. I just work at the *Columbia Free Press*. It's important. You should think about the issues more. You're still just stuck in sex, drugs, and rock and roll."

"Right on." Mark raised his fist in the power salute.

"Don't shrug it off. Social change is important. Don't be like Dave and talk about social change all the time, but then secretly take the easy way out."

"Yeah. I ran across his dad in Westlake's. He told me Dave was working for the Army in St. Louis—LogCom, Logistics Command. Which got him a nice stable income and a draft deferment." Mark covered his hurt feelings. "After all his talk about grad school and living the simple life, he sneaks off and goes to work for the military-industrial complex. Remember his talk about how too much government involvement in the economy was inefficient? Now he's part of it."

Jeff held his coffee cup in both hands right at lip level, taking machine-like little sips. "He left Allison behind, I assume?" Mark opened his mouth to speak, then shut it. Jeff set his empty coffee cup down. "Got to go." He paused. "This stuff Carol is doing is important. Get involved, Mark."

## Chapter 16

Mark kicked the Suzuki to life and rode through the evening rush hour traffic to the Suzuki shop on Business 70. The traffic's hot breath felt good in the cold air. But it felt better to step into the bright warm showroom with its perfume of new motorcycles. The guy in the parts room was singing along with the radio, "...I am a lineman for the county…" then he popped his Linda-haired head up from behind the counter. "Help you?"

"I need a set of points for a two hundred cc Suzuki X-6"

"What year?"

"'63."

While the guy looked through the parts bins, Mark strolled around the new motorcycles, clean and bright, yellow and black and chrome. Beautiful, but ever since he'd bought his Suzuki a year ago, his enthusiasm for motorcycles had diminished. Anticipation was sometimes better than reality. He looked at himself in a rearview mirror. And sometimes the anticipation of Jennifer is better than the actuality. "That's unkind," he told his reflection.

"Is this what you need?" The guy held up a set of points in its little clear plastic bag.

Mark examined it. "Yeah, that's it."

"You can roll your bike into the shop and install them here if you want," the guy said.

"Great. Thanks. It's cold outside." Mark rolled his bike into the shop bay and in a few minutes had the old points out and the new ones in. The owner even helped him set the gap.

Then he had just enough time to ride his bike back to the trailer, get the grease off his hands, and drive his Chevy back to Columbia College to pick up Jennifer. The radio said the snow would not materialize; instead it would be clear and colder, temperature in the twenties.

The circle drive in front of North Hall was crowded with cars this Friday night. The two girls at the reception desk looked him over officiously while the other guys waiting for their dates avoided each other's eyes.

"Jennifer Campion please, room two-oh-two."

In a minute Jennifer came down the stairs wearing her big coat with the loop buttons and a blue miniskirt. She had trouble signing out with her purse and her huge black and red Carnaby Street shopping bag in her hands.

"No problem signing out for the weekend?" he asked as they drove to the trailer.

"No," she smiled and took his arm. "Did Bill and Jeff leave for the weekend?"

Mark hugged her. "We've got the trailer to ourselves. Did you bring that Judy Collins album?"

"Right here."

The trailer was quiet and felt cozy with Jennifer there and both his roommates gone. Mark peered out the window of the trailer as though checking for spies. There were a few flakes of snow in the air. Jennifer busied herself putting her shopping bag of overnight things in the bedroom and hanging up both their coats. She set a little red and gold box of Constant Comment tea on the kitchen counter. "I love the smell of this tea."

Mark put a record on the record player and they sat at the kitchen table holding hands while the water heated for tea. "...to say I love you right out loud..." Jennifer sang along. "I do, you know," she added. Mark kissed her.

They sat sipping their tea and watching a few errant flakes

of snow blowing past the street light. "...something's lost and something's gained in living every day..."

"I love being inside, with you, when the weather's bad outside," Mark said. "I want us to have this same feeling of being at home together no matter where we are. Like London, say, with cold rain outside." He pushed her long black hair back behind her ear, took her glasses off, and kissed her. Their lips stuck slightly as he pulled back.

They made dinner and listened to Mozart. Mark read some Thomas Gray, then some Andrew Marvell poetry. She read some verse from Blake's "Auguries of Innocence" and then picked up the battered copy of *Selected Poems of Robert Frost* she was reading for Lit class. Mark pointed at the cover, Frost's craggy New England face. "The stuff he talks about. A cabin deep in snowy woods. How perfect it could be. Deep in the country, just you and me. So far away from everything, everyone, no one would ever find us."

She put the book down. "Who would we be hiding from? You talk about living deep in the country, seeing nobody, but we both like spending time with our friends."

Mark's eyebrows rose. "Just a figure of speech." He drew back to study her expression. "I guess it seems like a paradise that we can't attain. Instead I'll be in the Army with people all around. And you'll be far away."

She slid closer. "I love you, Mark. I do want to spend all the time we can together. Sometimes it's good to be by ourselves, but sometimes it's good to be with other people. Our friends and our families. I still haven't met your parents."

Mark nodded. "And I haven't met yours."

"But yours are right here in Columbia, mine are in Florida." She patted his hand. He felt his eyes evading, tried to keep them steady on her warm brown eyes.

"My mother is ill..." He turned his head to the side and stopped talking about that dark future. "I haven't been able to find the right time for you to meet her."

"I'm sorry. I knew something was on your mind a lot recently. I assumed it was your Thermo course," she said, still sitting close. "Did you pass the course?"

"Flunked it," Mark said with a smile. "So I'm taking it again this semester." He went into his room, got his grade report, and handed it to her.

"An A in Politics and Economics, two Cs, two Bs, and...an F," she read, then handed it back looking surprised and a little embarrassed by this sudden glimpse into his private life. "I know you've told me you love engineering, Mark, but you are so much better at the softer sciences that sometimes I wonder why you take courses like Thermo."

"Maybe part of it is the challenge. To force myself into the discipline to learn things that are not easy." He stroked her hair and changed the subject. "I didn't tell you that I really appreciate you and your brother getting that Ovulin. I know it makes it hard on you, but I really, really like the fact we can make love when we feel like it, without using rubbers."

She smiled a bright clear smile. "I think I'm getting used to it. Maybe the worst of it is past. I only really feel it at the beginning of the cycle."

"And another thing I appreciate you doing for me is watching *Star Trek*. I know you hate that show."

"I don't hate it."

"I won't ask you to watch it with me every week."

"Good."

"But, then again," Mark made a show of checking his watch, which he wasn't wearing. "Well, I hesitate to bring this up, but it is on this evening, starting in ten minutes."

They watched *Star Trek* and afterward Mark said, "Sometimes it's good to watch these simple stories, like this one: 'Requiem for Methuselah.' Think about being immortal, and creating the perfect woman." He hugged Jennifer. "Like you. And then finding out she has a mind of her own. Also, like you. It's a tragedy."

"Baloney."

Mark poured them each a glass of Mateus. "I know, it's just a network TV show, but I sometimes think about what the writers are trying to say. Like in this one, the sadness of outliving someone you love."

Jennifer hugged him. "That won't happen."

Mark sipped his wine and said nothing. He got up and turned the TV off and put on Bill's Lovin' Spoonful record.

"Another thing, Jennifer," he continued. "I won't keep asking you to drop acid with me. In fact I think I'm done with that stuff myself."

She got up and paced the living room. "I'm afraid of LSD. Afraid of what it would do to me and what it will do to you." She turned back to him. "Can I ask you something, Mark?" He nodded. "Is it your grades, or the draft, or your mother's illness that causes you to sort of compartment your life? Like keeping me out of some parts of it. If it's none of my business, we don't have to talk about it."

He started to make a glib reply, but changed in mid-sentence. "I want to keep the good things good. Keep the things I love always the same and keep the bad things out of my mind as much as possible. If I talk about them it makes it worse. I guess that makes me seem secretive, or compartmentalized."

Jennifer sat down on the couch again. "We've known each other a year," she said slowly. "I know you know you can trust me with your feelings, even the bad ones."

"Yes," he said as much to himself as to her. "I'll try not to do it so much. It's not because of lack of trust."

Then they smoked a joint, drank the rest of the Mateus, and talked about all the things they would do in the years to come. The places they would go—Nepal and the Greek islands, New York City, Australia, Egypt and Africa. And after every adventure, every trip, come home to a house deep in the country.

"It would be so neat to have a fireplace on evenings like this," Jennifer said.

"Neat?" Mark said with a smile. They sat on the floor in candle light. Mark had the pot spread out on the record album cover, rolling a joint. The dry leaves seemed to blend into John Sebastian's and Zally Yanovsky's grins.

"Remember that two story house we saw last fall when we were riding the bike around country roads? Mark licked the joint. "It was for sale. Twenty-seven thousand dollars. We could get some people together, buy it."It would be great—walking the woods, cutting firewood, reading..."

He felt her warmth, the scent of her Chantilly perfume. "We need time, time to be together, not just weekends. I want to have the time to talk about all the things we want to talk about. And to read a book slowly, all the way through, savor the language and the imagery. Not like now, read fast, pass a test."

They made love in his tiny bed in the light of a single candle. Afterward, they weren't sleepy so they got back up. Jennifer put a Leonard Cohen record on. "...you can hear the boats go by, you can stay the night beside her..."

Mark turned off the lights in the living room. In the bleak streetlight outside, the snow had stopped, the night looked clear and cold. Mark brought the candle out to the living room. The flame stilled and flickered, stilled and flickered. They lay together on the couch, not speaking, not making love, but fully and completely happy.

"...and you know that she can trust you, because you've touched her perfect body with your mind..."

## Chapter 17

The next day Mark made some tea in the early morning dimness. He played the Leonard Cohen album very softly "... tea and oranges that come all the way from China..." While the water heated he leafed through the poetry books on the couch. He looked up and Jennifer was standing shyly at the bedroom door, smiling as softly as the Madonna. She was dressed in white Levi's and an MU sweatshirt. "I smelled the tea."

They read and drank tea, went to IHOP for breakfast and lingered over eggs and bacon. They stopped by Sav-Mor to buy some food and beer and a bottle of Mateus, then went back to the trailer. The TV news said the temperature was twenty-seven degrees.

"It's going to be cold," Jennifer said wistfully. "Maybe we could just take your car."

"No, let's go on the bike. It'll be an adventure." They bundled up and rode east on I-70 in the bitter cold. After fifteen miles he turned north on County Road A. A few miles of two lane road and they reached the town of Mason. "There's a café," Jennifer shouted in Mark's ear. "Let's get inside and warm up."

The old café had high ceilings, a worn wooden floor, and a woodstove burning in the back corner. Stiff with cold, they sat down on cracked red vinyl bar stools. "Coffee?" The plain woman behind the counter poured it into heavy white porcelain cups. She was smiling. "You folks must be near froze."

"That's for sure," Mark said. "How far is it to Benton City?"

"About twenty miles straight up Route A."

Jennifer went to the restroom.

"Your wife's lookin' pretty peaked. Her gloves are way too thin."

Mark grinned. "Yeah, it's a lot colder than we thought it would be."

The lady rummaged around under the counter, looking for something. "Harold, get me a pair of those thermal gloves." A stolid man in overalls rummaged through the racks of shovels, buckets, bags of seed and fertilizer, pipe fittings, bins of nails and screws and turned up a heavy pair of brown gloves. "Not them, the white ones, next shelf under," the woman said.

Jennifer came back and wrapped her hands around her coffee cup. Harold laid a pair of thick white cotton gloves on the counter. "Try these, sweetie," the woman said. "Put them on over your leather gloves. This kind of weather, my hands get real cold. Feet too," she said.

"Yeah, she wears two pairs of socks in bed." Harold said. She gave him a look and he shuffled off to fiddle with the fire in the woodstove.

Mark and Jennifer finished their coffee. "How much for the coffee and the gloves?" asked Mark.

She pushed a key on the ancient mechanical cash register. "Fifty cents for the coffee. Take the gloves as a gift." The woman waved her hand at them. "Come back and see us some time, on a day when it ain't so cold."

The last few miles to Benton City were better. The afternoon sun was a bright smear of orange behind gray clouds. Mark had liked the way "your wife" had sounded when the woman said it. He wondered what it would be like to move into a house, that one, the old two story white house on the neat farm, to live and work in a tiny community like Benton City and spend winter days cutting firewood, and evenings in front of the fireplace drinking hot tea and reading the classics.

Larry Mitchell and his wife Brenda were elementary school teachers at Benton City Elementary School.

Larry had seemed eager to have them visit. Over-eager in fact, and had repeated the directions three times when Mark had talked with him the week before. It was easy to find the Mitchell's neat brick ranch-style house in this tiny town of fifteen hundred people.

* * *

Larry's Mustang was parked beside a blue Ford in the driveway. Dinner was roast beef, green beans and potatoes. It was too much food, and since Mark was having difficulty finding things to talk about with Larry, he ate much more than he had intended to. They played Scrabble after dinner and Brenda won. Larry did not take it well and compensated for that sting by a stream of overloud jokes. Finally, Brenda showed Mark and Jennifer to the picture-perfect bedroom they would be using, but they lay a long time, not able to fall asleep, not wanting to make love, afraid to even whisper in the silent house.

The next morning Brenda made bacon and eggs with toast. She wanted to show them the school where she and Larry worked, which Larry made clear he was not enthusiastic about. But there was nothing else to do on a Sunday morning, so Mark and Jennifer insisted and he capitulated with bad grace. "We usually go to church," Brenda confided as they drove down Main Street. "Just for something to do. That's where you get to talk to your neighbors. Most people who live here work on farms outside of town or have jobs in Columbia. There's nobody around during the day."

The school was a pleasant looking, no-nonsense brick building with a big Benton City Consolidated School District sign in front. Their shoes squeaked on buffed linoleum as they walked down the dark corridor to Brenda's room. The smell of the school was the same one Mark remembered from his own elementary school days. Brenda clicked on the lights in her classroom and chattered on about the children's projects on a side table, the children's art taped up over the windows, and the stories in the textbook she was using to teach reading. Larry planted himself in the chair behind the teacher's desk and stared out the window.

As Brenda walked down the rows of empty desks she would touch this one or that, almost as if the child were there. "Sammy is a happy kid, but this one, Alfred, is so quiet I worry. Arthur is the class clown, Donny is a melancholy little guy, Marcie is a little bit of a bully and a tattletale, and Angela is a studious girl, like I was. She absolutely amazed me last November with her project on the solar system. Her parents had helped her make a mobile."

Outside, whirls of wind blew little cyclones of dry leaves into the corner of the building. Clouds were coming up over the western horizon. They moved down the hall to Larry's classroom. He reluctantly opened the door, but remained in the corridor while Brenda, Mark and Jennifer made a quick circuit around the room. Jennifer paused at a terrarium near the window. Mark saw it held a tiny tortoise stolidly attempting to walk up the glass without any progress whatsoever.

In Brenda's Ford, they made a circuit past the Quik-Stop and the auto parts store, the gas station, the feed and seed store, and another Quik-Stop. Then they were out of town. They drove down straight roads around flat square fields tilled bare and waiting for spring planting. Larry turned down the long driveway that led to an old two-story farmhouse, abandoned and falling into ruin. He insisted they explore it. "No telling what kind of valuable stuff we'll find." He pulled up in the weedy yard in front of sagging steps. "Besides, it'll make a good photograph." At dinner the night before, Larry mentioned he had taken up photography, but he had not offered to show them either his camera or any of his photos.

They hurried through the cold wind to the porch. The front door gaped open. "Larry can use the darkroom at school," Brenda said. Her look indicated she had been told to be supportive of his hobbies. Mark wondered what else he might be using the darkroom for.

While Brenda wandered through the parlor and Larry banged around in the wrecked kitchen, Mark and Jennifer cautiously made their way up the narrow staircase to a bedroom. The wallpaper was still bright, except for a large water stain in one corner where the roof was leaking. It had been a child's bedroom.

Jennifer touched a row of blue bunnies in the wallpaper. There was a horizontal mark along one wall. "That's where the crib used to be," Jennifer said. She and Mark looked at the abandoned room and its cheerful wallpaper now stained and peeling. Mark could feel the people that had lived and been happy here. He noticed Jennifer's eyes were brimming. "Where do you think these people are today?" she whispered.

Mark started to make a bad joke about pumping gas at the Quick-Stop, but caught himself. He took her in his arms, but she did not return his hug. After a moment he pulled back and they stood side by side at the window, staring at frozen fields that stretched away to a featureless horizon. The clouds were growing thicker. "This kind of farming is a dying way of life," Mark said.

Jennifer looked at him and at the bleak scene outside the dirty window. "I don't think I can live deep in the country. And I don't think you could either."

Larry's banging and clattering continued. He seemed to be kicking each bit of rubble he encountered. Then came the sound of smashing glass. Mark and Jennifer made their way downstairs where they found Larry standing in the living room admiring the remains of a broken window. "Finished it off," he said proudly, ignoring Brenda's look of disgust.

The four of them trudged back to the car, Larry whining, "This place is just going to get torn down anyway. This kind of farming is dying, big farms are taking over. Nobody will ever live in this house again." The four of them stood beside the car looking this way and that. The wind was cold; clouds now formed a solid gray cover to the horizon behind the Benton City water tank. They tried to think of something to do but nothing sounded interesting. Eventually Mark made up a flimsy excuse that he and Jennifer needed to get back to Columbia early to do some studying, and the Mitchells accepted the excuse.

The Suzuki ran smoothly down the blacktop roads, but at the last curve before the intersection with the highway at Kingdom City, the engine started sputtering and eventually quit. Mark pushed it up into the entrance to a farmer's field. "Points get wet. Can't get the cover sealed up right." He and Jennifer walked half a mile to a truck stop on the highway and phoned Bill. When he got there they loaded the Suzuki into the trunk of his black '63 Chevy and drove back to the trailer.

"So, how was your trip?" Bill asked.

"Bleak. I don't think Larry is making a very good elementary school teacher."

"Or a very good husband," Jennifer added.

"At least not in that small town," Mark said. He helped Bill get the bike out of the trunk of the car and they went inside for hot cups of Constant Comment tea.

"It's a shame," Jennifer added. "Because it's obvious Brenda likes it all, the teaching, the children, living in a nice house in a small community, and being married."

"She just picked the wrong guy to do it with," Mark said.

"Is Larry that guy with the green Mustang?" Bill asked.

"That's the guy."

"No offense, but I always thought he was kind of a jerk."

"He is a jerk," Jennifer said. "He got what he said he wanted and now he doesn't like it." Mark nodded, but he remembered cruising around with Larry one September two years ago. Larry had just gotten back from a summer in Ft. Lauderdale, working as a waiter at some beachfront hotel. He was sun-tanned and cool. They would shoot pool at the table downstairs in the Student Commons while Larry's date Candy sat watching and looking luscious.

* * *

Mark ran across Rod at the Heidelberg two nights later. The senior member of the skydiving team, who looked like the ex-Marine he was, ran a hand over his buzz-cut hair and ordered beer for both of them.

"You handled that malfunction in Florida pretty well. I don't remember if I told you that."

"It happened fast," Mark said. "My training took over, I was just acting by instinct."

"That's what good training is for." Rod grinned. "When the tough times come, and they will, you react, and you react right. There's never time to think about it."

"Thanks." Mark drank a slug of beer.

Rod laughed out loud. "So what's the problem? You look like somebody ran over your pet dog. Grades? The draft? Women?"

"All the above."

Rod laughed again, loud and long, drawing dirty looks from other booths. "I can't give you advice on women. I went over to Vietnam, got divorced as soon as I was back. But the other stuff, grades and the draft—I'll tell you what I think: you make up your mind and then you do it. You just grit your teeth and you get it done. There's no sense whining and complaining. And nobody can do it for you."

Rod finished his beer and nodded to the waitress. "Another

round, sweet thing."

"Easy for you to say. You've done your military time. You came home."

Rod admired the fresh glasses of golden beer. "Home? You can never go home. Just ain't possible, no matter how much you want it. Best if you don't even try. Back in Vietnam, when the time came for me to go on R&R, my wife wanted to fly over to Hong Kong from Sacramento and spend a week together. She'd go shopping for clothes and jewelry. After six months in the bush, this was just after Pleiku, all I wanted was to go with my buddies to the bars and hookers in Thailand." He laughed again. "I wrote to Mary and told her, 'I'm going to Bangkok. When I get back to the States, we'll get on with our lives if you want to. And if you don't want to, that's alright too.' I never got a single letter from her after that. When I got off the plane in Sacramento, the divorce papers were waiting for me. I've never spoken to her since."

"Sorry to hear that," said Mark.

"Don't be. To tell you the truth, I don't miss her, and she probably doesn't miss me now. While I was overseas I changed, and maybe not for the better. We're better off apart." Rod finished his beer. "Got to go. Let's go skydiving. How about this Saturday?"

"It's winter, Rod. If it's thirty degrees on the ground it'll be zero degrees at ten thousand feet."

"Don't be a pansy-ass. I've got old man Karsch coming out to fly the plane at ten Saturday morning, but can't find anybody else who wants to go."

Mark grinned. "Alright. I'll be there. Ten o'clock Saturday."

* * *

Saturday morning was cold, freezing cold under a high overcast. But Rod was there as planned. Old man Karsch, bundled into an insulated flying suit with full head cover and ski mask, taxied the plane over from its parking place. Rod and Mark got aboard and old man Karsch shook his head and mouthed something about idiots, then taxied out to the deserted runway and took off. They spiraled upward in roaring silence. Mark was shivering, but the frigid wind also felt good—clean and clear, blowing all uncertainty away.

At five thousand feet the pilot turned upwind, leveled the plane, and came across the drop zone. Rod signaled, Karsch cut the power, and Rod stepped out on the strut and pushed away into freefall.

Karsch looked back at Mark expectantly, but Mark got to his knees and shouted in Karsch's ear. "I changed my mind. I want to go higher, twelve thousand."

The pilot shook his head but pushed the throttle back in and the plane climbed steadily higher. Mark leaned close again. "As high as we can go. Fourteen thousand if we can make it."

"You crazy?"

"Go on up," Mark said. The icy wind against his face felt like clarity itself.

The plane roared toward the formless gray ceiling of clouds still far above them. The rate-of-climb indicator was sinking slowly as the plane approached its service ceiling. Mark stared at the flat countryside below them, a pattern of dark squares frosted in white.

Eventually the altimeter said fourteen thousand feet. "That's it!" the pilot shouted into Mark's ear, pointing at the rate of climb indicator. "She won't go no higher." Mark nodded and waited while Karsch lined the plane up on the drop zone.

After a moment more, Mark nodded to the pilot. He pulled the throttle back and settled the plane into a glide. Mark stepped carefully out into the roaring wind. He hesitated on the strut, not in fear, but in anticipation. Almost three miles of clear air below his boots. Then he pushed off and fell away into silence.

The rush of air cradled him in its frigid palm. Below him

Columbia was indistinguishable in the mottled black and white winterscape. The horizon was impossibly distant. His mind was empty, yet fully engaged. He felt no emotion, only the rushing icy wind, the limitless horizon, the gray and white world flat and motionless below him. His altimeter wound steadily down as he fell alone through the sky. Straight down, drawing a line toward the earth.

When his altimeter said twenty-five hundred feet he formed himself into stable position and pulled the ripcord. His chute billowed out with a swoop and he hung in silence, drifting toward the frozen drop zone. He saw Rod waiting by his car, then watched old man Karsch expertly land the plane and taxi to his tie-down spot.

Mark did a neat stand-up landing, wrapped his chute in his arms, and put it in the back seat of his car.

Rod sauntered over. "Nice up there isn't it?"

Mark nodded.

# Chapter 18

Mark knew something had gone out of him, frozen out by an empty room in a desolate house under a glowering winter sky, driven out by a long fall through winter air toward a black and white world below. Burned out by Rod's words at the Heidelberg, "You can never go home, not really."

He blocked everything from his mind. Every night for the last two weeks of the semester he spent all his free time at the farm. In the mornings he drove to campus, attended class, and studied in the library. Then he drove back to the farm to help with washing dishes, making meals, housecleaning. Early afternoons, as his mother napped, Mark would find his father sitting on the couch in the living room, pretending to read a book from the shelf. Some days he could be cajoled into going outside with Mark for some farm work. Once in a while the clear sky, the cold air, the crackle of a bonfire, or snow on the cedar trees would reanimate his father for a time. They would talk about the work they had done on the farm over the years, but then he would start to remember a spring day when he and Mark's mother had planted that walnut tree and he would sink down into silence again.

Evenings in his room, Mark worked stolidly through his coursework, preparing for final exams. Finals week came and for once he was prepared. After his last exam, Machine Design, he got in his car and drove to the trailer. Bill had apparently already left for the inter-semester break. Mark turned the thermostat up, sat down on the couch, and stared at the trailer park outside the dirty window.

The phone rang. It was Jeff. "Hey Mark, haven't seen you in a while. What have you been doing?"

Disoriented, Mark glanced at his watch trying to think of why Jeff was so chatty. "Just the usual. Studying," Mark mumbled. He cleared his throat, at a loss for what to say.

"I know you've got a lot on your mind," Jeff said. "Just thought I'd keep in touch."

Mark glanced at his watch again, saw it was three. "Got time for a beer at the Heidelberg?"

"No thanks," Jeff said quickly, but still seemed reluctant to get off the phone.

"Well, keep in touch. I want to know what it's like at McDonnell."

"We'll get together some weekend when I'm back in Columbia." The phone line hummed. "There is one other thing," Jeff said finally. "None of my business really, but…"

Mark waited, dismayed.

"You'd better call Jennifer soon. Before it's too late."

"Too late?"

"Stephanie called me, said Jennifer was really hurt by you distancing yourself. Hiding, she called it."

"Final exams…"

"That's bull and you know it. She's going to leave you behind, Mark. I think she wants something more than what you're giving her."

"Well, I disagree," Mark snapped. "We, I, it's been, there's a lot more…"

Jeff's tone turned placating, "I'm just telling you what Steph told me. It's entirely up to you. Anyway, I've got to get going. I'll call you when I'm back in town." He hung up.

Mark paced around the room for a while, looked at the three Busch beers in the refrigerator, then closed the door and sat back down by the phone.

The Columbia College switchboard operator put Mark through to Jennifer's room. Stephanie answered. "Hi Steph, this is Mark, is Jennifer there?"

There was a long silence on the line. A car went by. "She's in Florida, Mark. She left yesterday."

"I thought semester break didn't start until Friday."

"Her last exam was yesterday."

"What's going on Steph?"

"Figure it out!" Stephanie snapped. "You never call. You think she's going to sit around waiting on your convenience."

"That's not it at all." Mark felt his anger simmering. "She and I...we need time apart. We weren't..."

"She got those birth control pills for your sake. You don't know how bad they made her feel. But she did it. For you. She waits here for you to call and sometimes you do but most times you don't. Mark, for a smart guy, you sure act stupid."

"I never meant to hurt her."

"But you do it all the time."

"When will she be back?"

"I'm not your social secretary. Call her at her parents' house in Florida." The line went dead.

He got in his car and drove around for a while, then came back to the trailer and sat down by the phone. It was already dusk, with a cold wind from the west. He turned on all the lights in the trailer but it still felt gloomy.

With a long deep breath, he dialed Jennifer's parents' home in St. Petersburg.

Jennifer answered. After some awkward moments, Mark got around to what he wanted to say. "Despite all this, I love you, Jennifer."

"I hear you say you love me, Mark, and I think you mean it, but you don't *include* me in your life. You keep your life so fragmented. I don't want to just be part of your life. It's not enough. All your talk about 'deep in the country' is running away to hide in some idyllic place where time stops and nothing ever changes. It doesn't exist and never will. And I don't want that and never will. Life is change, Mark. All the changes, for good and bad, all along the way, and the joy of having someone to share it with. That's love."

Mark quit rubbing the worn green fabric of the couch's armrest. He tried to think of something to say but his mind couldn't seem to form words. The soft sigh of the phone line lay between them.

"I think we should stop seeing each other," she said. He continued to sit staring at the rough woven green fabric, saying nothing.

After a time, there was a click and the dial tone.

He hung up the phone and sat there watching a couple of boys, their coats discarded on the sidewalk, chasing each other around. After a while he drove to the farm. He could hear the TV softly playing in his mother's bedroom as he tiptoed up the stairs and went into his room.

* * *

The new semester started. Mark went through the days and nights like a zombie. One Wednesday as he pushed his way through the crowd on the sidewalk in front of Jesse Hall, he saw Allison skipping down the steps, long thick brown hair flying in the wind, big breasts bouncing. "Hey, Allison!" he shouted, then wondered if she would be happy to see him.

But she broke into her familiar big chipped-tooth smile, pushed her way through the crowd, and gave him a big hug. Her hair blew across his face, smelling wonderful. "Mark, it's great to see you, you look great."

"So do you," Mark said truthfully. "You're back from New Mexico."

She linked her arm in his and they walked toward the Student Union. "Yeah, I've been back almost a month. I've got lots to tell you. Do you have time for a cup of coffee at the Heidelberg?"

"Sure."

They made their way across the quad and into the restaurant. "Guess what," Allison said, waving a folder at him. "I'm going to New York. I've been accepted by NYU."

"That's wonderful," Mark said. "Journalism?"

"Communication media." The Heidelberg was quiet in mid-morning. Students surged past outside the window.

"You still in Engineering?" Allison asked.

"Yeah, slogging away. How was New Mexico?"

She smiled and shook her head slightly. "Well, part of it was great, sunrises on the mountain top, the silence of the New Mexico desert. It really is a magic place. And lots of beautiful pine forest up north near Taos. But the people in the commune..." She squinched her face and continued, "So petty, so immature. They are a bunch of jerks really, and totally incompetent to do any sort of farm work, even gardening. I guess that's my farm-girl background speaking." She laughed her full laugh.

Mark squeezed her arm. "You look different."

"Different how?" She was smiling, her big brown eyes were on his.

He felt alive for the first time in weeks. "More focused, kind of like the way I remember you that evening we took the airplane up to see the sunset."

"Sunsets," she corrected him. "That was wonderful. That's the real me. I'm happy most of the time. I like to stay busy. I can't sit around all day smoking dope."

Clouds scudded past the row of trees now dusted with the first green buds of spring. "I still feel kind of bad about that night you and I..." Mark said, " and I hope you're not..."

She squeezed his arm. "Quit worrying. Free love, remember? It's the sixties." They both laughed, then her face turned serious.

"It was the sixties," Mark said, "and they are ending. You were so sad that day."

"I won't ever listen to 'White Bird' again," she changed the subject. "Back in New Mexico I decided I wanted to spend my time at something a little more substantial than making and selling bead bracelets." She looked out the window at springtime. "But at the same time, I still believe everything we talked about, everything we did, was right—the protests, the counterculture—we needed change, radical change. I wouldn't trade these times for anything. We were the perfect age at the perfect time. But nothing lasts forever. I've got to work at something. I need to accomplish something."

"Sounds like you'd rather write *Journey to the East* than read it," he said.

She nodded. "I think so."

Mark squinted. "I feel that way myself. I want to work, to accomplish something." He held up his hand. "These have been good times. But also bad times." He mentioned his mother's illness and breaking up with Jennifer.

"I'm sorry, Mark."

Mark nodded. Some eighteen-year-olds who had sat down at the table next to them were whining about dorm rules. Mark was happy to change the subject. "I know you'll succeed, Allison," Mark said. "Been back to Moberly recently?"

Allison's expression darkened. "For a long time I didn't think about Moberly at all. A few months ago, after I'd left the commune and was sort of just drifting around, I stopped in a little country store in a town called Cimarron. I had this vision, a memory of a summer when I was about ten years old living in Moberly, and we had gone over to my grandmother's farm for a Fourth of July dinner of fried chicken, green beans, corn on the cob and watermelon. Us kids set off fireworks after it got dark. There was a pay phone at the back of the store and I called home collect. My mother answered in her familiar accent and we talked for a while. Then she told me how ill my father had become. He had been diagnosed with liver cancer over two years ago but he hadn't wanted to tell me about it. The Stoic Midwestern farmer. I got in the car and drove straight home." Allison brushed a tear aside. "The white porch was the same, the lawn was the same. I could see a corner of my mother's garden behind the house. It was February and the soybean fields were disked and ready for spring planting."

"I knocked and opened the front door. My mother came into the living room and we hugged each other. We never used to hug. As I followed my mother into the bedroom to see my father, my heart was pounding. He was sitting in bed, a red flannel shirt on, so thin and white I barely recognized him. He said, 'Hi Allie,' and we touched hands, an unfamiliar gesture. His voice was still the same, though: 'The ceiling kind of fell in on me…' He said it so apologetically."

"I realized I had probably only been in their bedroom a half dozen times in twenty years. The drugs kept him pretty sleepy most of the time. He would doze for an hour, then wake for ten minutes or so, then doze again. I read to him sometimes. I realize now that I picked articles about people recovering from serious disease because that's what I wanted—I wanted to hear the doctor say he was miraculously recovering, that he'd see another springtime. I wanted that so badly. He put up with my reading, though it was hard for him to concentrate. I noticed my mother had sewn a new flower print cover for the chair that had sat right there for as long as I can remember. Sometimes while he dozed I'd look out the window at the garden, thinking of nothing, sometimes praying, sometimes crying a little. Without saying it, I thanked him for all he had done for me. And it was a cold, hazy, still day, sitting there, when I realized he had given me the greatest gift he could give me."

"He had let me go away to Columbia to live my own life.

That old farm was his life and I'm sure he would have liked for me to stay right there. He was in love with the land in that inarticulate Midwestern way, but he had loved me more. Enough to not ever talk about giving me the farm. It's a great burden, receiving something that someone loves, but that you don't love. I thanked him silently for understanding that."

"I helped my mother with housework. One day, I remember it was cloudy and cold with a steady wind blowing in across the fields, I put on my old jacket and boots and walked down the fencerow to the woods. I watched the bare trees swaying in the wind. I walked through the woods to the little pond and squatted in the dry reeds studying the pattern of bubbles and cracks in the ice. I felt closer to my mother then than I had ever before."

Allison was crying, her glossy brown hair hiding her eyes. "I wondered, how can this happen? We take for granted that our parents will always be the same, unchanging, until suddenly one day it all changes. I guess I was wondering why there was no time left to share with my father." She breathed a sigh. "But I was not thinking I should have stayed in Moberly all these years. I knew I was right to have left. But there is a part of me that will always be at home in that little house, on that old farm, in that little town. I can't articulate it. It is something I can't touch, and if I try too hard it slips away. It's deep in the country, the heart of the country, it's my mother's face, the familiar smell of the house, the slope of the fields in back. I'll never live there, but I'll never completely leave there either." She wiped tears off her face with a paper napkin, then looked out the window at the windy spring day. Then she smiled and took Mark's hand and squeezed it hard. "Remember when you took me up in the plane and made the sun rise?"

"I remember."

"I think of that often. I like sunrises. New beginnings."

After a little while they told each other they needed to get going. Mark stood in the spring sunshine and watched her disappear into the crowd on Ninth Street.

## Chapter 19

The phone ringing in the living room woke Mark. He was been dozing in the blue chair in his mother's bedroom. She was sitting up in bed, dressed in her tulip-print dressing gown, but her eyes were closed. On TV, Lola Albright was singing, "You'd Be So Nice To Come Home To." Mark's father clomped down the hall and told Mark there was a phone call for him.

"Hey Mark..." a familiar voice on the line. "It's Keith, man."

"Keith? Where the hell are you?"

"St. Louis," Keith said, "at my parents' house. I just got my stuff out of my old trailer in Columbia and brought it here to store."

Mark breathed in a long breath. "Damn. You scared us. We thought..."

"It's a long story, I'll tell you about it, but not now."

In the kitchen Mark's father began to boil water for tea. He took down three cups, one at a time, with slow movements. His head was down, his shoulders bowed.

"I signed up for four years in the Air Force," Keith said. "I've got to drive to McGuire Air Force Base, New Jersey, to be inducted. How about going with me? You could fly back."

" Okay. When?"

"Now. Drive over here. Then I'll follow you to the airport, park your car, buy a one-way ticket back to St. Louis." Mark scribbled down directions to Keith's parents' house, then hung up, his mind already on the trip.

"No tea for me," Mark told his father. "A friend of mine needs help moving to New Jersey. I'll be gone a couple of days."

His father nodded, put one cup back in the cabinet, and stood watching a robin hop across the lawn in the wind. Outside, the grass was turning green, hinting of spring. In the past, Mark thought, my mother and father would be outside enthusiastically digging and planting in the garden on these early spring days. He hurried out.

* * *

Keith followed Mark to the airport in a brand new British Racing Green Triumph TR4.

"Wow," Mark said. He tossed his carry-on bag behind the passenger seat and got in. Keith kept the top down as they zipped through traffic to his parents' big house. "My parents bought it for me after I told them I was coming back to join the Air Force. It's a bribe and I like it." Keith showed Mark to an immaculate bedroom furnished in old-lady kitsch, then they adjourned to the kitchen where Keith pulled a couple of bottles of Tuborg beer out of the refrigerator. They toasted each other. "We've got the place to ourselves for a while. My dad's down at our bowling alley checking the new pinspotting system. My mom's on vacation with her girlfriends in Barbados."

"Nice place." Mark took a long pull on the cold beer.

"This is their pride and joy," Keith snorted. They took their beers to the living room and sat on the white carpet.

"We thought you'd gone to Canada."

Keith grinned his long-toothed grin. "I was on my way. I drove to Los Angeles. Lived in the car. Played guitar for tips. Sunset Boulevard is great, man... saw Morrison at the Troubadour, saw The Byrds." He grimaced. "I even saw Sonny and Cher, that bubblegum rock you like."

"I'm touched."

The luxurious house was silent, smelling of carpet cleaner. The only sound was the bubbling of the aerator in the aquarium.

"Then I started north, up the coast."

"Going to Vancouver?"

Keith nodded. "Yeah. But you know, making my way up the coast, I found I really liked being on the road."

Keith started picking the silver foil off the neck of his beer bottle.

"So different from back here. In class all the time. Studying. In Canada I could keep doing it. I wouldn't have to lie low. I could go where I wanted, do what I wanted. Just playing for tips was already making me enough money for gas, food, and an occasional motel room. I can play better than most of the guys in the bands I was hearing. If I joined up with a band, we could..." Keith shrugged and grinned his familiar grin. "Oh well."

"What stopped you?"

"I drove all the way up the West Coast to Port Angeles, the dock where the ferries leave for Victoria, Canada. My old Corvair was knocking pretty bad by then. Across the sound, invisible in the fog, was British Columbia, and freedom. I decided to abandon the car in the lot, buy a pedestrian ticket, cross over, and disappear." He tilted his bottle to his lips. "It was cold on the dock, a mist of rain in the air. I got back in the car to warm up. The ferry boat emerged from the fog and people filed down the passenger gangway. I got out of my car and locked it and walked over to the line of people at the ticket window." Keith's voice had sunk to a whisper barely audible over the soft bubbling of the fish tank. "I was staring at my old white Corvair sitting there in the lot. After a few weeks they'd haul it to a salvage yard. They'd know I'd run away to Canada, but it wouldn't matter by then. But the funny thing is, I started feeling sorry for my car. It looked so...lonely... sitting there in that parking lot. And then I started adding it all up, figuring everything I'd be losing by leaving. After a while I stepped out of line, got back in my car, and started back for Missouri. The old Corvair finally broke down for good in Spokane. I sold it to a salvage yard for ten dollars, then played guitar in the town square until I had enough money for a hot meal and a bus ticket back here." He finished his beer and got out two more.

"I remember that old Corvair very well," Mark said, "and that trip to Wyoming. And that time last spring when you and Gail, me and Jennifer drove down to the Lake."

"Rest in peace—she's crushed for scrap metal now." They toasted the old Corvair.

Keith put a Django Reinhardt record on and they ate cold chicken and potato salad from the refrigerator. Keith put two plates and two forks in the dishwasher and started it. "With only two plates and two forks?"

"My parents wash the dishes after every meal."

Mark and Keith adjourned to the living room with two more Tuborgs. Keith put on a Carlos Montoya flamenco guitar record.

"I guess your parents were glad to see you back."

Keith shrugged. "Saved them from making up a story to tell people at the country club."

"What's this?" Mark said, pulling a book titled *The Urantia Book* from the shelf. Mark opened the book to chapters of dense print, but an illustration caught his eye. "Flying saucers?"

Keith grinned, embarrassed. "Yeah, Urantia. It's a religion. They think there's something sacred about Uranus, the planet Uranus. My mother's into it. Pretty wacko, huh?"

Mark shrugged and slid the book back in beside *Wildflowers of North America*. "No more wacko than any of the other religions."

Later, Mark woke in the old-ladyish spare bedroom. He had dreamed he was back at the farm, sitting in his mother's bedroom while she slept in front of the TV. Peter Gunn was on, Lola Albright singing. He drifted back to sleep.

* * *

The next morning they rolled through St. Louis and out onto I-70 eastbound. Keith had the top down for a while, but it was too windy and noisy, so they stopped in the farmland of Illinois and put it back up. Keith was grinning. "On the road, man, getting our kicks on Route 66."

"Remember that day last September, when we drove down to the Lake in your Corvair?"

"Oh hey, turn that up." Keith interrupted. "I like that song." Keith sang along with "Na Na Hey Hey Kiss Him Goodbye" for a minute. "It'll be goodbye for me soon."

"You don't seem too worried. But I guess some guys get sent to Germany rather than Vietnam," Mark said.

"Or Italy," Keith replied. "Drink lots of wine, eat good pasta, look at the Ferraris in the showroom windows. And the women…" He fell silent.

"What happened to Gail?" Mark asked.

Keith shrugged. "We said we'd write to each other." Keith had maintained an insubstantial relationship with Gail, a tall, silent, pale girl, all three years he had been in Columbia. Mark realized that for all the times the four of them had double dated, he knew nothing about her.

It was dark by the time they got to Pittsburgh.

They checked in at a Days Inn and walked down the street to a neighborhood bar and restaurant for hoagy sandwiches. Afterwards they went to the bar and sat on barstools and drank Iron City draft beer. "Not bad," Mark said.

"Think I'll end up like these guys?" Keith tilted his head toward row of guys in blue work shirts and leather jackets at the bar. Mark shrugged. "Doubt it. And anyway it might be good."

"I promised my parents I'd finish my degree after I got

out of the Air Force. That's why they bought me the car. They're still pretty bitter about me leaving school. My mother especially." Keith grinned his toothy grin. "The thing is, I liked being on the road." He glanced around the dim bar. "I like it." His eyes were opaque behind his glasses.

"Didn't miss Columbia?..."

Keith shook his head. "Not a bit. Didn't miss Columbia or Webster Groves, or the University, or Gail."

"Not coming back to Missouri after your Air Force time, then?"

"Nope. With the GI Bill I can go to school wherever I want. If I want to go back to school at all. I loved California." Keith ordered another beer. "Did you ever think about dodging the draft, moving to Canada?"

Mark studied the straight lines of bubbles rising in his beer. "No. I guess I'm just too much of a Columbia kid—I'll usually do the right thing, the conventional thing."

They were back in the motel by ten. Near dawn, Mark woke. Keith slept quietly in the other bed. Mark got up silently and looked out at the parked cars in the motel parking lot. The freedom of the road. Martin Milner and George Maharis in that '62 Corvette convertible. Absolute freedom.

Mark closed the sheers. But so lonely.

* * *

Keith pushed down hard on the accelerator and the TR4 jumped out into traffic. He went through the gears fast. "See You in September" loud on the radio. Keith smiled his hawklike smile and whipped through traffic, while singing along with the radio.

"Here's one some of your bouncy bubblegum," Keith laughed. But he sang along with Mark, "...summer Sunday, up with the dawn, my, my, my, what a beautiful day..."

They rolled east through Pennsylvania. The sky was clear

but the rundown houses, empty stores, the brick factories, the used car lots and the gas stations, made it all seem gray.

"I told you about LA," Keith said. "Easy living, music everywhere, sunny and warm every day. After I get out, I'm going back there and lie on the beach, play guitar, live life." Keith pushed down the accelerator and the TR4 shot around a semi.

The New Jersey countryside rolled past. The traffic was much heavier now. But Mark was seeing the calm streets of Columbia, remembering Keith playing guitar at the Hofbrau, and junior year, getting to know him junior year in the Statics and Dynamics class they had both been taking. Happy hour at the Berg, smoking cheap dope with him in his microscopic trailer while he went on and on about Reinhart and Parkening. Walking the quadrangle with him and Gail, drinking beer at the Shack and the I.V..

Maybe a few years from now I'll hear about him playing lead guitar with The Byrds at the Troubadour or The Doors at the Whiskey a-Go-Go. Or maybe, despite all his talk, he'll come back to Webster Groves and manage his family's bowling alley for the rest of his life.

I don't really know him. He studied Keith's familiar profile out of the corner of his eye—his wire frame glasses, thinning yellow hair, long-toothed smile.

At a seedy motel outside McGuire Air Force Base, Keith checked in for the night. "One night, twenty dollars cash," the clerk said without looking up. Keith paid, got his key, and they got back in the car. "I'll take you to the airport."

They drove down dirty streets clogged with traffic. "There's the front gate." Keith pointed at a sign arching over a street lined with bars, pawn shops, strip joints, and tattoo parlors.

"Looks just the way I thought it would," Mark said. Keith down-shifted and they pulled away as an Air Force transport plane screamed in for a landing.

At the bar in the airport they each drank a Busch, not saying much. After a while Keith walked with him to the gate. Mark shouldered his bag and stuck out his hand for Keith's bone-crushing handshake. "Thanks for coming with me," Keith said.

"Take care of yourself, Keith," Mark said.

Keith's grin was distant, his mind already on what lay ahead. He clapped Mark on the shoulder. "See ya, buddy."

Mark never saw him again.

# Chapter 20

At the farm Mark parked his car in his usual place and stepped out into a cold spring filled with the sounds of frogs calling from the little ponds. He tiptoed upstairs and reread a little of chapter one of *Islands in the Sky*, trying to occupy his mind until he could sleep. But for a long time the dim motel room in Pittsburgh, the grungy New Jersey Air Force Base, and Keith's distracted goodbye at the airport intruded.

The next morning, his father's clomping around the house on the hardwood floors woke him at six. His sister fixed breakfast while his mother sat at the table sipping coffee. They ate bacon and eggs and toast. Cool spring air flowed in the window. Mark's mother shuffled to the window and closed it. "I love spring, but it's a little chilly this morning." She carefully sat back down. The sun was bright on the lush grass. Robins hopped across the lawn.

"Want to do some pruning this morning?" Mark suggested cheerily. "Still cutting brush along the treeline by the big pond?"

His father agreed immediately. "But I'd like for you to do the dishes first. Your sister needs to go to the University this morning." Mark looked blank. "Registration for fall semester." Mark realized with surprise that his little sister would be a freshman this year.

After Mark had done the dishes and his father had gotten his mother back to her bedroom, they loaded the trailer with two chainsaws and the fuel can and started off. It was a clear, cool morning; green and gold and wet with dew. The feel of the light and the air cheered them both. There was little talk between them. They both knew the routine. The steady physical work soothed them in a way thought could not and for a while Mark's mind was at ease. But when they came back to the house for lunch, his father checked on his mother and told Mark, "She won't be joining us for lunch. Some days are better than others. This morning was good, but now…"

* * *

That evening Mark watched *The Huntley-Brinkley Report* on Channel 8 from the old armchair in the family room. "...the biggest anti-war protest yet has nearly paralyzed downtown Manhattan." There was footage of police and protesters scuffling, a helicopter shot of Times Square full of people, and a close-up of banners reading "End the War." People were shouting, an American flag was burning, police pushed the protesters back, a bystander picked the flag up and tried to put it out, but it was too late. Protesters and police were running, sirens wailed.

"Time for dinner," his father called down the stairs. Mark turned off the TV and clumped up the stairs. His mother sat stolidly in her chair saying nothing. Mark and his father made conversation around her as she tried to eat a little. She would look at one or the other of them from time to time. Her familiar brown eyes cleared for a moment and she asked Mark, "When do classes start?"

Mark forced a smile onto his face. "Monday."

After dinner his mother retired to her room and Mark silently helped his father with the dishes. "I'll spend the night here," Mark told him.

"Good," his father said heavily. "Your mother appreciates seeing you."

* * *

Mark retreated to his room and stared at the pages of his Mechanical Design textbook, trying to force himself to comprehend, but he could not. After a while he gave up and went to bed. In the darkness, the familiar shapes of his room should have comforted him, but instead he felt a looming loneliness. He wished Jennifer could be beside him now. The way they sometimes lay together in the bedroom at the trailer, enjoying each other's presence in silence. His mind would not be calm. Finally he whispered, "My mother is dying, soon she will be gone, and there's nothing I can do about it." Maybe saying his fears out loud would help. But it did not. A tear leaked out of his eyes and he brushed it away. "But I will spend time with her. And I'll help my father and sister." His resolution helped a little but tears continued to fall until he drifted into sleep.

* * *

Sunday evening Mark stopped by campus and went into the Student Union and downstairs to the last phone booth in the row of dark confessional-like wooden booths. He pulled the folding door closed, and a tiny bulb cast a buttery light on the old black phone. He stared at the white circles for a time: ABC, DEF, GHI… then dropped a dime into the slot and dialed.

"Hi Jennifer, this is Mark," he said, heart pounding.

"Yes, Mark." Her tone was neutral.

Mark tilted his head down and pulled the phone in tight. "Yeah, I've been thinking…" He paused. "I've missed you. I haven't really been communicating lately. I've had a lot on my mind, with school…" He couldn't quite bring himself to mention his mother. "But I want to see you, spend time together, be happy. Like we used to be."

He sat listening to his heart's steady thump.

"I've missed you too, Mark. But you need to talk to me."

"I should, I will."

He waited and she waited. Finally Mark said, "My mother is ill, very ill." It sounded strange to say it. He was glad for the phone. Telling Jennifer face to face would have been impossible. "She has cancer and it's not getting better."

"I wish you had told me that long ago."

"I should have." He paused. "Your birthday is tomorrow. I'd like to see you...?"

"Pick me up at seven thirty. Steph and the girls are taking me to dinner first."

* * *

At the trailer, Mark ushered Jennifer in and opened the bottle of champagne he'd bought. He and poured it into three mismatched glasses and toasted, "To your twentieth birthday." Jennifer and Mark and Bill raised their glasses. "Happy birthday."

"I have a surprise," Jennifer said to Mark while Bill was fiddling with the TV. "I signed out for the whole night. I told them I was staying at Steph's cousin's parents' house." Mark grinned and held her close. "That's great!"

The TV came on. "I hope I'm not causing a problem." Bill changed channels and settled onto the floor in front of the set. "*Star Trek*. Sorry."

Mark's expression was apologetic, but Jennifer was smiling. "That will be fine."

"You look beautiful tonight," Mark whispered as the episode began. Her touched her long silky black hair. She was dressed in a miniskirt and a green sweater.

Zarabeth is imprisoned in an ice age, thousands of years in the past of her planet. She is alone. Spock and McCoy are sent back in time by mistake and are lost in a blizzard. She takes them to her cave, saves their lives. Spock wants to stay with her, but he and McCoy must travel forward in time together. Spock goes with McCoy, leaving Zarabeth alone for the rest of her life. As the *Enterprise* warps out of orbit, Spock says, "It happened, but that was five thousand years ago and she is dead now. Dead and buried long ago."

Mark found his eyes wet and noticed Jennifer's were shining too. He took her hand and they retired to his room, stripped off their clothes, and got into bed where they lay together in darkness not making love. "It's just a silly TV show," he whispered. "But thanks for watching it with me."

She kissed him. "So sad, to be endlessly alone."

"Lost in the past," Mark said quietly. They were silent for a while. "I want to explain why I didn't tell you about my mother's illness..."

"You don't have to."

"I want to." Mark said. "I want our time together to be good. If I talk about bad things with you, it brings that sadness into our time. When I'm with you, I can pretend for a while that my mother's illness doesn't exist, that the war and the draft don't exist."

She comforted him, "We can face the bad times together."

He turned to face her in the darkness. "And I don't want your sympathy to change the feelings we have for each other. I was afraid of that, too."

They dozed. Mark woke in the dark stillness. Without seeing if Jennifer was awake or asleep he continued, "I try to be cheerful and helpful at the farm. I see my younger sister doing the same thing in her own quiet way. I think I see her clearly now, for the first time. She's four years younger than me and she's close to our mother, probably closer than I am. I see my sister's happiness being taken from her. And I can't help her either."

Jennifer stirred. "I'd like to meet your mother sometime."

"I'll take you out to the farm next weekend."

* * *

Bill was moving around the trailer next morning while they lay under the sheets in the stuffy bedroom. Eventually they heard him go out the door, start his car, and drive away. Mark dressed and leaned out the front door and found it was a warm and overcast spring day. As the scent of Constant Comment tea filled the trailer, Jennifer came out to the living room looking very beautiful, her long black hair combed and glossy. "It's warm outside," Mark said, "warm and still." He closed the door and turned on a light to make the room feel brighter.

On the couch, teacups in hand, Mark continued the conversation of the night before. "Mother's death will be harder on my sister than it will be on me." The fragrant tea and Jennifer's presence held back the dread and loneliness he had felt alone at night in his room at the farm. "I wish it was all over. I want to speed through these difficult months to some happier future time. But at the same time I want to slow time down, to savor every minute that is left." He looked into her dark brown eyes. "...times winged chariot. But I'll try to make these last few weeks you and I have together as good as it can be."

She nodded. "About that night last winter, when I walked out of here. I'm sorry about that. Those birth control pills just twisted my emotions up."

Mark kissed her. "Forget it. I know you started taking those pills for my sake and I appreciate it. And I love you," he said.

"I love you too," she replied, and Mark felt something slip into place between them that had not been there before.

* * *

After class on Friday, Mark got in his car and drove down Highway 63 to where police cars' flashing lights slowed traffic and directed it to one lane. A long column of students in threes and fours walked down the shoulder, some carrying posters printed with big red letters: "*One Voice Manifesto*." Mark had read in the *Free Press* that they would be stopping for the night in a little park by the highway, so he inched past them, drove to the park, and pulled his Chevy into the row of cars and vans on the grass.

The barbecue pits were already smoking as serious-faced volunteers prepared an evening meal for the marchers. He saw Jeff arrive, adorned with a huge backpack.

"I can't talk now," Jeff said. "Got to set up committee meetings and prep Carol for her speech tomorrow." He discarded his pack and disappeared into the crowd. Mark hung around the barbecue grills and was handed a burger. While he was eating, someone got a bullhorn going and began to harangue the crowd. "As the first land-grant university in the Louisiana Purchase, the University of Missouri has a moral obligation to lead the way to a new social compact. We demand action on the eight principles in the *One Voice Manifesto*. Evolution, not revolution. What is needed is consensus and clear action!" There was scattered applause.

Mark tracked Jeff down talking urgently to Carol as flunkies looked on respectfully. "Leave it in your speech. You are the one who wrote the manifesto and got momentum behind it. You called for the non-violent demonstrations that got the University to change their visitation rules." He stood close to her. She stepped back, kept her expression impassive. "You were the one who shamed the University into stopping the harassment of professors who don't support the war. All non-violent. While over at SIU and KU there are riots and burning buildings. You need to take credit for this so that the politicos take you seriously." Carol found a place by one of the campfires that were warming up the evening. She sat down and Jeff sat beside her. "And now, *One Voice*," Jeff said, "it's pulled us together, articulated our goals. Tomorrow the state legislature will be listening. This is important."

There was a breathless silence. Carol looked around at the expectant faces. "Yes, it is important and we've got a lot of work to do. You've got your committee assignments so I suggest we get to them. Jeff and I need to work on my speech." Mark almost expected the faithful to break into spontaneous applause, but instead they shuffled off to form little circles around other campfires.

Jeff caught sight of Mark. "You finally joining us, Mark?"

"I can't spare the time."

"Bullshit! There's nothing more important than getting involved." Carol took out a University notebook and began writing. Her golden hair glowed in the firelight and once again Mark was struck by her extraordinary beauty. Jeff took Mark's arm and stepped him away from Carol. " All your talk about changing society, about alternate lifestyles, about freedom." Jeff shook his head. "This is how you do it." His gesture took in the park. "But you insist on staying a bystander. A pretender."

"We need you over here," someone called, and Jeff bustled off.

Mark drove back to his trailer and tried unsuccessfully to study. The next morning dawned cold and clear. Mark drove thirty miles to the state capital and stood in the crowd listening to Carol's speech. It was good, but the wind was cold and the crowd was thinning by the time she finished.

* * *

Wednesday afternoon when Mark came out of the Engineering building, the clouds were spitting cold rain. He trotted across the quadrangle and dodged into the Heidelberg for a cup of coffee. He found Jeff at their old table by the window leaning back, eyes closed, a cup of coffee and the St. Louis *Post-Dispatch* spread out in front of him.

"Thinking deep thoughts?" Mark said, sliding into the booth. "What the heck are you doing here on a weekday?"

Jeff opened his eyes. "Nice to see you too." He read a headline from the paper, "'Humphrey Addresses Farm Bureau

Conference.' We arranged that."

Mark glanced down the article. "Pretty impressive."

"Carol's making it happen," Jeff said intensely. "And this is just the beginning. We're hoping to create an evolution in state policies, right here in Missouri," said Jeff, levelling a meaningful look at Mark. "But with national implications. Missouri could become a model for a new social compact. You should get involved. This isn't just some student sit-in at Jesse Hall."

Mark ordered a cup of coffee. "I read the manifesto. It's good. Eloquent, impassioned but reasonable."

Jeff frowned at the newspaper. "But we need to keep the momentum up. I've been trying to recruit others who want to do serious work, but most of them will only listen to Carol."

"You can take this much time off from your job?" Mark said.

Jeff gave Mark a disgusted look.

"What's that about?"

"You ready for a beer?" Jeff went to the bar without waiting for an answer.

They sat sipping Hamm's, watching students hurrying by in the cold wind. "How's Jennifer?" Jeff said, not taking his eyes off his beer.

"Fine. Better than ever." Jeff didn't seem to be listening. "So..." Mark said, "you working on any interesting designs at McDonnell-Douglas? Or is it all classified?"

Jeff shrugged and took a minute sip of his beer.

"Something must be bothering you."

"None of your business," Jeff snapped. His expression instantly softened. "Sorry, I'm under a lot of pressure at work."

Mark put his feet up on the seat opposite. "How so?"

"Don't repeat this, okay? Especially not to my parents. They think everything is fine. But being a junior engineer is bullshit. It's grinding work, calculations all day long in a big windowless room full of desks. And the deadlines are murder." He sipped. """I don't think I'm cut out to be an engineer."

"That's nonsense," Mark said, his concern growing. "Don't sell yourself short. The first few months are bound to be tough, but things will settle down. You always studied hard, worked hard and got decent grades."

"Yeah, I've worked my ass off for the last four years, at stuff I frankly don't care that much about, and what's it getting me? Just the chance to keep working my ass off." Jeff downed his beer. "I've lost interest in electrical engineering."

Mark was floored by this confession. He snagged a waiter and ordered two more beers.

Jeff moved his glass around in a small square on the tabletop. "I may quit working for McDonnell."

Mark was stunned. "You've been there less than six months." The beers came, and Jeff stared at his glass. Behind him the crowd was increasing as happy hour began. Someone started the jukebox.

"Don't do anything you'll regret," Mark said earnestly. "You worked hard in school, now you've got to work hard at McDonnell. You can do it, I know you can."

"I can't do this anymore," Jeff said, and to Mark's horror he saw tears welling up in his friend's eyes.

"Hey, take it easy," Mark stammered. He folded the newspaper into neat thirds. Jeff regained his composure and checked his watch. "Well, I've got to go."

"Driving back to St. Louis now?"

Jeff surveyed the bar. "Guess so."

But Jeff did not drive back to St. Louis that afternoon, or the next morning either.

* * *

While Mark pondered Jeff's revelations, Carol was in Washington D.C. She walked through the lobby atrium of the Rayburn Building feeling tightly exultant. She had an appointment to meet with Senator McCarthy and she felt prepared, focused and entirely optimistic. Inside the tall wooden door to McCarthy's office she told the secretary who she was. A staffer welcomed her, told her it would be a few minutes and offered her coffee. They found they were both from Chicago and traded reminiscences. Then she was shown into McCarthy's inner office. He looks just the same as he does on TV, she thought, shaking his hand. The gray hair, the dark eyes, the look of thoughtfulness and concern.

"I'm pleased you've come to see us, Ms. Bianchi," he said, and sounded like he meant it. They sat down at a table. Coffee was brought. This was the moment her efforts over the last year and a half were focused on. She went through her position quickly and succinctly. McCarthy wrote nothing down. She handed his staffer a suggested political action plan for how to build support for the position she was outlining. McCarthy asked a number of interesting questions and Carol thought she answered them well. On her way out she was given the business card of McCarthy's chief of staff, with its gold eagle emblem.

"Thank you for coming to see me Miss Bianchi." McCarthy shook Carol's hand and turned away, greeted the next group of constituents warmly, and showed them into his office.

As she walked to Union Station she was sharply aware of the cherry trees in bloom, the sun on her face and the scent of the city. She had a glass of Pinot Grigio at the airport and another glass on the TWA flight to St. Louis. There were only two other people in first class. She sat looking at the sunset outside the airplane window and wondered why it all felt too simple.

# Chapter 21

Mark and Jennifer found Bill sitting at the kitchen table in the trailer, a pint of Sealtest chocolate milk in front of him. He pushed a sheet of paper across to Mark. "Our lease on this trailer ends at the end of this month. They want to know if we're renewing."

Mark and Jennifer sat down at the table. "I'll graduate in the middle of August. You too, right?" asked Mark.

Bill finished off the milk and tossed the container into the trash.

"Think they'd give us a three month extension?" Mark pressed.

Bill shrugged. "Maybe, but with Jeff gone, we don't need this much room. Or do we?"

He looked from Mark to Jennifer and back to Mark. The three of them sat in awkward silence for a moment, each looking a different direction.

Mark took Jennifer's hand. "Jennifer is going back to Florida right after she graduates to spend the summer with her parents, then Florida State next fall," Mark said. It sounded artificially cheerful even to himself. "I'm looking forward to visiting Tallahassee," he added lamely.

"I checked out a little two bedroom place on Matthews Street the other day," Bill said. "It's tiny, but close to campus and the gas station. I assume you're planning to work at the gas station?"

Mark nodded. "If we can rent month-to-month, tell them

we'll take it."

Bill stood up. "I'll go talk to them now." He left whistling.

Mark opened the front door and sat down beside Jennifer on the couch. They watched Bill's black Chevy drive off, windows rolled down, KXOK fading away. Jennifer opened her Art Appreciation book while Mark slumped down beside her on the couch. "Don't you need to study?" she asked.

"Yes," Mark said, staring around the room as thought he'd never seen it before. The beige carpet and the worn green couch, Bill's little 19" TV, the rabbit ears always in the way. We only see things when we are leaving or arriving, he thought. He looked at Jennifer reading, one leg folded under her, her black hair hiding the sides of her face. The high overcast and still warm air filled the day with a sense of waiting—waiting for things to end.

"You'll graduate soon," Mark reiterated. "Then back to St. Pete."

She nodded. "My parents are diving up for my graduation. I'll ride back to St. Pete with them." Her words hung in the air.

* * *

Finals week and the library was crowded. Most of the study carrels were full; people shuffled endlessly up and down the aisles. Some guy down the row kept blowing his nose.

Mark turned back a page in *Principles of Mechanical Design* and read it for the third time, still not comprehending. His mind insistently drifted to that night in the bedroom of Keith's trailer in Roach Valley trailer park. It was the first night he and Jennifer had made love. They had undressed in total darkness and made love slowly with little skill but much consideration. Later in the darkness, she sighed a small sigh and whispered, "I'm falling in love with you."

He studied and did the best he could on his finals, not expecting much. Most of his grades were alright, but he found an F by his student number outside Professor Bradley's door.

No matter. He would take the course again in summer school. He strolled out into a warm afternoon feeling like he had just surfaced after two months underwater in a submarine. He heard himself whistling "Grazing in the Grass" as he walked to the bookstore to sell his books.

A pale green Mustang hardtop pulled up to the curb. It was Larry grinning up at him. He turned the car radio down. "Hop in."

Mark slid in and Larry popped the clutch, nosing the Mustang back into traffic on Lowry Street. He turned the radio back up for "Bad Moon Rising."

"Hey babe!" Larry yelled at two girls walking along Rollins. He slowed the Mustang down beside them. The tall girl in the blue dress with peter pan collar sneered. Her friend kept her eyes forward and walked faster.

"Let's go party," Larry added.

"Get lost," the tall girl said. Larry wheeled back into traffic.

"Pretty smooth, Larry. She likes you, I'm sure." Mark turned the radio back down. "Still married?"

"Sometimes." He dropped the Mustang into second and squealed the tires.

Larry spotted his next targets half a block ahead. A GTO was ahead of them, slowing. Larry pulled up close behind him to urge him on and he did. But the car behind them hit his horn and Larry kept rolling. "Tri Delt tee shirts," Mark said. "They usually aren't approachable. Besides, if you ever do pick up a girl in this car, you're not going to have much luck on the vinyl-covered two by four that passes for a back seat. Unless Brenda doesn't mind you bringing your dates home."

Larry was checking his hair in the rearview mirror. "How's my hair look?"

"Like some kind of second-rate astronaut," Mark said.

Larry wheeled the Mustang around the block and pulled up

beside a couple of girls walking and laughing together.

"Hey babe, let's go get a beer," Larry called out the window.

The nearest one gave him the finger. Larry accelerated away.

"I think that gesture indicates she thinks you're number one," Mark said. "Let's quit this and get a beer at the Shack."

"One more try." Larry pulled even with a girl walking along, her boobs bouncing under a tee shirt with a peace sign, nice tight jeans and long brown hair.

"Hey babe, what time is it anyway?"

"It's daytime, man," she said breezily.

Larry's grin got wider. "Well then, got time for a quick fuck?"

"Yeah, man, but not with you." She kept walking.

The Shack was empty except for the counterman staring out the window. Its cozy smell of spilled beer and hamburger grease, its ramshackle wooden booths and the cathedral light of the glowing Hamm's Sky Blue Waters sign had always given it a cloistered feel for Mark. A place of refuge and confession.

"How about a Shackburger?" Larry said. "I haven't had lunch yet."

He placed their order and brought back two beers.

Mark raised his glass. "To the end of the semester."

"To sex," Larry countered.

"You're getting it every night with Brenda, so why chase after every girl on the street?" Mark asked, already knowing the answer.

Larry ignored the question as rhetorical.

Mark rubbed condensation into Pi K A carved on the table top, one of hundreds of initials, names and dates incised into every inch of wood surface.

"Variety, man," Larry said unapologetically. "Every fuck you pass up is forever lost. There are a million women out there."

"That's not what the pastor said at your wedding, as I recall." Mark interjected drily. "Something about cleaving only to... and of course, the 'until death do us part' part."

"That's for the sake of convention, for our parents, our friends and neighbors."

Mark laughed out loud, which Larry didn't seem to find amusing.

The counterman mumbled something and Mark got their greasy hamburger baskets. They both chewed ruminatively. "You should marry Jennifer," Larry said. "She expects you to."

"How do you know she expects it?"

"All women do."

"That's bullshit," Mark said, trying to find some position that would be even slightly comfortable on the canted wooden bench. "I'm no playboy, but I think Hefner's got it right. Sex is for fun. But relationships are even more fun."

"Sure," Larry said sarcastically.

"Marriage is something out of the middle ages," Mark lectured, "contracts to ensure treaties, property rights and lineage."

Larry's attention was wandering. "Speaking of bullshit, are you still into that hippie crap?" He flashed two victory signs. "Peace and love, brother, free love." Then he checked his watch. "Got to get going."

"So you can get home before Brenda does?" Mark couldn't help jabbing him.

Larry ignored him.

* * *

"You're driving very slowly today," Jennifer said. Mark glanced down at the speedometer—forty-five miles per hour. He sped up. "Guess my mind was elsewhere. Thanks for coming out to the farm to meet my parents."

She smiled. "I'm happy to."

The day was unseasonably cold and windy. Inside, the house seemed over-warm and was filled with the scent of roast beef. "Maybe after lunch, if you want to, we can walk down to the pond. Sorry the house is so hot. My mother is usually cold, so..."

"You don't need to apologize."

Mark's mother was sitting up watching the irises rocking in the wind. Her hair, thinned to almost nothing by chemotherapy, was pulled to one side and held with a red barrette, giving her a strange, childlike appearance. Her prominent eyes seemed glassy, but she smiled as Mark and Jennifer entered.

"Beautiful irises, Mrs. Exner," Jennifer said. Without a look at Mark she took the only chair. Mark stood around while they exchanged pleasantries for a moment. "Could I have a cup of tea?" Jennifer asked Mark.

In the kitchen he found his father already had the old metal tea canister out on the counter, and the was water boiling. Mark left him to it and wandered to the living room where he could watch his father's reflection in the window. As he listened to the familiar click of cabinet doors, the water boiling, and the clink of cups on the counter, he saw his father in a different light than ever before: just a person doing the best he could, with his own fears and joys, strengths and weaknesses. His head was down, his shoulders bent under the invisible load he carried. Mark stood for a long time examining this person he had known and not known his entire life.

Jennifer and his mother were sitting quietly when he and his father returned with the tea. "We had a nice talk," Jennifer said. The four of them drank tea and chatted, and for a time everything seemed normal. Grief is selfish, Mark thought once again. I feel hurt because my mother is leaving me, not because her life is being cut short.

Lunch was pleasant enough, although Mark's mother

ate almost nothing and was clearly tiring. After lunch Mark and Jennifer washed the dishes, then bundled up and hurried across a field deep green with spring. The irises his mother had planted near the small pond were in bloom, along with scattered clusters of cheerful yellow daffodils.

As they watched the wind blow fans of ripples across the pond, Mark asked Jennifer, "What did you two talk about?"

"Mostly about you, but I think she would rather I keep it to myself for a while." Jennifer was tucking one ear down into her collar, then the other. "My parents will be here this Saturday for graduation, and right after the ceremony we start back to St. Pete," Jennifer said. She held his arm tightly. "Will you come to graduation and meet them?"

"Of course."

They stood watching the wind fan ripples across the surface of the water. Mark pointed. "My mother planted those irises ten years ago. Now it looks the same, but it feels different. Columbia, and the University too. You're leaving. It's all ending."

As they walked back to the house Mark continued, speaking as much to himself as to her, "I want everything to stay just as it was, and I want us to always be together, and be happy. But…nothing stays the same forever."

In the car he pulled her close, breathing in the scent of her Chantilly. "Thanks," he whispered. On the way back they drove past a big green and yellow John Deere planter seeding corn. Life goes on, Mark said to himself. The scent of turned earth comforted him.

* * *

Carol sat in her apartment's immaculate kitchen drinking Sumatran coffee from the elaborate Braun coffee machine on the counter. The taste was lost on her, her mind elsewhere. She had been sitting at the table for an hour. She glanced at her watch. Her seminar on Asian politics had started forty minutes ago.

The phone began to ring. She ignored it for a time but it continued. When she picked it up, Jeff burst out, "I've got to see you. Right away."

"Not now." She checked her watch again. "If you're in town Saturday..."

"I'm in town now. I need to see you for a few minutes right now."

Fifteen minutes later Jeff knocked on her door. She made more coffee and they sat down at opposite sides of the round kitchen table.

"What's so urgent?"

Jeff blew steam off his coffee. "We're losing momentum. I talked with staffers from all the Missouri representatives I thought were backing us. Nothing is happening." He saw Carol's expression sinking into a frown and continued more slowly. "Farm Bureau has organized a big campaign to counter our efforts. All about patriotism and the American farmer. All bullshit..."

"...but well funded, I'm sure," Carol interjected.

"We need to call a meeting," Jeff continued. "Right away, get some people down to Jefferson City." he ground to a halt.

Carol set her cup down. "You take a day off from work, drive over here, barge in here just to tell me that?"

He raised his chin. "I've quit my job. I'm going to work full time on our referendum."

"Are you crazy?" Carol stared.

Jeff got up and began to pace. He launched into a monologue about his job, about what he could do for *One Voice*, about the entire student movement. "Build coalitions with SIU and KU. They're more active that we are, more radical. I know I can—why are you shaking your head?"

"You need to drive back to St. Louis and get your job

back, immediately," Carol said. "Tell them you had a family emergency you had to take care of, tell them anything. They'll..."

"No they won't," Jeff snapped. He slammed his cup down on the Formica, coffee slopping. "They fired me. Said I wasn't performing. I'm still in the six month probationary period so they don't have to do any paperwork. I'm out, as of last Friday." She moved around the table away from him. Jeff's expression hardened. "I don't care about that job. Best thing for me anyway. I hated that job. This is what I want to do, politics."

"No you don't," Carol said. Her face twisted into an expression Jeff had never seen before. "*One Voice* is dead."

Jeff tried again to approach her but she warded him off and poured herself more coffee. Bewildered, Jeff found himself mopping up his spilled coffee with a paper towel. He sank into his chair as Carol began to pace. "I'm not surprised at the sand bagging these stupid Missouri legislators are doing. And this Farm Bureau thing, that's no surprise. Lot of vested interests like the status quo. I'm sure they call us a bunch of kids behind our backs. I expected that from these local guys, but not from McCarthy." She looked through the window at the pool, lip trembling. "He wouldn't even see me last week. I waited all afternoon. Finally his internal affairs aide told me he'd relay my message to the Senator." A tear rolled down Carol's cheek. "Wouldn't even see me."

Jeff stepped forward to embrace her, but she pushed him back, hard. "Get off me!"

"Quit pushing me away!" Jeff shouted. He backed away and leaned on the back of a kitchen chair until it creaked. "That's your problem, Carol, you won't let anybody near you." They glared at each other. "My problem?" she said sarcastically. "Sounds to me like you're the one with the problem, fired from your job."

"No, you're the one with the problem, Carol. People don't

tell you, because you never listen to anyone. The joke around the *Free Press* office was that the manifesto was one voice all right, your voice. Nobody else had a say in any of it."

"Get the hell out of here!" Carol screamed.

Jeff stood, stricken. "We can rebuild, you and me..."

"I told you to get out! Never come here again!" She stormed off to her bedroom, slamming the door. Jeff heard the lock click.

She sat on the bed until she heard Jeff go out the front door. The apartment was entirely silent. She continued to sit there on the neatly made bed. The mirrored sliding doors of the closet reflected an image of someone she felt she didn't know any more. One of the closet doors was open and her eye slid over her clothes, neatly separated—dresses at one end, skirts and blouses at the other. Two rows of shoes on the floor. The neat rows blurred as she cried. She let herself cry for a long time, then she turned it off, picked up the phone, and called her father's private number.

# Chapter 22

At the airport Mark sat in his car, breathing the scent of cut grass, and watching jumpers get aboard the Cessna 180. It taxied down the runway and a moment later roared by overhead. After a while the distant buzz of the plane's engine sank to a whisper and the jumpers went out. Mark tracked the three specks as they maneuvered together, then separated. A few seconds later three white and orange chutes bloomed one after another in the blue.

There would be some new jumpers today. Rod was teaching a half-dozen students across the street in the Army Reserve Center. After his active duty time, Rod had stayed in the Army Reserve and had a key to the building which he treated as his own. Rod had been in the Eighty-Second Airborne Division in the Army. After Vietnam, he'd enrolled in the University on the GI Bill pay. Two years ago he had teamed up with Robert Karsch, another reservist who owned a plane, to form the University Jump Club. Karsch rented the plane to the club and Rod taught skydiving to pay for his own jumps.

Mark decided to do the right thing today. Study first, then go skydiving. The building was immaculate inside, waxed linoleum floors and metal doors painted with block numbers. Mark put his orange Thermodynamics book squarely in front of him and glared at it. Then he got out his notebook and opened it to a blank page. He stared at the blank page, the book, the neat rows of desks, the clean blackboard. Outside the window was a neat lawn, a trimmed hedge, and a perfectly-painted wooden sign. Every weekend Reservists were here doing maintenance as their Army commitment. It keeps them out of Vietnam, Mark thought. Maybe that's what I should have done.

He shook his head. Those half-measures don't work, not really. Either do something or don't do it.

In chapter eight he read four pages slowly, going back over each paragraph several times. Then he turned to the problems. Air expands in a turbine from two thousand degrees Fahrenheit and fifty-five pounds per square inch absolute to twenty pounds per square inch.

He could hear the plane taking off, down the hall the muted voices of Rod and his students.

Initial flow velocity is two hundred feet per second and exit velocity is eight hundred feet per second. Calculate the work output of the turbine if the process occurs isentropically. He turned to the gas-expansion tables, calculated the difference, and plugged it into the formula. He checked his answer, but it didn't match. He went back and found he'd made a calculation error, corrected it, and got to the right answer.

Mark tried to focus on Maxwell's equation, but his mind kept forming the picture of how this building looked from twenty-five hundred feet overhead. The tarred roof with air conditioning units. Nearby, Interstate 70, the big State Farm Insurance building, houses on tree-shaded streets. The blue sky drew him, but he told himself to study hard. His father's voice whispered to him. With an enormous effort of will, he pulled himself back to his book and the next problem. After three attempts he managed to work through it to the correct solution.

He went to the drinking fountain in the corridor, then returned to the silent classroom and stood looking out the window at the occasional car passing on the street. He became aware of a cricket chirping. The day was sunny and mild. A muddy Buick drove slowly by, an elderly man and his wife. In fifty years that may be me driving down these streets, Mark thought, going to get my lawnmower blade sharpened at Schaperkotter Hardware. The days will follow one after another regardless of how much I worry. The breeze will rustle the leaves of sycamore, elm and oak just as it does now. Despite my worry, things will be as they will be. How we spend the time is what matters. He gathered up his book and notebook and clicked off the light.

Mark walked down the neatly waxed hallway, shoes squeaking, out into the sunshine. He could hear the faint drone of the plane overhead, but could not see it, lost in the blue.

He found Mrs. Karsch in her usual spot, sitting in a lawn chair under the sunshade by their van. "I'm going to sell my gear," he told her cheerfully. "Maybe one of today's new students will want to buy it. All of it, main and reserve, boots, jumpsuit, helmet, goggles, altimeter, everything."

"Quitting?" She gave him her usual look—quizzical and cheerful.

"I love skydiving, but my mother is ill and I need to spend more time with her."

Mrs. Karsch was a warm and motherly figure, Mark realized. Why hadn't I noticed that before? "Could you pass the word around?"

"I'll do better than that. Just put your stuff in the van. I'll sell it for you. A couple of the new students have already asked about buying their own rigs so I'm sure we can sell it. Come out here in a week or two and we'll give you the money."

"Thanks." Mark loaded his gear into her cluttered van. He paused. "It's really been great; I'll miss all of you."

She smiled and waved as he walked away.

* * *

On his way back to the trailer he stopped at Safeway. A woman pushed a loaded grocery cart through the parking lot, a little girl skipping beside her. The flower boxes were brimming with daffodils nodding in the spring breeze. Down the block, in the little pond near the water tower, frogs called in chorus, announcing spring.

He stepped through the electric eye doors and into the familiar scents of Safeway. At the magazine rack he looked through the magazines, and remembered being ten years old, reading *Astounding Science Fiction* magazine as fast as he could while his mother shopped. The colorful covers flooded back into his mind—*The Pirates of Zan* by Murray Leinster, with its Kelly Freas cover showing a pirate climbing into a spaceship airlock, a slide rule gripped in his teeth. Mark scanned the rack from end to end, but now there was only *Redbook, Cosmopolitan, Life, Sports Illustrated*, and *Field and Stream*.

Mark had picked up four cans of tuna when Randy Vaughn walked up looking the same as the day he'd graduated from high school. "How you doing, Mark?" Randy leaned his broom against a freezer case and they shook hands. Randy had the same short, neatly combed brown hair, the same black-framed glasses, blue slacks, penny loafers, and white short-sleeved shirt. His narrow black tie was pinned with a silver tie bar.

"I'm fine, fine. How about you?"

"Just great." There was a moment's silence. "Linda and I are getting married next week," Randy volunteered.

"Congratulations." Mark tried to put enthusiasm into his voice. They shook hands again while Mark tried to remember what Linda looked like. Randy and Linda had been high school sweethearts. There had been no question they'd get married some day.

On those Friday nights Mark hadn't been able to get a date, he'd envied Randy. But now? Mark imagined himself behind Randy's smooth, honest face and black-framed glasses. Mark saw himself working here in Safeway, driving home in a Chevy Impala.

"I'm assistant manager now," Randy said to fill the silence. "After only four years."

"Great, great."

"You graduate from MU yet?" His tone was derisive. The tone of a Columbia kid who never intended to go to MU.

"August," Mark said.

"Then what?"

Mark shrugged. "Army. I can't see any way around the draft."

Randy looked around as though someone might be listening. "I'm III-A, a deferment for married guys. That and my bad eyesight." He touched his glasses apologetically.

"Well, that's good."

There was a page from one of the checkout girls and Randy's head went up like a dog hearing a whistle. "Got to go," Randy said, edging away. "But let's get together sometime soon. We bought a house on Ridgeway. It's got a big back yard. We could barbecue some steaks."

"Sounds great," Mark said as Randy bustled off with a wave.

Mark paid for his tuna. Randy and Linda would have good lives. They were honest, ordinary people—hard working, loving, and loyal. They would go to the same church their parents had, live in Columbia all their lives. They'd raise two well-behaved kids who would go to Hickman High School just like they had. He saw Randy's son, looking just like him, walking down the same halls, wearing black-framed glasses and jeans an inch too short.

Mark stepped out into the sunshine. He'd see Randy from time to time in the years ahead. They'd greet each other like old friends, but they would know nothing of each other's lives. Just Columbia kids who had known each other for a short time a long time ago.

* * *

Mark picked up Jennifer at her dorm and they drove to the trailer with the radio on WHB 710 AM, and the windows down. He told her about running into Randy. “”I guess we sometimes envy what we don’t have. I’ve spent the last two years demonstrating for change, but what I sometimes want is for things to stay exactly the same, always.”

Jennifer gave him a hug. “Classic conundrum. How about a cup of hot tea?”

They went into the trailer. “Yeah, let’s have a cup of tea.” He handed her a form letter typed on University letterhead. “I won’t be graduating this spring,” he told her. “Flunked Heat Transfer and it’s a required course for graduation.” Mark shrugged. “I’ve signed up for the course again this summer. I’ll graduate in August. The draft board changed my status to 1-A, but they’ll let me graduate before I get inducted.” She came over and put her arms around him.

They drank their tea, read poetry to each other, went to the bedroom and made love in the dark.

“I need to go back early tonight,” she said. “My parents are coming in tomorrow morning. My graduation ceremony is in the afternoon. Afterward, I thought we could all go to dinner.”

Mark drove out to the farm and put on his only jacket and tie and met Mr. and Mrs. Campion at the ceremony. Afterward they went to the Daniel Boone Hotel, where Jennifer’s parents were staying. In their suite on the fourth floor, which was heavy with the scent of painted wood, there was a basket of fruit on a side table and wine, scotch, and beer bottles and glasses clustered on the glass coffee table. “Busch isn’t it?” Mr. Campion pressed a cold bottle and glass into Mark’s hands. Mark found he was enjoying himself, despite his anxiety.

He met them at Jennifer’s dorm the next morning and helped them load Jennifer’s things into her parents’ white Oldsmobile Vista Cruiser. Stephanie had already moved out. He tried to envision Jennifer living in this room, going downstairs to meet him for their dates, but he couldn't. Jennifer's parents were waiting in the car.

"I used to watch for your car out this window," Jennifer said. The room was empty now. "You'd usually park right over there." He took her in his arms and they kissed and it seemed like the first time he had kissed her. Then they walked downstairs and out into the spring day.

Her father shook hands with him, her mother hugged him. "You'll come visit this summer won't you?"

"Yes, after summer school is over."

Jennifer got in the back seat beside the pile of her clothes. They kissed again. "I'll miss you, I love you," he said into her ear.

"I love you too," she whispered to him. "Call me, tell me about…everything… and study hard." She looked up at him and he gently closed the car door and waved as it pulled away.

He jumped into his car, drove back to the trailer, and loaded his three cardboard boxes of books and towels and kitchen stuff into the trunk, threw his clothes on the back seat, and started his car up. Then he turned it off and went back into the trailer and sat down on the couch with the front door open. The day had turned hot and silent. Mark tried to think about the hours and days of this last year, all the times in this trailer, the good times and the bad, but the wraiths of memory would not appear.

He walked around trying to conjure them up one last time. Down the narrow hall, his room was bare except for the cot-like bed. The empty closet stood open. He'd taken down the Summer of Love, Hendrix, and Joplin posters and thrown them in the trash. He sat on the old couch for another moment, then gathered up the last three bottles of Busch out of the refrigerator, put them on the seat of his Chevy, and drove away.

It took him less than fifteen minutes to move into his room at the shabby apartment Bill had found. When his things had been put away, Mark opened a bottle of Busch and sat on a metal lawn chair in the shade by the front door and succeeded in keeping his mind empty.

Mark had considered moving back to the farm for the summer, but couldn't bring himself to do it. He felt guilty, but keeping an apartment would give him some space. Mark needed space where he could at least pretend for a few hours that life was good. He had told his father he would not graduate until August. His father, deep in the silence of sorrow, had only nodded.

He drove to the farm every afternoon. Mark's mother was seldom conscious any more. Her bed faced the window that overlooked the garden that she had lovingly tended for as long as Mark could remember.

The irises were in bloom in the June sun. Clouds rose up in the sky in the rounded cumulus of summer. The humid wind from the south caressed the green, rustling trees. And past the tops of the trees, far to the south, past her vision now, lay the distant horizon and the daydreams she had had since the beginning of her life. She felt herself drifting off toward that hazy horizon. The drugs clouded her mind. Mostly she just lay there torpidly, but occasionally a voice or an image would appear. Sometimes it was Mark's father speaking to her, or the nurse asking her something, and sometimes it was Perry Mason or Della Street.

Mark and his father reassured each other that the drugs kept her from feeling any pain. Mark felt all the love he had for his mother, and an equal guilt for it being too late to express it.

* * *

That summer, the same as the past summer, Mark worked part time in a gas station across Ninth Street from campus. His summer routine was to go to his two classes in the morning, work at the Standard station until four, then go to the farm, and then back to the apartment to study. In addition to the Heat Transfer course he needed to graduate, he had signed up for an American Literature course. He had little interest in the course, but it was easy and he needed the grade.

His aunt and uncle had come to stay at the farm to help. A nurse came every day to check on his mother's medication. The doctor came twice a week, but there was nothing more that could be done.

Before dinner Mark would sit in the blue chair in her bedroom, the TV tuned to *Perry Mason*. As the dirge-like music would begin, Mark would gratefully sink into the black and white world of Perry, Della Street, and Paul Drake. Mark saw that his mother's eyes were sometimes on the TV, but more often on the light coming in the window. After dinner, Mark would drive back to his apartment and study until he could sleep for a few hours.

* * *

Through the haze of pain suppressants, Mark's mother could see only colors and shapes, shades of light and dark. She could hear the TV and the cadence of voices, but not the words. Deep in her mind she knew it was summer and that she was in her bedroom, in her house, at the farm. She knew her garden lay just outside, although she could no longer see it. From time to time she would hear her husband's familiar clomping footsteps on the hardwood floor in the hallway or his voice nearby. She also knew that there was a monstrous pain inside her shriveled body, but she did not feel the pain. The drugs held it down with a heavy hand. Sometimes she could see the blue of the sky through the window and the white of clouds. The tomato plants need rain, she thought. She realized her gardening gloves were nearly worn out and made a mental note to buy a new pair of gloves when she was at Westlake's Ace Hardware next time.

It was afternoon. The horizon beyond the garden was hazy with summer humidity, golden just as it had been on summer afternoons when she was a girl growing up in Nevada, Missouri. She saw herself when she was twelve years old, sitting outside on the lawn at their old house on a mild June day like this one. She was daydreaming of distant horizons. She heard her mother's voice calling her in for lunch. As she rose to her feet she found she kept on rising, light as air, floating up into the brilliant blue sky. Below her now was her own house at the farm in Columbia, her room, her garden, all of it falling away from her as she rose up into the endless blue sky.

When Mark got to the house that afternoon, his uncle met him at the door. "She's gone."

## Chapter 23

A robin chirped. Mark woke in an aquarium-green glow of morning sun through the hedge outside his apartment's tiny window. He lay there serenely until a wall of memories rose up around him. He pushed them back, feeling their overwhelming power just as the crewmen of the Patna in *Lord Jim* felt the ocean through the steel bulkhead that separated them from sinking. He dressed and drove to the farm where he found his aunt making eggs and bacon. Mark sat down to breakfast with his family. There was nothing much to say.

"The funeral is at ten," his father informed them.

"I'm taking an American literature course this summer," Mark told his aunt as they sat in the living room waiting to leave. "I only need to take a Heat Transfer course to graduate, but I thought I'd add a literature course."

"How is it?" his aunt asked without interest.

"Boring. Literary stories age badly. Pulp fiction will be read long after they are forgotten." She nodded, not hearing him.

He wandered into his room, sat down at his desk, and pulled *Secret of the Martian Moons* off his shelf. He looked at the familiar cover, willing himself to be pulled into the picture the way he had when he was twelve years old. It almost worked for a few minutes. Outside his window, the summer breeze rippled the daylilies in their orange row along the driveway.

He slid the book back onto the shelf with the others and ran his fingers along the row of colorful spines. I've read and reread these books since I was ten years old, usually right here in this room. They are a meditation. A portal through which I can travel back to a simpler time, when I was a kid and the future stretched out before me, limitless and untroubled.

He opened another and read a bit at random. In literary fiction, dysfunctional characters have interior monologues about trivial things, he thought. In pulp fiction, interesting characters do imaginative things. He put the book back on the shelf. These books don't change, but we do. Allison gone, Steve Griffin in the Navy, Keith in the Air Force. Tim dead, Dave and Jeff working. My mother gone.

A moment in time together, then everything changes.

* * *

Mark rode with his father and sister to Memorial Cemetery. His aunt and uncle followed in their car. It was a hot and humid summer day. They filed into a quiet room furnished to emulate a church, but without religious artifacts of any kind. There were small piles of white and yellow brochures on the polished wood table near the door—helpful tracts about how to deal with losing a loved one. They all sat in silence for a time. There was no ceremony. Mark knew his mother had wanted it that way—no religion. The urn containing his mother's ashes was on a table covered with black velvet. Four rows of folding chairs had been set up. Friends of his father's came and went, offering condolences and leaving sympathy cards in the basket near the door. Mark sat and kept his mind focused on images of the sunny morning outside, the breeze blowing through the oak and walnut trees. After a while, he needed the sunshine and walked out of the silent room. There was Bill Whitten sitting in the back row. He shook Mark's hand, then pulled him into a hug.

"Really sorry, Mark. I know it's tough on you, but hang in there," Bill said. Mark was touched. Good old conservative, studious Bill. Today he wore a dark suit, a narrow tie with a silver tie clasp, and polished black wingtip shoes.

After a while the family drove back to the farm. His sister and aunt made lemonade and they sat in the living room while Mark's father scattered his wife's ashes in the garden.

After lunch there didn't seem to be anything to do. Mark's father had retired to the spare bedroom, Mark's aunt and uncle were off running some errands; his sister was in her room.

Mark drove back to his apartment and opened to chapter six of his Heat Transfer textbook. He knew he needed the routine and normalcy of the campus and the classroom, and work at the gas station. He spent an hour working Heat Transfer problems, and felt better. After lunch he put on his blue work shirt with the Standard Oil emblem over one pocket and went to work.

A week went by. Mark maintained his routine of going to class, working at the gas station, studying, and driving out to the farm for dinner. His aunt and uncle left and the house felt very empty.

One afternoon when he arrived, he found his father and sister gone on errands. Propelled by emotions he could not name, he stepped silently down the hall to his parents' bedroom, cautious as a cat. The room looked the same—the bed was made, the pictures on the wall were the same, the blue chair and the dark red carpet were in their familiar places. Outside the window the irises still nodded in the summer wind.

Mark drove back to his tiny green room and studied Heat Transfer for four straight hours, then fell into an exhausted sleep.

* * *

One evening at the apartment, instead of studying, he opened a beer, clicked on the tiny black and white TV, and stared as Walter Cronkite's face slowly materialized. "...disclosed they had used wiretaps for surveillance of the so-called Chicago Eight at last year's Democratic National Convention in Chicago. In Laos, Prince Souvanna Phouma announced he has allowed U.S. bombers to bomb suspected North Vietnamese Army supply trails in Laos and further stated that bombing raids had been conducted into Cambodia for the same reason. The Pentagon denies that allegation. At the Paris Peace Talks, the Soviet Union and most Eastern Bloc nations have now recognized the provisional revolutionary government as the legitimate government of South Vietnam..."

Mark switched the TV off and stared at the blank screen. He took a short nap but woke dreaming of Perry Mason's dark eyes looking down on the empty bedroom at the farm.

His routine helped exhaust him for sleep at night. Most nights he sat in his tiny room studying, but then he began turning the TV on after dinner so he could follow the coming Apollo 11 launch. The first lunar landing was scheduled for next week. Mark had thought about this event his entire life as he devoured science fiction books. Within days he would be seeing the real thing, but somehow it didn't seem real. Nothing seemed real. He existed in his own lunar landscape of black and white, insulated from the world. Bill kept his conversation minimal. He asked if Mark wanted him to work some shifts for him, but Mark declined the offer. Frank, the owner of the gas station, asked Mark if he wanted to take time off, but Mark told him he'd rather work. In the evenings and mornings before class he would open his Heat Transfer textbook and work stolidly.

He sleepwalked through the days, a zombie.

* * *

The car at the pumps was a brand-new jet-black Chevelle two-door hardtop. The front fenders had small chrome emblems—396 over crossed checkered flags. The driver cut the engine and told Mark, "Five dollars worth of high-test." He got out and leaned against the side of the car while Mark got the gas going and cleaned the windshield. The guy was dressed in jeans, a white tee shirt, and loafers with white socks. His hair was cut short. The guy slipped his sunglasses off. "I know you, don't I?"

Mark tossed the blue paper towels in the trash and took a closer look at his boyish face marred by a few acne scars. "You're Glenn McCray aren't you?" Mark said, remembering his face from high school. They shook hands, power to the people style.

"Yeah. You're Mark Exner. I just got out of the Army," Glenn said. "Only been back in the world two weeks."

Mark finished gassing up the car, took the five dollar bill, and put it in the cash register. McCray didn't seem to be in any hurry to leave.

"I'm closing up now," Mark told him. "Want to drink a beer?" He nodded at the Heidelberg next door.

"Can I leave my car here?"

Mark nodded. "Or pull it up beside my Chevy."

Glenn grinned. "Want to drive it around the block before I park it?" He tossed Mark the keys.

Even with all the windows down the interior smelled new. He turned the key and the big engine came to life with a loping rumble. Glenn lit a Marlboro. Mark took hold of the Hurst three-speed automatic. "Put your foot on the brake," Glenn told him. "It'll lurch when you drop it into gear."

Mark slid the shifter back and felt the solid *thwock* of the automatic locking in. He let off the brake and the car moved forward aggressively. Mark checked traffic and pulled out onto University Avenue in front of the BPA building, accelerating. He let off and at the stop sign the big disc brakes slowed the car fast. There was a long block ahead of them, no traffic all the way to the intersection of College Avenue.

Mark jammed the accelerator to the floor and the Chevelle jolted forward with a scream of tires. Mark kept his foot in it and watched the tach wind up past four thousand RPM, the speedometer passing seventy-five before he let off and braked hard to the stop sign. They sat at the stop sign while a station wagon went by the other way. Glenn was grinning, cigarette cocked in his mouth. The rush of adrenalin washed out the simmering anger Mark had felt for days. He made a U-turn in the intersection and came back to park the Chevelle beside his Chevy. He pushed the thumb button on the Hurst and pushed the shifter up into park. The engine idled, gently rocking the car. Mark turned the key and handed it to Glenn. "Yeah!" Mark said.

In the cool gloom of the Heidelberg they found a booth and ordered a pitcher of Hamm's. Glenn laughed. "She's a goer isn't she?"

Mark shook his head. "Man oh man." He spread his hands. "Didn't mean to push her so hard."

"That's what she's designed for, to go fast."

"What did you do in the Army?" Mark asked.

"Eleven boom-boom."

Mark looked puzzled.

"Infantry," Glenn elaborated. "My MOS, military occupational specialty, was eleven, infantry. I let the draft take me so that I'd only have two years of Army time. But if you're a draftee, you go straight into the infantry. Cannon fodder."

"You came through okay."

Glenn made a good luck sign. "I figure, if I'm going to be in the shit, be in the shit all the way." Their beer came and he filled two glasses. "First tour was tough. Most platoon leaders, the lieutenants, are morons. They usually last about ninety days after they get to Vietnam; they're either shot or their own men frag them." Glenn shrugged. "The sergeants are the real leaders, good guys. If you listen to them and learn the ropes, promotion's fast. I made E-6 in two and a half years. Now I'm running the show for my platoon." Glenn's grin made him look ten years old.

"So you're just here on leave?"

Glenn shook his head. "Nope, I'm out. They offered me a big bonus to reenlist, but I turned them down. I had a bunch of saved pay, combat pay and paid-up leave. I walked out with eight thousand dollars in my pocket."

Mark whistled.

"Paid sixty-two hundred, cash, for that Chevelle in Oakland and drove here."

"Now what? Back to MU?"

Glenn laughed. "Nah. That time is past for me. I wasn't any good as a student the first time, and I'd be worse now." He laughed again. "Too much like going back to high school, you know?"

"GI Bill. You could take whatever courses you wanted, just mess around, have a date every night."

Glenn laughed long and loud. "To tell you the truth, Mark, since I've been back all the women look like old housewives or junior high school kids. The hookers in Thailand are better."

They contemplated their beers.

"So what's next?" Mark asked.

"Know of any jobs around town? I'm pretty good with an M-16." Glenn grinned his boyish grin. Mark laughed. "You could pump gas. Like me."

Glenn laughed. "Thailand, that's where it's at. It's paradise. Hookers everywhere, and good-looking too. Pot, beer, whiskey...it's paradise. And the food's great. You wear yourself out." He looked away. "And why not, three weeks of paradise, then back to the shit. Nobody lives forever." Glenn raised his glass and Mark followed suit. "Back in 'Nam one day, my second tour, my buddy Scow and me were riding a five ton in a resupply convoy going up to Danang. Late afternoon some trucks were almost out of diesel so the lieutenant calls for the convoy to stop and radios for tankers to bring some diesel." Glenn sipped meditatively. "Lieutenant's jittery as hell. Chicken shit kind of guy. But a stopped convoy is a target just waiting to get hit. And his bosses at I-Corps will bust his butt for stopping outside a safe zone if he sits there too long. The usual locals are walking along the road, going about their business. We don't let them get close to the vehicles; the VC'll throw a grenade under a truck before you know it. Scow's waving them back but they're ignoring him. The old guys and women don't want to walk around on the paddy dikes, they want to walk on the shoulder of the road." Glenn drank his beer and refilled his glass. "Anyway. Lieutenant's up at the front of the line. Scow and I are at the back. I hear a burst from an M-16."

"Not an AK-47?" Mark asked.

"No. They sound completely different. An M-16 has this real high snapping sound. I go running back to the last truck and there's Scow reloading. He'd shot a couple of the women. 'They got too close, man,' he says as I get there. Lieutenant didn't hear with all the truck engines idling. 'Help me get rid of these gooks,' Scow says. The rest of the locals had disappeared as soon as Scow opened up. We dragged the bodies off into a ditch. They looked like a discarded pile of rags with a straw hat nearby. 'You going to tell Top?' I asked Scow when we climbed back into a five ton. 'What for?' We sat inside the canvas, hot as hell, until the tankers got everybody refueled and off we went."

Mark thought about murder, unpunished, unknown.

A couple of girls came in as Glenn stood up. "Got to get going, Mark. Good to see you." He slid a ten dollar bill out of his billfold and laid it on the table. "See you around." Mark noticed the girls were watching him as he walked out, his self-assurance drawing their eyes.

Mark heard the rumble of the black Chevelle diminish. No regret. Mark poured the last of the beer into his glass. Maybe I should just go ahead and enlist right after I graduate and get it over with. Volunteer for Vietnam, get right in the middle of the shit, and right in the middle of R&R in Thailand. No thinking required, just live for the moment.

Mark went back to his green room, clicked on the window air conditioner, and opened his American Literature book to Sarah Orne Jewett's story, "The Dulham Ladies." The grad student teaching the course had called it an ironic and sympathetic picture of small-town Maine society in the nineteenth century. Mark read as much as he could, but the archaic descriptions lay there on the page.

He closed the literature book, got out his Heat Transfer book, and worked problems until his mind tired. Then he opened a beer, drank it fast, and opened another one. The whisper of the window air conditioner became the steady rumble of truck engines idling, the crackle of M-16 fire, a jukebox in a Bangkok bar, the rumble of a 396 Chevelle engine.

The next morning Mark arrived at the station with a hangover. Sam, Frank's pompous assistant, hooked a thumb at a Cadillac and a Lincoln Continental waiting to be washed, and Mark set to work with anger crawling all over his skin like a thousand insects. At noon Frank added up the receipts for the day, and he and Sam left the station to Mark. After they had driven away Mark went to his Chevy, got out four cans of Busch, and stocked them in the Coke machine. He opened one and sat in the decrepit military surplus swivel chair staring at the leaves on the trees across the street. Maybe the alcohol would settle his anger, but he doubted it. At one forty-five Mark rolled the rack of used tires into the service bay and pulled the rolling door down. A white Ford station wagon pulled up to the pumps.

"We're closed!" Mark shouted from the office. A guy with a boot camp haircut got out of the car and sauntered into the office, removing his sunglasses.

"Jeff!" Mark exclaimed. "What the hell! Are you in the

Army?"

"Yeah, I enlisted. Just finished Basic down at Fort Leonard Wood."

Mark's mind couldn't absorb the idea of Jeff in the Army.

"There's a good movie at the Uptown," Jeff said. "What time do you get off?"

"Right now. Let's go." Mark took the beer out of the Coke machine and locked up the station.

# Chapter 24

After watching *The Thomas Crown Affair* at the Uptown Theatre, they went to Hulen Lake and swam out to the raft. The bleached wood was warm in the late afternoon sun. "Be great to live like Steve McQueen," Mark said. "I liked that scene where Steve McQueen and Faye Dunaway are having breakfast outside on the rooftop. Have lots of money, big house with servants."

"I thought your plan was to take Jennifer deep in the country. Hide out from the world."

Mark closed his eyes against the sinking sun. "Well, none of those plans matters much until we get our Army time over with, right?"

Jeff sat up. "Guess what?"

Mark was silent, fearing the worst.

"After I finish AIT, I'm not going to Vietnam. I'm going to Germany. I've already got my orders."

Mark snapped up to a sitting position. "You lucky son of a bitch." He pounded Jeff's narrow shoulders. "Germany for Christ's sake—one big party. And I assume McDonnell will hold your job for you until you get back."

Jeff picked at the sun-bleached wood and let loose another surprise: "I quit McDonnell."

Mark shielded his eyes from the glitter of the water. "Jesus! Why'd you do that?"

"I hated it."

"But it could buy you that Thomas Crown lifestyle."

"I never really wanted that lifestyle. I wanted to be an engineer partly because my parents expected it and partly to get out of my shell, meet some new people, really accomplish something. But the job never got to be fun and I never did meet anybody in St. Louis. I just went to work and then back to the apartment every night and watched TV. That's why I started spending weekends back here in Columbia, working with Carol on that political stuff."

"Whatever happened to her anyway?"

The sun had turned orange in the Western sky. "She's in San Francisco now. I called her father's investment company in Chicago, to get her number. Strange name. Pacific Partners it was called. I was going to call her but..." Jeff shrugged. "Sorry to hear about your mother's death."

"Thanks," Mark said.

The waves tapped the underside of the raft. The scent of warm wood was fading as the sun sank. A couple of boys swam out to the raft and ducked under it, giggling and splashing.

Jeff chuckled. "I used to do that. We lived right up the street here." He paused. "I don't really mind being in the Army, now that I don't have to worry about Vietnam. Everything is cut and dried, no decisions to be made. And when my time's up I'm coming back to MU, to grad school on the GI Bill. I want to spend my life in contact with people, not locked away at a desk doing calculations." A determined note had come into Jeff's voice. "I want to get married, raise a family, live right here in Columbia."

Jeff stood up too. "I remember you telling me I should be a little less honest with women. You were probably right at the time. But not now. I want to meet a woman I can be completely honest with, really share our lives." He glanced at Mark. "I was probably too honest, Mark. And you were never honest enough."

The sun touched the horizon.

* * *

After work the next day Mark forced himself to go out to the farm. He had lunch with his father and sister, everyone working hard to act normal. Afterward Mark went out to the shed.

"Give me a hand, will you Mark?" his father said. They took the tractor and trailer to the young walnut trees and spent an hour pruning and hauling cut limbs to a brush pile.

"Once we get some rain, I'll burn this. The ash is good for the soil."

They worked until nearly five. Tired, but feeling better than he had in months, Mark helped his father put things away in the big shed.

"Staying for dinner?"

"No thanks," Mark said. His father trudged to the house.

Mark hesitated, watching barn swallows swooping against the sunset. He and I keep our grief to ourselves, he thought. Maybe that's bad, but that's the way we are. In the fading light, Mark noticed a red frame protruding from a dusty tarpaulin. He tugged it back into place and realized it was his old go-kart. He flipped the tarpaulin off and it all came back to him—working with Tim Bryant on this old go-kart, getting it running just for the fun of it.

Mark touched the old Briggs and Stratton engine they'd bought secondhand. They had fixed it up, put it on the kart, and gone out on the abandoned highway to see how fast it would go.

"Good times," Tim used to say.

"Listening to the old songs on the radio," Mark whispered. "Lesley Gore—'She's a Fool.' The Rip Chords, The Hondells, Jan and Dean, Randy and the Daytonas." Mark laughed out loud. "Little GTO, you're really looking fine, three deuces and a four-speed and a three-eighty-nine."

His smile faded. Life goes on. But the good husband and

father Tim would surely have been, was gone from the world.

In the dusky light Tim's ghost grinned at him, Buddy Holly glasses and braces on his teeth, unchanged from the day Mark had met him in high school—likeable, naïve, shy, in love with cars, just like Mark. They'd cruise around after school, Mark in his '57 Chevy, Tim in his '57 Plymouth, drag racing from light to light on Business 70—oldies on the radio, doing things on the spur of the moment, just for the fun of it.

Tim, dead and buried.

Mark pulled the tarp back over the go-kart, got in his car, and accelerated hard up to seventy-five miles-per-hour like they used to in high school, cars side by side. He imagined Tim's yellow Plymouth taking the Stadium Road exit, tapping his horn twice.

* * *

Mark floated up to consciousness in the deep green light of his room. The tiny window was screened by a hedge backlit with golden summer morning light. He drifted back to sleep, completely at ease, with his small room fitted around him like a tent in the wilderness. But then a dove called and sorrow washed over him, pushing him down into its depths. He pulled himself up, showered, dressed, gathered his books, and walked to campus through air liquid with humidity. Walking kept him from drowning in an ocean of sorrow.

When Mark shambled out of the Arts and Science Building after his American Literature class, he was surprised to find Bill sitting on the wide steps reading a paperback copy of *The Pentagon Papers*.

"Hey, this is not like you," Mark said. "Next thing I know you'll be joining the protest marches, like the Berrigan brothers. Your father was a priest too, right?"

Bill put the book down and leaned back against the stone steps. "He was pastor of a little neighborhood church in

Webster Groves. He died a few years ago."

"Sorry," Mark said. "And by the way, thanks for coming to my mother's funeral."

Bill nodded. "People try to help in many ways. My father tried. Less dramatically than the Berrigan brothers. The protests and sit-ins and demonstrations are one way." Bill rubbed his hand along the worn stone step. "But there are other ways. Less dramatic."

"Maybe that's the direction you ought to go," Mark said.

Bill stood up, clearly embarrassed. "Maybe. But first I'm going to be an engineer for thirty years or so. Did I tell you I took the job with the naval shipyard in California?"

"Congratulations."

Bill checked his watch. "Got to get to the lab. By the way, you don't mind if I bring Martha over to the apartment tonight do you?"

"You need me out of there?" Mark said. "I kind of want to watch the moon landing tonight."

Bill shook his head, embarrassed. "Oh no, nothing like that. We want to watch the moon landing too."

Mark laughed. "A Forestry major like Martha is interested in the space program?"

* * *

The moon landing would occur about nine in the evening, Columbia time. After work at the gas station, Mark bought a six-pack of Busch and ate a TV dinner at the apartment with the tiny black and white TV running. Then he set to work reassembling his motorcycle engine. He and Bill had taken it apart a couple of days before to overhaul it and Mark was getting tired of stepping through a tangle of parts spread out on newspapers on the apartment floor. Walter Cronkite was stalling for time, interviewing various NASA dignitaries. Mark worked through a few cans of Busch while he laid the transmission gear assemblies into their bearing races, got the case closed, and reattached the piston cylinder and head.

At eight thirty the front door opened and Bill and Martha came in carrying another six-pack of Busch. Mark clicked the overhead light on so they could navigate through the sea of motorcycle parts on the floor. Beers were passed around. Bill sat down in the only other chair and Martha sat on his lap.

Finally the *Eagle* dropped down out of orbit and blurry black and white images of lunar dust rose up. The TV confirmed that they had safely landed. Mark grinned and opened another Busch. The three of them watched in silence as Neil Armstrong hopped awkwardly down the ladder to the lunar surface and made his famous announcement with its small flaw. Mark and Bill and Martha applauded.

"I've been reading stories my whole life about the first lunar landing," Mark said. "Now it's actually happened." He looked around the room, a grin on his face. "A toast: to the final frontier...."

"...where no man has gone before," Bill answered. They drained their beers and Martha got out another round.

"But now nobody can write stories about it anymore can they?" Martha said. She was a solid, no nonsense girl with the most beautiful straight blond hair Mark had ever seen. A Forestry major, Mark had never seen her wearing anything other than tee shirts, worn jeans, and work boots.

"Turn it up," Bill said. "They're going to replay it." Once again the space-suited figure of Neil Armstrong hopped down the ladder to the lunar surface. Mark thought of his books in his bedroom at the farm, their covers depicting spaceships settling onto the lunar surface. Now I've seen the real thing. The thought warmed him.

"Man on the moon," Mark breathed. "I hope the space program will get going now. We should have a colony on the moon and a space station within a decade; first ship to Mars in twenty years."

"And commercial space flight to low earth orbit," Bill said. "I'd sign up for that."

"Me too. Definitely," Mark said. He felt elated and it wasn't just the alcohol. "We have momentum now. The entire Mercury program, Gemini program, and Apollo program have only taken eight years. I remember how thrilled I was when President Kennedy made that speech, '...we choose to go to the moon in this decade...'"

"I remember where I was when President Kennedy was shot," Martha said. "I was in class in junior high. It was a rainy afternoon. We were literally stunned. They put the radio broadcast on the PA system for a while, then they let school out early that day."

"I remember," Bill said. "It's only been six years."

"I'd pay for a ride to orbit," Mark changed the subject briskly. "A few years from now I'll be rich so a hundred thousand for a ride to orbit will be no problem." He found he was sitting on his American Literature textbook and tossed it to one side. "Literature is great, but it's for fun, not for work. I want to work with machines—beautiful machines like spacecraft." He and Bill were both grinning while Martha rolled her eyes. Bill gave Martha the chair and slid the motorcycle engine over enough to sit on the floor.

At dawn the next day, Mark woke and lay in the morning silence until images of the farm rose up in his mind and started tears flowing. He put his mind on Neil Armstrong and Buzz Aldrin on the moon until the tears stopped. But as he dressed, a dove began to call softly in the green light outside, and sorrow settled over him again like a shroud.

Walking to class cleared his mind. He paid careful attention in his Heat Transfer class, but decided to skip American Literature because they were going to discuss Flannery O'Connor and he wanted to go the apartment and finish getting his motorcycle running instead. It took him less than thirty minutes to get it running. He changed into his gas station shirt and rode the Suzuki. It felt good having the bike running again, and running right. And it felt even better cruising down Ninth Street on the bike, savoring the humid summer day.

The Standard station's business followed the cycle of the school year. Summer was always slow. Frank and Sam would work only until noon, then leave either Mark or Bill there to tend the station until closing time.

Mark always took his Heat Transfer text and his American Literature text with him, but never opened either one of them. Most of the time he'd sit in the old Army chair, feet on the desk, thinking of nothing.

He opened his Lit book. With minimal effort he could get an A in the course. Writing about literature had always been easy for him. He glanced down the assignment sheet—Bret Harte, Henry James, Katherine Anne Porter, O. Henry, Sherwood Anderson, Eudora Welty, Sarah Orne Jewett, for chrissake. What tripe! He snapped the book closed and breathed in a great breath of air scented delicately with oil and new tires. The stories in the text were deadly boring. Stone Age artifacts. Page after page of very closely observed and elegantly described trivia. Absolutely static, I should put that in my next paper, he thought. No, I need the grade, so I'll keep my true opinions to myself. He had put no effort into the course so far and was making a B, so let well enough alone. The science fiction stories he read and reread were so much better. He drifted into a reverie that started in his room at the farm, but newsreeled back through the semester—the campus in springtime, Jennifer in candlelight, LSD colors flowing in an endless wave, the cool air of autumn on his motorcycle riding down country roads to the farm. Then the images darkened: his mother gone, the farm silent, Tim killed, Keith gone to the Air Force, Dave working, Jennifer in Florida. And the draft coming at me like a freight train.

He swung his feet down off the desk as a pale green Pontiac Bonneville pulled up to the pumps.

Mark sauntered outside while the driver got out. A guy in madras shorts, loafers with no socks, a green golf shirt, and aviator shades. He slid the sunglasses off and reality shifted for Mark. It was Dave.

For a moment neither of them said anything. Then Dave stuck out his hand and Mark shook it, then pulled him in for a hug and they slapped each other's backs.

"Where in the hell did you disappear to?" Mark said.

"St. Louis." Dave grinned.

They stood there looking at each other for a moment, both shaking their heads. Then Mark stepped back and looked at the car. "New."

"Yeah. Bonneville 400. Three hundred and eight miles on it."

Dave popped the hood and Mark admired the big, clean V8 and four barrel carb. "Seven fifty CFM, three-speed automatic," Dave ticked off the important points about the car, "power windows, air conditioning, stereo FM."

"Man oh man," Mark breathed. They retired to the battered Army surplus chairs in the office and settled in, admiring two girls with MU notebooks crossing Ninth Street.

"Not much going on here," Mark said. "You know how slow it gets in summer. Want a beer?"

"Sure." Mark unlocked the soda machine and got out a couple cans of Busch.

"About last winter," Dave said slowly, avoiding Mark's eye. "I should have let you guys know I was moving to St. Louis, but things were moving kind of fast..."

"You had me worried," Mark said. "But I didn't want to contact your parents in case you hadn't told them..."

"It all just sort of happened by chance really. Allison had gone home for Christmas and New Year's. I was in St. Louis visiting my uncle over the holidays. The draft board had already rejected my request for deferment for grad school. My cousin said they were hiring people at LogCom there in St. Louis."

"What's LogCom?"

"Army Logistics Command. Buying and shipping tanks and helicopters to Vietnam." Dave stared at the row of fan belts hanging from the racks in the service bay. "My cousin took me down there to talk to them and they made me an offer."

"You just stayed in St. Louis?"

"Pretty much. I started working right away. I just took a day off to come back to take my finals." He tilted his beer to his mouth and put his sunglasses back on. "I guess I really just didn't want to discuss my decision with you guys, or with Allison." He took the sunglasses back off and studied the sky above the oak trees on campus. "I guess I was afraid you guys would think I'd sort of chickened out."

Mark felt very uneasy about this confession. "Well it looks like things worked out."

"Allison?"

"She went to Taos," Mark said evenly.

"Good," Dave said. "She'd been talking about doing that."

"Found any hot women over in St. Louis?" Mark asked to change the subject.

"A few."

"You don't seem very enthusiastic about it."

"I'm not." Dave lifted his head as the breeze came through the open door. "I was serious about getting into grad school. I really wanted to explore that region of knowledge where philosophy intersects economics and politics. I think I..." he stopped suddenly.

"That job got you out of the draft at least," Mark said.

Dave said nothing.

"I mean, you're contributing to the war effort."

"Bullshit," Dave said softly. "It's just bureaucratic crap, paper-pushing a chimpanzee could do."

Mark didn't want to hear this either. He downed his beer, tilted the old swivel chair down, and stared at the scarred desktop. "I'm just going to let the clock run out, let the draft board get me."

There was silence for a time.

"Sorry to hear about your mother's death," Dave said.

"Thanks."

"Want to drive down to the Lake?"

An image came into Mark's mind so clearly he could feel Jennifer's sun-warmed body next to his, crowded into the back seat of Keith's Corvair, driving back from an afternoon at the Lake through the long summer evening—the windows down, warm air blowing past, singing along with Andy Kim on KXOK, '...baby how'd we ever get this way...'

"The Lake?" Mark said. "No, I don't think so."

Dave finished his beer and tossed the can in the trash. He stood. "Well..."

"I heard from Steve Griffin a week ago," Mark said to keep him from leaving. "He's in Oakland, doing his Navy time, says the Bay Area is great, topless bars everywhere."

"Let's go," Dave said, straight-faced.

"You don't have to work?"

"I took a few days off."

"Well, you've got the perfect car for a road trip." Mark finished his beer with a flourish. "Besides, there's nothing to do around here. Columbia's not the same anymore, everybody we knew is gone, all new faces on campus, in the I.V., the Black and Gold, the Heidelberg. It's not our time anymore."

"If we left tomorrow morning," Dave said, "we'd be in Oakland Wednesday, two days there, start back Saturday, get here Sunday. I'd be back at my desk Monday morning."

"I can get Bill to work my shift for me," Mark said.

"I'll pick you up at seven tomorrow morning," Dave said authoritatively and slid into his car.

# Chapter 25

They took turns driving. Morning turned to afternoon, and evening into night as they crossed the Kansas prairies to Denver, then north to Cheyenne, and west again on Interstate 80. The road was a Felliniesque ribbon of asphalt, unrolling endlessly in the Pontiac's headlights. Eventually they wound down the Western slope of the Wasatch Range past Salt Lake City and into Nevada.

Mark longed for the freedom he'd felt two years ago when they'd driven down to Galveston for Spring Break, but now he felt only homesickness for his tiny green room on summer mornings and his routine of work and class and the farm.

Mark started out of a doze; his watch said four AM. Dave was at the wheel, staring straight ahead, the speedometer steady at eighty-five.

"I'm surprised you decided to go on this trip," Dave said. "Aren't you retaking some course you flunked once already?"

"Yeah, Heat Transfer. I could have graduated in June if I'd just passed that course, but I didn't."

"Well, this spring's been a tough time for you, I'm sure." Dave kept his eyes on the highway. "How's your dad doing, and your sister?"

"My dad will be alright. He's the tough, silent type. My sister seems fine now but there may be delayed effects. I don't even know who her friends are or what she does. I help my dad some, but we don't talk much."

Dave mulled this over for a few miles. "I understand delayed effects." Now he seemed to want to talk after a thousand miles of silence. "I feel guilty. Last January I should not have left town without talking to Allison. She deserved better. But I was under pressure. The draft board had rejected my request for deferment for grad school." He grimaced in the soft glow of the dashboard lights, and made his familiar shrugging motion. "I try to convince myself that going to work for the Army is right and consistent with everything I've been saying the last few years. My parents tell me I did the right thing. But inside my own head I'm not so sure. Maybe I did the right thing or maybe I just did the expedient thing." The same shrug again. "Now I've got a draft deferment, ten thousand dollars a year, a nine-to-five job, all kinds of health and retirement benefits. But no grad school and no Allison."

"Don't beat yourself up too badly," Mark said. After a minute he added very softly and carefully, "Allison was hurt... but, you know..."

Dave didn't hear him. "Allison. I guess I just wanted to get it over with fast. A clean break." He drew a long breath. "I couldn't trust myself to look her in the eye and tell her I was leaving. And that I was leaving her behind because it just would have been too complicated having a live-in hippie girlfriend with me in St. Louis. Too hard to explain to everybody. I don't think she wanted to get married. I know I didn't. But she and I were..." He glared at the fan of headlights in the darkness. "We were as perfect together as anything I have ever experienced. So I let her go and maybe I shouldn't have."

Mark was silent.

"The road," Dave said softly to the white dashes sliding under the car one after another. "The way, the Tao."

They lapsed into silence. Eventually morning came as they drove up into the Sierras and down the long slope to the Bay.

* * *

They reached Steve's apartment in Oakland at four and crashed in their sleeping bags on the floor. Steve woke them when he got home at five. "Get up you deadheads." He pressed Budweisers into their hands and they drank the beer in an exhausted haze. They made disjointed conversation until the phone rang and Steve had to get back to the base.

The next morning Mark woke from a dream of his silent green room in Columbia. After a while he roused himself, and nudged Dave out of slumber. They sat hunched over coffee cups; Steve had already left for the day.

"Mario Savio in Berkeley," Dave read in the Berkeley Barb.

* * *

They joined a throng of people making their way down Telegraph Avenue toward Sather Gate. The golden light of morning flowed over them like honey, raising Mark's spirits, but Dave's expression remained dark. Too much confession, Mark assumed.

"The Free Speech Movement is passé," Dave pronounced. The crowd thickened as they approached Sproul Plaza, where hawkers of every sort were working the crowd, selling marijuana, peace signs, ankhs, beaded necklaces, bongs, roach clips, rolling papers, tee shirts, and pamphlets promoting every imaginable cause. They shouldered into the crowd far enough to hear someone on a loudspeaker, but the words were unintelligible. Around them people were chit-chatting. In the press of bodies, Dave grabbed Mark's elbow. "Let's go." They retreated to a coffee shop on Telegraph Avenue. "Free speech?" Dave snorted. "Now it's just an excuse to sell tee shirts."

"You and Carol used to have a passion for that stuff," Mark reminded him. The espresso was good, but expensive. He'd have to watch his money. Mark fingered the slip of paper in his pocket with Carol's address on it. He'd called her parents in Chicago, gotten her number in San Francisco, and left a message on her machine. He wasn't quite sure why he wanted to contact her. He hadn't mentioned it to Dave yet, but as he opened his mouth to tell him, Dave said, "Let's go over to San Francisco."

"Yeah, Haight-Ashbury," Mark said. They'd talk about Carol later.

"Haight-Ashbury?" Dave raised his eyebrows. "Even more passé than free speech."

He was right. They found that the Age of Aquarius had departed. Heroin junkies lay in doorways, panhandlers chanted, "Spare any change?" People on the sidewalk seemed grim, or stoned, or both. Peace and Love were gone. They walked up Masonic to the panhandle of Golden Gate Park between Oak and Fell Streets, where pale yellow sunlight filtered through the eucalyptus trees and there were no people around. They sat cross-legged on the ground and passed a joint back and forth until it was gone.

"I always thought that drugs like psilocybin, mescaline, LSD, peyote, all the psychedelics, were about exploring new states of consciousness," Mark said. "But those guys back there," he hooked a thumb toward Haight Street, "that's just old-style inner-city hard drug stuff."

"It changed last June when Robert Kennedy got shot," Dave intoned. "Actually when Clean Gene got passed over at the Democratic Convention. No, actually when Nixon won the election. The sixties ended in November 1968." He fingered a eucalyptus leaf. "They ended for me in January when I took this job."

Mark closed his eyes in the warmth of the sun. "Things have changed fast. My roommate Bill has been dating a girl named Martha. She doesn't know anything about the protests, political activism, freedom of speech, or the counter culture. She's in school to get a degree so she can get a job."

"Nothing wrong with that," Dave said. He slipped his

sunglasses on.

"Maybe not," Mark said. "Sometimes it seems like all that stuff happened long ago. Things have changed. A new reality. You were smart to go to work for the Department of Defense and get that deferment."

"Maybe," Dave said. "It doesn't feel very satisfying."

"Look at it this way. You don't have to worry about the draft. And, the job gets you money and money gets you beautiful things—like your Pontiac."

"Speaking of beautiful things," Dave got to his feet, "let's go to one of the topless clubs and see some naked girls."

"Right now?"

"You told me you've only got about a month of freedom left, so you'd better enjoy it."

They walked up Columbus Avenue and went into the first club they saw. They pushed through two sets of doors in total darkness, and emerged in a red-lit bar, where two completely naked girls were dancing on a long platform right behind the bartender. The jukebox was playing "Elenore."

"This puts a whole new perspective on that song." Dave smirked as they dropped onto empty barstools.

"What'll it be guys?" the bartender asked. They ordered beers. The girls were about his own age, Mark noted, not bad-looking with pretty good bodies.

The next song was "Sugar, Sugar" by The Archies. Dave laughed. "Bubblegum! Your kind of music." They drank their beers down quickly and ordered another round. Mark found his attention wandering away from the girls' repetitive movements and stony expressions, but then their naked bodies pulled his eyes back. He found he'd finished his beer and Dave was ordering a third round. Mark ponied up some cash for the jukebox and they listened to "Who'll Stop the Rain" and "Put a Little Love in Your Heart."

"I always liked that song," Mark shouted to Dave.

"I like her," Dave nodded toward the cute blonde gyrating right in front of him. The jukebox went on to "Bad Moon Rising," then "Gimme Gimme Good Lovin'."

"Crazy Elephant," Mark shouted to Dave. "Good stuff."

"Absolute crap," he answered. "Let's move on." The tab was thirty-five dollars. They left two twenties on the bar, and stumbled out into the street, which seemed bleak and monochromatic.

"I'm worn out," Mark said. "And half drunk."

"Then you're ready for the next stop." Dave pointed at a sign. "Carol Doda at the Condor Club. That's where topless started."

"She's the one with those gigantic..."

"Forty-four inches of pure silicone," Dave said reverently as they went in.

But Carol didn't perform until ten at night, so they had one beer, then drove to Fisherman's Wharf for an early dinner at Alioto's. "Got to do the tourist stuff, right?" Dave said expansively. He brightened more as they were shown to a window table in the uncrowded restaurant. White tablecloth and silverware, the sun sinking behind boat masts, the world was as it should be.

The red snapper and Pinot was wonderful. Darkness settled over the marina as the fog swept in. Dave picked up the check and they lingered over coffee. "My treat. I'm the working class, you're still the starving student."

Mark looked at his watch and broached the subject of Carol. "I got her number from her father's investment firm. I'm going to meet her in half an hour."

Dave's look stayed skeptical through Mark's explanation. "Why don't you come along? It'll be good to see her again, talk over old times. Besides, I'm curious as to why she left Columbia so unexpectedly. Left all that political action behind."

Dave looked at his watch. "Unexpectedly? Maybe. Or maybe all that political action was just about her. Talk was cheap back then, but those days are over. A new reality, right?"

Mark looked at the fog hazing the lights outside. "Maybe. Of all the people I've known, she seemed the most sure of herself. And I guess I want to see what happens to us after we leave school."

"Here's an example," Dave pointed a finger into his chest. "Maybe not a good one." His tone was unexpectedly bitter. He set his coffee cup down. "I don't need to see another one."

Embarrassment? Mark realized that Dave seemed embarrassed over Carol's high relative position and salary. As they walked out into the foggy night Mark tried once again. "It's just for old time's sake...reminisce about the late, great sixties, about Columbia..."

"You want me to pick you up after your little chat?"

"No, I checked the bus route. It'll get me back to Steve's place."

The foggy night seemed to restore Dave's spirits. He flashed a dark and knowing look at Mark. "I'm going to City Lights bookstore, then maybe a jazz club."

* * *

The lobby of Opera Plaza Condominiums featured vintage posters of Metropolitan Opera stars. The security guard at the lobby desk told Mark that Carol was expecting him. Mark rode the elevator up to the sixth floor and found Carol standing in the open door at the end of the hall. She was dressed in jeans and a tee shirt, her silky blonde hair was cut short now, but her stunning beauty remained the same. She gave Mark a quizzical look and a quick hug, then pulled him inside with the self-assurance Mark remembered. She had two big glasses of white wine already poured. "You look different," she told him.

"You look great," he replied. They toasted and she sat on

the white sofa while he admired the red lights on Sutro Tower glowing through the fog.

"You were our Mario Savio," Mark told her, "our Mark Rudd..." and then, slyly, "...our Angela Davis."

She flashed him her brilliant smile. "How many times did I tell you guys not to compare me to her?" She drank a healthy portion of wine. "How've you been? Still in grad school?" "

"I'm still an undergraduate. One more month. Then the Army."

She looked puzzled. "Army?"

"The draft. That little inconvenience." Mark tried a light tone but failed. "You were more our Tom Hayden than our Mark Rudd," Mark said. "Not a hot-head. You had the passion, but it was balanced with thoughtfulness and practicality."

"Don't make me out to be too much of a saint."

Mark tried a grin that didn't seem to reach her. She turned her glass of Pinot Grigio in the lamplight. "Lot of talk back then." She leaned back on the white couch, looking more than ever like a fashion model.

"You left MU all of a sudden," Mark said.

"Well..." She got up, made a round of the room, paused to straighten a picture on the wall, poured herself another glass of wine, and topped his off. "After all our talk, nothing was happening." She sat down and gave Mark a sharp look. "I made a second trip to Washington, to see McCarthy. This was after the election. He wouldn't even meet with me." She shrugged and got up to pace again. "My father had always wanted me to take a position with a financial management firm, so it was an easy transition." She sat down straight-backed. "Besides, I'd been wondering for a long time how much energy I really wanted to keep putting into that stuff. I pretty much had to do everything myself. And what had we accomplished anyway? Some changes to campus rules, an abortive referendum to amend the state constitution, some planks for a failed presidential hopeful. A year after Prague Spring the Soviets still had thirteen divisions of troops in Prague and Dubcek under house arrest, but McCarthy's staffers just wanted to talk about Senator Proxmire's milk subsidy. So stupid!"

Carol downed her wine and poured herself some more. "Sorry." She kept her back to Mark.

"Beautiful place," Mark stammered, cursing himself for his inanity. This was not the reminiscing he had imagined.

She began pacing. "It's just a place to sleep. I'm on the road three weeks out of four. The housekeeper is probably in this condo more than I am. You're lucky I just happened to be in town while you're here."

Mark tried to bring the conversation back to the old days. "Despite what you may think, you did accomplish things back in Missouri."

"Some campus rule changes? Some articles in an independent newspaper? A march on the state capitol that resulted in nothing?"

"It opened people's minds up. I can remember reading your *One Voice Manifesto* in the *Columbia Free Press*. That cold windy November day is etched in my memory. I stood on the porch of the old house where the CFP offices were and read the whole thing through. It fired my mind, made the issues alive and pertinent."

She began prowling again. "Change the world," she snorted. "It was…" her voice dropped to a dramatic whisper "…important. It's not."

She straightened the same picture. "Business, commerce, conducted by big and efficient companies has done more to improve social welfare than all the do-gooder protests ever did or ever will. Read Hayek or Chandler." She looked Mark right in the eye. "Thanks for the compliments, but my career now is much more relevant than marching through the streets with hand-lettered signs."

A different kind of silence filled the room.

"Well..." he said. "Just thought I'd drop by to say hello. I'd better be going."

She came over and put a hand on his arm. "I don't mean to sound so harsh. I'm glad you stopped by." Her tone softened. "I remember our march on the state capitol. It was early spring, the trees were still bare, but the grass was green. We camped in a little park by the highway." Mark waited for her to say Jeff's name, but she didn't.

"We were in a circle around a campfire. I wrote out my speech with a BIC pen in an MU notebook." She stopped. "Seems so long ago."

"I was in the crowd the next morning when you gave your speech on the steps of the capitol building—the *One Voice Manifesto*," he said.

"People listened politely, even applauded." Carol shrugged. "But when the speeches were over, and we'd had our little meetings with the state officials, we caught rides back to Columbia, and went to class, students again."

Mark kept a smile on his face.

She laughed, "Remember Wollheim? And the Lindblom textbook he loved so much? I see now that those professors are all just a bunch of academics debating things they've never experienced and never will. They are so..." she made a condescending gesture "...inconsequential." She got up and poured a tiny bit of wine in Mark's already full glass.

Her phone rang and she took the call in the other room. While the call went on, Mark wandered the room, then slipped his jacket on and rode the elevator down to foggy Van Ness Avenue.

* * *

The next morning while Mark was pouring his first cup of coffee, Dave told him, "I don't want to hear how much money she's making."

"Good morning to you too," Mark muttered.

"It's our last day here," Dave said briskly. "Let's drive up to Point Reyes National Seashore, see some coastline instead of city."

They picked up a map at the ranger station and set off on foot through the cypress forest to the iceplant-covered dunes. It was a magical place—foggy coastal savannah giving way to a rocky shoreline battered by great waves. They stood in the wind, savoring salt spray and the roar of the waves, then retreated behind rocks for their lunch.

"So is the beautiful Carol still involved in politics, or is it all about money now?"

"She quoted me Hayek," Mark said as he chewed a gas station sandwich they'd brought along. "Said business does more social good than all the street marches put together." The wind whistled over the rocks and roared in the twisted trees.

"Well, she knows her economics, I'll give her that," Dave said. "But she's a little rich girl who sees no contradiction in living well while talking revolution. She expects everyone to do what she tells them to and usually gets her way. Comes from being the only child of a well-to-do, politically active family, and a mother who reads Ayn Rand." Dave shook his head. "She'll do well."

"She is doing well."

"But she never really gets very close to people."

They finished their sandwiches and put the debris in the backpack they'd brought. Mark stood up but Dave continued to sit in the lee of the rocks. "I'm not sure I get very close to people either," he muttered, his eyes on the pinyon trees swaying in the wind. "I've been at LogCom six months and I know I don't want to get close to those people. Bunch of whining, unionized idiots. Our division director is good, graduate degree from Harvard, really understands public policy, but the workers are worthless." He shrugged. "But I'll work there a year at least. I don't want to go into the Army. And I like the pay, the vacation, the health insurance coverage."

"Health insurance?" Mark gave him a look. "That doesn't seem like a high priority."

Dave avoided his eye. "Been having headaches. Started going to a specialist..."

"So what's the diagnosis?"

"Don't know yet. I try to take it easy, no more psychedelics, just pot and beer."

"Give up women too?"

"Might as well have. St. Louis is full of really boring and ugly women."

"Maybe you should try to get in touch with Allison."

Dave smoothed the cold sand with his hand. "Over is over." He wiped the sand off his hand and stood up. "You ready to start back?"

When they got back to Steve's apartment he was putting his uniform back on, his face knotted into a scowl. "Got to get back to the base," he told them. "Some screw-up in ship loading, and she's got to depart at oh eight hundred tomorrow." The phone rang and he dived for it. "Yes Sir, I'll be there in ten minutes." He hung up and bent over a notepad, scribbling fast.

Steve settled his cap on his head, becoming someone they didn't know. "I'll probably be out at the base all night," he said. "Take care you guys, keep in touch."

The door banged closed behind him.

In the silent fog the next morning, Mark and Dave piled into the car and drove down empty streets to Interstate 80.

## Chapter 26

Mark closed his bluebook and handed it to the proctor at the back of the classroom. Outside, the noonday sun was bright and the air was hot and humid. He sat down for a minute on the worn limestone steps and watched the maintenance guys cutting the grass on the quad.

I should feel pretty good, Mark thought. The last exam of my last class, Heat Transfer, hadn't been that bad. Choose any four out of six problems. He knew he had two exactly right and the other two mostly right. Other guys drifted out of the building one by one and wandered off down the sidewalk without a word. The relaxed but simultaneously exhilarated feeling he'd had at the end of other semesters didn't come. Instead he felt an undefined anxiety. A guy wearing white Levi's a little too short for his black socks and loafers clipped his slide rule to his belt and strode away purposefully toward Jesse Hall. A humid breeze stirred the elms and red oaks overhead. A summer day—the last day of my last year at MU.

The maintenance guys shut off their lawn mowers and sat in the shade smoking cigarettes. For a moment Mark imagined himself on one of those lawn mowers, working a mindless eight-to-five job, his wife working at Sears, living in a double-wide out at Sunrise Estates, buying new tires for his pickup truck at Como Tire. No stress, no worries about the future because there was no future.

For a week it might be nice, then the boredom would be

overwhelming. Mark walked to the bookstore, sold his books, and walked to his apartment.

* * *

Mark liked the mornings at the apartment the best. He would wake as the summer sun lit the small window of his bedroom, filling his tiny room with green light. If there was a breeze, the moving shadows of the leaves would capture his eye. He felt like he slept deep in some hidden pool, rising up to the surface each morning. He drifted in an empyrean realm of light and fire. He sometimes tried to imagine himself in the Army, but that seemed even more unreal.

He'd shower and put on his gas station shirt, then ride his motorcycle four blocks to the Standard to work until two in the afternoon. That left the afternoons free for lying by the pool at Martha's dorm. There was never anyone else there. Bill had gone to St. Louis to stay with his mother until graduation, August tenth. Mark had heard Bill say nothing about Martha, and that, too, fit this new life of drifting.

At the pool Mark would strip off his tee shirt and lie in the sun until he got too hot, then dive deep in the pool, all the way to the bottom of the deep end, then drift to the surface, watching the blue and white hexagons flickering on the pool bottom, endlessly breaking and reforming. In the heat and sun, his memories of Carol, and Steve, the Haight, and Berkeley seemed like images from a history book.

One afternoon there were thunderstorms, so he stepped into the Heidelberg. He sat alone at the bar watching a Cardinals baseball game being played in some sunny city. The beer was unappealing, but the soft patter of the announcer formed a mantra in his mind, drawing him farther into lassitude. "... high, outside, that's one and two for Chavez..." Westlake's Ace Hardware was offering a pre-Labor Day sale on barbeque grills.

* * *

On the afternoons when he didn't lie by the pool he would drive to the farm and help his father with the methodical work of trimming trees. Mark liked the routine. Two hours of work in the steambath heat, maintaining and amiable silence. A shower, dinner, sit in front of the TV for a while watching *Perry Mason* and *Have Gun—Will Travel*, then retire to his childhood room to sleep.

Bill returned to Columbia unexpectedly the next day. "Got bored. I'm going to work until graduation day, it's only six more days." In the evenings, he and Bill took up the habit of sitting in front of the apartment in the rusty lawn chairs, watching the afternoon turn to deep green dusk. They would drink a Busch, sometimes two, before darkness and mosquitoes drove them inside.

"My father died when I was fifteen," Bill told Mark one evening. "Heart attack. He was only forty-three. He'd been pastor at the church for nearly ten years. He tried to build the congregation up, but few young people join the church these days and the old folks in the congregation were steadily dying away. He prayed hard, worked hard, took everybody's problems into himself. It killed him."

"I'm sorry to hear that," Mark said, and with the words, realized he was sorry. He'd always taken Bill for granted. An engineering geek, three point grade average, scholarship, part time job in the engineering lab, graduating two semesters early. Every week he'd be on the floor in front of the TV for *Star Trek*. He interviewed early in the spring, had his career planned since he was a junior. And he'd probably stay with the same company his entire career, marry soon, have a couple of kids, live comfortably, keep his faith.

"Does that old guy still work in the lab? The guy who helped me with that motorcycle part last fall."

"Yeah. He'll never retire, wants to die on the job." Bill grinned and sipped his Busch. "Really nice guy, knows how to run every machine tool in that lab. Really good with his hands."

"I sometimes envy guys like him," Mark said slowly. "Good at what he does. Got a steady eight-to-five job, lived here in Columbia all his life."

Bill looked puzzled in the gathering dusk. "That's not what people expect you and me to do."

"Yeah. I wouldn't mind going to grad school," Mark mused. "But my grades are crap. Did you get a draft deferment?"

"Yeah," Bill said. Swallows darted across the sky above the elm trees. "You and Jennifer used to talk about travelling the world. Is that what you plan to do, after the Army?"

"I don't think that far ahead anymore."

* * *

The next afternoon at the station, Frank left at his usual time. Bill had stepped out to run some errands, leaving Mark alone. Mark was canted back in the creaking Army surplus chair at the desk in the office, enjoying the warm breeze, when a white Ford station wagon pulled up to the pumps and Jeff got out.

Mark got to his feet and went out to the pumps. "Hey Jeff, back in town before you ship out for Germany?"

Jeff frowned and tapped his fingers on the roof of the car. "Yeah, leaving day after tomorrow."

"You don't seem very happy about it." Mark slapped him on the back. "How about a little going away party. My apartment is microscopic, and there are no women around, but…"

"Something's happened," Jeff interrupted. He looked around the empty sky, at the oak trees across Ninth Street, everywhere except at Mark. "My dad got a call yesterday from Dave's father. Dave's had a stroke. He's in Barnes Hospital over in St. Louis."

The noise of the afternoon seemed to drain away into an unnatural silence. "How serious?"

"Don't know. Let's drive over there."

"Yeah... yeah." It was Mark's turn to drum his fingers on the top of Jeff's parents' station wagon. "Bill will be back in a few minutes, then I can leave. I'll pick you up at your parents' house. Maybe thirty minutes." He scanned the street for Bill.

* * *

They didn't talk much on the drive. There was nothing much to say. Mark couldn't find the visitor's parking lot, so he parked in a lot in Forest Park and they walked through pleasant shade to the hospital entrance. They were still at the information desk in the lobby when a familiar voice behind them said, "Hello there young fellers." It was Dave's father's voice. And there he was, the same unstylish glasses, the same gentle smile, as though nothing had happened. Just the way Mark remembered him sitting in his Barcalounger watching a Cardinals baseball game at home. But a cruel god had touched his son with darkness. Mark felt his heart pounding. They shook hands and rode the elevator up to the tenth floor.

Dave's mother was sitting in a chair at the side of the bed near the window. She set her library book down as they came in. Dave lay there like a ghost, his black hair in stark contrast to the white sheets.

"Hello stranger," Mrs. Gardner said jokingly to Mark. He mumbled an answer, but the real stranger lay in the bed. Mark was intensely aware of the sights, sounds and smells of the hospital. The starched nurses uniforms, the machinery, the concerned but confident expressions. We demand that doctors and nurses look knowledgeable, Mark thought, we need answers and they are our only source. Mark looked at Dave's Buddha-like face. He had already passed beyond some incomprehensible barrier. The past Dave had shared with him and Jeff had all vanished.

"Hi Dave," Mark said too loudly. He calmed himself and tried to neither shout nor whisper. "How are you doing?" Stupid phrase.

Dave said nothing. His face was the same, but the expression was so calm, so different. For Mark, the knowledge that their roads had irreversibly separated was like a weight bearing down on him.

Mr. and Mrs. Gardner left the room and Jeff and Mark sat looking at the window, at the floor, at each other.

Mark thought of all the hours the three of them had spent together since they'd gotten to know each other their first year of high school. Cruising around after school in Dave's two-tone green '58 Chevy, sitting in front of Jeff's house talking about the infinite promise of the future. Now that continuum was broken.

Outside the window, the familiar Missouri summer light seemed a betrayal.

Dave's parents came back eventually and the four of them talked to fill the silence. Awkward small talk about this and that. After a while Mrs. Gardner went back to her book. A nurse came and Jeff and Mark moved out to the hall with Mr. Gardner and they exchanged more small talk and worn jokes.

"I'm on my way to Germany day after tomorrow," Jeff said. "But you can contact me through my parents."

After a while longer, Mark and Jeff left. The humid air outside felt thick as warm water after the hospital air. The grass in the park silenced their footsteps, the old oaks rippled in the wind overhead. Mark brushed the bark, trying to break the wall of glass that seemed to lie between him and reality.

They drove back to Columbia in a different kind of silence.

Mark opened a beer and sat on the lawn chair in front of the apartment watching the swallows swooping in the dusk. Dave now drifted in another world. The people he knew and that knew him, the Coltrane and Getz records he loved, the books he had read, Allison, Zen, his old TR3 parked under the oak tree, and the new Pontiac barreling through the Nevada night—all gone. His body will continue to breathe and sleep and eat. But shared times, the common environment of custom and routines and knowledge that construct a life, have all disappeared.

Mark raised his beer can to an absent Dave, "Your regrets, the stuff we talked about on our way to California, I hope they've been lost too. And I hope in some way that the road, the Tao you always talked about, still lies ahead for you. I hope that maybe the enlightenment you were seeking may still be within your reach."

* * *

Mark moved through the summer days, zombie-like. The heat and humidity had pulled a veil of silence over the streets of Columbia. Mark maintained his routine of work, farm, TV, sleep. He stopped going to the pool. The aquamarine oval in the hot sun had lost it's appeal. His mind slowly orbited the fact that his closest friend was gone. Better to be killed like Tim in some distant place rather than to be here and not here at the same time.

Several days later Mark drove to St. Louis and sat for a couple of hours by Dave's bedside. Mr. and Mrs. Gardner would absent themselves from the cool and sterile room.

Dave moved occasionally, but attempted to say nothing. Mark looked at his immobile face, at the summer sky outside. "You used to tell us that only this moment, this moment alone, truly exists," Mark whispered to the still form. "The past and the future are only constructs of our own thought. I hope you are right."

But instead of the calmness of inner contemplation, the image that rose up in Mark's mind was of the comfortable house on Oakland Gravel Road, a Cardinals game on TV, the dutiful son Dave had been, mowing his parents' lawn on a summer afternoon. Mark pushed the sadness away. Grief is selfish, he reminded himself once again.

* * *

A week later when Mark visited again, Mr. Gardner told him they were taking Dave home to Columbia the next morning. There was nothing more the doctors could do. "He's getting better," Mr. Gardner said, promoting the fiction. "He's getting stronger every day." The three of them sat in plastic chairs by the bed and carried on a desultory conversation about the school system in Columbia, the price of hay, the fact that fall clothes were already on display in shop windows on Broadway. Then they lapsed into an amiable silence as uncomplicated as the heartland itself. Mark thought of a Cessna droning overhead in a perfectly clear sky summer sky, and the deep green horizon of oak and walnut trees shimmering on a summer day hazy with humidity. Hospital staff came and went. Outside the gray-tinted hospital windows, summer clouds moved across the sky.

* * *

That evening Mark opened a beer and sat on the rusty lawn chair in front of his apartment, watching swallows swooping in the evening light. When the beer was gone he got in his car and drove to the farm with the car windows down and the liquid air of summer smooth and scented with cut grass. He ate a silent dinner with his father and sister, then helped with the dishes and sat in the living room with his father watching a rerun of *Have Gun—Will Travel*. In his room he sat at his old desk in the glow of the lamp and reread most of Alan E. Nourse's *Trouble on Titan*, letting the familiar story soothe his mind until it was empty and he could sleep.

For the first moment of waking the next morning he was content. His mind had absorbed the comfort of his childhood room. He drifted for a bit in a timeless place, soothed by images of the familiar all around him.

He rode his Suzuki down the quiet country roads through a morning already heavy with bright humidity. The road flowed by, dreamlike, but the feeling of speed and freedom he used to feel, no longer came.

On his lunch break at the gas station he lettered a FOR SALE sign on a piece of cardboard from a box of oil cans and by noon a guy had given him $200 for his Suzuki. After closing, he stepped next door to the Heidelberg and drank a draft Hamm's at the bar to celebrate, but the place was empty and the Cardinals game on the TV unappealing. He walked back to the apartment, got in his car, and drove to the farm.

The next day after work he crossed the empty quad and went into the silent Engineering building. He checked his final Heat Transfer grade in his Heat Transfer course and found a C by his student number. The class had been taught by a vapid graduate assistant, not the ferocious Bradley, which had made it seem like an entirely different class. I've graduated, he thought. He examined his feelings but could find no change, no elation, nothing.

One afternoon at the farm a week later, he came in from the fields with his father and found his sister had a put a letter from the University on his desk. Inside was a certified transcript dated August 1969, indicating he had been awarded a Bachelor's degree in Mechanical and Aerospace Engineering. Enclosed was a form asking if he would attend the graduation ceremony. He checked the box no.

The days drifted by in routine and silence.

Walking back to his apartment after work one afternoon, he found Rich Behr standing motionless on the corner. There were no cars in sight in any direction.

Mark slapped him on the back. "Lost in thought Rich?"

Rich came back to the present with a start. "Mark. Hey. How you been?" They crossed the street together and strolled along in the shade of the old elm trees.

"Got something here," Rich said, his tone reverential. He pulled a tinfoil square out of his pocket. Inside were a dozen small purple tablets. "Purple Owsley," Rich said. "The best LSD there is. The original."

"How much are you charging for them?"

"Five dollars each."

Mark stared at the tiny purple dots in the tinfoil. "No thanks. I think not."

"Better get some now, this stuff will go fast."

"No thanks," Mark repeated.

They reached Matthews Street. "Well, see you around, Rich." Rich stopped to scan the street, then the treetops waving in the summer breeze.

Mark chuckled, "Looking for something?"

"Where are you going?"

"I live here, Rich." After a moment Rich started uncertainly back the way they'd come.

# Chapter 27

The next morning when Mark stopped by the apartment on his lunch break, Bill had his black '63 Chevy backed up to the apartment door, and was loading the trunk with cardboard boxes.

"Graduation is today," Mark said. "You're not going?"

Bill closed the trunk. "I'm going, but right afterward I'm going back to St. Louis." He ducked into his room. "Got to get changed and meet my mother. You want to join us for lunch?"

Mark thought about it for a minute. "No, thanks. I'll grab a bite here then get back to the station."

Bill stuffed his shirttail into his suit pants and stuck out his hand. "Well, I probably won't see you before I leave."

Mark shook his hand. "When are you going to …where was it?"

"Richmond, California. The naval shipyard. I need to be there on the twentieth."

Mark wrote out his farm address on a piece of paper. "Keep in touch."

Bill grinned, put the paper in his pocket, and pushed up his black-framed glasses. "Yeah. We had some pretty good times at the old trailer, didn't we? But you need to take *Star Trek* more seriously."

Mark smiled, remembering Bill on the floor in front of the TV. "Funny thing is, I do take it more seriously now."

Bill got in his car and backed down the alley.

"See you around, Bill," Mark whispered. "You're the last. Everybody's gone now."

* * *

At the gas station, business was brisk. Frank chatted with customers while he their filled their tanks. Sam pumped gas with pompous efficiency. Cars rolled past searching for parking places. Parents filed along the sidewalk in a steady stream, on their way to the quadrangle, the men in dark suits, women in pastel dresses with hats and white gloves. As Mark changed the oil in a Buick, he could hear speakers droning away on the quad. After a time there was a great cheer and soon a smiling throng spilled out along the sidewalk, taking pictures, shaking hands, hugging.

When his shift ended, Mark walked across the street to the empty quadrangle and sat on a stone bench in the shade watching the cleanup crews stacking the rows of wooden folding chairs. He told himself he should go talk to the Army recruiter about getting signed up for Officer Candidate School while he still had some choice in the matter, but somehow it seemed easier not to think about the future at all.

He floated through humid silent days in solitude. His routine was comforting: work at the gas station, swim at the dorm pool, sit in a lawn chair in front of the apartment or go to the farm and sit with his father watching reruns of *Peter Gunn*, and *Perry Mason*. He had called Jennifer and told her about Dave. "Should I come up there for a few days?" she asked.

"No. I feel okay, and there's nothing we can do, any of us." He sat holding the phone until she asked if he was still there. "Is there something I should be doing?" he asked.

"Come see me."

"Soon. But for now, I need time to myself."

Mark received a letter from her every week, she was staying with her parents over the summer, visiting friends, but mostly just waiting. He told himself she deserved a summer vacation before she had to drive up to Tallahassee when Florida State started.

She told him she loved him and he told her he loved her, and he did. But he felt no desire to go see her or have her with him in Columbia. He kept her letters in a stack on his desk at the farm and reread them from time to time, like the books on the shelves.

* * *

Mark stopped by the Heidelberg one evening and saw Debbie at the other end of the bar. She didn't see him. Mark left his full beer and crept out the back door. That was the last time he went into the Heidelberg.

The next afternoon when Mark was alone at the gas station, sipping a beer and reading *Playboy*, a white Ford van pulled up to the gas pump and a long-haired guy stumbled out, stoned and giggling. A girl in a skirt and tee shirt, her boobs bouncing under the peace sign, emerged from the side door of the van. "Two dollar's worth of regular," the driver told Mark.

They'd parked so far from the pump that the hose would barely reach, but Mark managed to get the nozzle in the tank and put the gas in.

The guy laboriously pulled coins out of his pocket one by one and laid them out on top of the gas pump. This took a long time. When he was done, Mark found he had arranged two dollars in dimes, nickels, and quarters, the coins neatly grouped together by denomination. "We're going to New York," the guy volunteered. Big concert near a small town called Woodstock." The girl squealed with laughter. "Big concert, small town," he repeated, mesmerized at his own words. After that had subsided, he told Mark, "It's going to be the biggest music festibal…fes-ti-val. Santana, Sly and the Family Stone, Canned Heat, The Who, Hendrix…"

"…the Dead," the girl continued for him. "The Band, Joe

Cocker…" She looked around, suddenly disoriented, then steadied herself on the door to the van standing open. She climbed inside and looked at Mark. "You want to go along?"

Mark thought about it. "Why not." He put the money in the cash register, pulled the rollup doors down, and locked the front door. Frank really doesn't need me to work, there's no business in the summer, he's just doing me a favor, he thought. My father and sister don't need me at the farm. Jennifer's in Florida and everybody else has already left Columbia. "Let's go." He climbed in the side door and stretched out on one of the cushions.

I'm just here, waiting. Frozen in time. That breathless moment of silence just before everything changes. Across the street, the tops of the tall oak trees were motionless.

The guy in the driver's seat finished rolling a joint, lit it, and started the van. "Close the door, man."

Instead Mark got up, climbed out, and gently closed the van door. "No, I've changed my mind. All that's over for me."

"Well…peace, man," the guy said. He ground the van into gear, let out the clutch, stalled the engine, restarted it, and lurched off down Ninth Street at ten miles-per-hour. Music from the eight-track drifted through the air: "…come on people now, smile on your brother…"

A few days later Mark came into his apartment from his evening vigil in the lawn chair and clicked on the TV while he ate a TV dinner. The news showed a helicopter view of a mass of people in a muddy field. "...the New York State Thruway is closed due to a huge traffic jam near the upstate town of Woodstock, where a music festival has been underway for two days..." Mark raised his can of Busch in a toast to the screen, then went back to his Swanson fried chicken.

He told himself he should move to the farm, he was there most evenings anyway, but he made no move to do so. He liked waking in the apartment, drifting back to consciousness in the glowing green. In the evening he stopped smoking pot, and instead would cruise aimlessly in his car. He did not look at the girls he passed, nor did he stop by any of the familiar bars. He just drove, the familiar streets of Columbia with KAAY or WLS on the radio, windows rolled down on the soft night air. The same way he and the other Columbia kids had cruised around on summer nights in high school. Down Business 70 to University Avenue, to Stadium and back to Providence Road. Tim's yellow '57 Plymouth, Steve's white '59 Chevy, Dave's green '58 Chevy, Jeff in his blue Volkswagen. At McDonald's they would lean on their cars, talk about cars and girls. The years seemed to have passed in an instant.

He thought about visiting Dave and his parents, even went so far as to drive past the house one afternoon. But he did not stop.

Instead he drove to Paquin and pulled into the gravel lot of the old apartment house where Dave and Allison had lived. Inside, the building smelled like fresh paint. Allison's apartment door was locked, but Dave's door stood open. He went into the empty room and looked out the low window at the froth of green oak leaves and his Chevy parked where Dave used to park his TR3. The ceiling fan was turning, clearing paint fumes.

Mark touched the place where the brick and board bookcase had been, where Allison had put up the Fillmore concert poster, the corner where the mattress had lain covered with the old Indian blanket. The room was silent except for the whisper of the fan and a faraway cricket.

He saw Steve Griffin shake a Marlboro out of a pack with a practiced gesture. "Political philosophy is fine, but military power and the will to use it are what solves disputes..."

"...and starts them," Dave countered. Outside, the oak tree's bare branches moved against the glow of the street light. "*The Way of Zen*, by Alan Watts; *The Tao*, by Lao Tzu, that's true power." Allison laughing, chipped front tooth, singing along with the Beatles, "...gonna be a revolution, yeah...you know..."

Falling free through infinite crystal blue sky, from his first parachute jump to that last, highest, fall from leaden clouds toward a frozen earth.

Sitting in the wooden booths at the I.V. drinking pitchers of Hamm's, talking about the new girls in town and hearing about Steve's trip to South Carolina and Keith's trip to Wyoming. Shooting pool downstairs at the Student Commons. He and Dave riding their motorcycles out to the old strip mines north of town, and racing their bikes down country roads brilliant with fall colors. Taking half a hit of psilocybin and sitting on the couch in the trailer, watching the rain glittering on the window, reading a Fritz Leiber story. High on windowpane LSD watching purple and yellow mandalas turning slowly in the Formica surface of the kitchen table. Reading *The Moon is a Harsh Mistress* and drinking Constant Comment tea on a snowy weekday morning when he had the trailer to himself, no classes until afternoon. Walking across campus in the cold autumn air, arm in arm with Jennifer—in love. The way his heart skipped when he caught sight of her coming carefully down the airplane steps in the golden afternoon light, tanned and perfect in blue miniskirt and red blouse.

Drinking beer at the Shack on Friday afternoons, pumping gas and changing oil and clowning around with Bill Whitten at the Standard station. Happy hour at the Heidelberg, Keith playing "Suzanne" on his guitar at the Hofbrau. Sunday afternoons at the airport, skydiving with Dave. Talking engineering with Jeff over bad coffee in the Student Commons. The summer he and Tim Bryant had bought the old go-kart and got it running. The wintry day he and Jennifer had ridden his motorcycle up to Benton City. All the evenings he and Jennifer had talked about Marvell, Blake, Gray, and Byron, and all the evenings they had made love in his room at the trailer, candlelight making the LOVE poster glow.

Talking with Bill Whitten about working for NASA, watching the moon landing. Arguing with Dave about politics and philosophy and economics. Drinking beer with Jeff at the Black and Gold and talking about women and the future and leaving Columbia behind. And the war in Vietnam with Steve over beers in the dimness of the Shack. Getz and Coltrane and Brubeck at Dave's apartment—talking about Zen, the Tao, and enlightenment. Coffee with Carol and Jeff, after Wollheim's class, comparing Lindblom, Marcuse, and Friedman, Carol so intent, Jeff so smitten. The afternoon he had read Carol's *One Voice Manifesto*, and the afternoon he'd learned Professor Wollheim had quit.

The dark winter day he'd come up the stairs of this old house to find Allison crying. They had made love while the silent snow fell. Allison, back in town, on her way to New York and a new life. Dave, gone forever. Tim, dead. Keith and Steve and Jeff gone to be soldiers.

He pulled the cord on the ceiling fan and watched it coast to a stop. In the gathering dusk the room became just an empty room in an old house in a small town in the Midwest.

* * *

Driving back to his apartment he noticed the sidewalks were crowded with students in new MU tee shirts. In front of the Shack and the I.V., guys were milling around eying the girls. There were crowds in front of the Heidelberg and the Hofbrau too, their front doors standing open to the mild evening. Laughter echoed over jukebox music. Students crowded the sidewalks, jostling and joking. Mark thought about stopping in the Heidelberg for a beer, but kept going.

The next morning at the station, Frank called Mark over to his desk. "You've graduated, so you'll be leaving, right?"

"Any day," nodded Mark. "Whenever the draft board sends me my notice." He glimpsed several job applications on the desk.

"In fact," Mark said, "I should probably quit now so you can hire a new guy for the new semester.

Frank shook his hand. "I appreciate that." He handed Mark a check which included a small bonus.

He felt great walking down Ninth Street, his few obligations falling away, one by one.

At the apartment he boxed his things, threw his clothes in the back seat of the car, and took a bag of trash out to the dumpster. But before he drove away he lay on the mattress in the silence of his room, looking at the green light at the window, and floated free in invisible water.

* * *

At the farm he put his things away, then walked to the little pond. The water reflected the blue of the sky. He sat on the bare dirt and watched water bugs zig-zag across the smooth surface. There were no signs of his mother's irises, but he knew the bulbs were there and the purple blooms would appear again next year.

When he got back to the house, Mark found his father in the garden weeding around the iris plants. He noticed his father was smiling.

"Beautiful weather," his father said. "Still warm but you can feel the beginning of autumn in the air. It's when things change that we appreciate them the most." He nodded at the irises. "Your mother loved this garden." His father pulled one glove off to wipe the sweat off his brow. "I know you're not enthusiastic about going into the Army, Mark. But, I want you to know, I'm proud of you for the doing the right thing, even when it is not the easy thing, and even when you don't fully agree with it."

Mark nodded, dumbfounded. They each quickly turned away, embarrassed. "Thanks, Dad," Mark mumbled and withdrew to the house.

His sister was on the phone. "...so many kids in that class, a full auditorium. But it's great. Really interesting." Mark realized she was talking about her classes at the University.

In the day's mail he found an official envelope addressed to him. The letter inside said, "Greeting: You are hereby ordered for induction into the Armed Forces of the United States, report date September 25, 1969."

He went to the phone and called Jennifer. "I got my notice. My report date is two weeks from tomorrow."

"I can come up there," she said.

"No, I'm coming down there," Mark said. "I'll start for Florida this afternoon and be there by noon tomorrow."

# Chapter 28

Mark put his suitcase in his car and walked out to the garden where his father was patiently spading the vegetable bed. Reality was now sharp and clear—the scent of sun on the fields, the rich smell of the turned earth turned by his father's spade, the long golden light, the mild breeze, sounds of birds and insects already subtly changed from deep summer, and hinting at autumn. "I got my draft notice," Mark said. He was surprised at how easy it was to say, the dread he had felt for months was gone. "I report in two weeks."

His father nodded and removed his gloves. "I thought that might be what that letter was." His father clicked off the voice of Dan Devine on the transistor radio.

"I'm going to spend the time with Jennifer in Florida," Mark said. His father nodded and set his spade down. "She seems like a very fine young woman. It was good she got to meet your mother."

"I left the phone number on the table by the phone. I'll call you when I get there." They both nodded the same nod and Mark went to his car.

Reality was sharp and clear. When he closed his car door, his sister was standing by the front door of the house. "Thought I'd say goodbye," she said.

"Thanks. I'll be back in two weeks. I report for active duty in St. Louis."

"Well, drive carefully and call us when you get there."

"I will. See ya."

Despite the long drive ahead of him, he detoured through Columbia, down Stadium to campus, where students filled the sidewalks in front of the Heidelberg and the Hofbrau. He drove down Broadway past Puckett's, Barth's, Neate's, all the stores he'd passed a hundred times without seeing them. Their brick facades now seemed supernaturally clear. Then he turned on Stadium Boulevard and drove all the way out to the little airport. This weekend there would be blooms of orange and white nylon in the clear blue sky, and above them the distant drone of the Cessna. He turned onto Interstate 70, envisioning how it looked from 5000 feet in the air. At the Providence Road exit he tapped his horn twice and waved to an invisible Tim speeding up the exit ramp in his yellow Plymouth, and then he was out in the flat farmland of Missouri. He drove for a while and when he looked in the rearview mirror next, Columbia had disappeared from view.

* * *

It was paradise at Jennifer's parents' house in St. Pete. They welcomed Mark warmly, clearly expecting him to become a son-in-law soon. He was given the tiny guest house across the pool from the main house. He had his own lanai, bedroom, sitting room, and bathroom. Every day after Mr. Campion left for work and Mrs. Campion for her bridge club or shopping, the humid mornings became very still. Mark would lie in the comfortable bed in his tiny house, watching the blue reflections from the pool on the ceiling. Jennifer would come to his door looking very fresh and beautiful. Sometimes they would make love. Every day they would prepare a big breakfast and take it poolside to eat under the sunshade with WBAE playing easy listening music.

They lived each hour as it came with no plans, no appointments, no obligations. Most afternoons they would drive out to the ocean and lie in the sun at St. Pete or Madeira

Beach. Sometimes in the heat of the afternoon they'd make love in his bedroom with the air conditioner whispering and the tropical heat of Gulf Coast Florida outside.

A big comfortable house to live in while someone else took care of it. Unlimited free food and drink. Sex, love, every sensation seemed to be filled with scent, sound, taste and feel. Every moment was gorgeous. But as they walked the beach in the in the warm sea breeze of late afternoon, he knew every moment was finite. An end would come. They watched late afternoon thunderstorms gather far out on the green Gulf horizon;, lightning would flicker in the peach-colored bellies of the clouds.

Sunday morning they went with Jennifer's parents to the Madeira Beach Club and sat poolside with her parents' friends drinking Bloody Marys and laughing at anecdotes about people they didn't know. Sailboats rocked on the green Gulf water, the warm breeze rippled the yellow and white umbrellas over the tables, the beach stretched away to either side. They would eat Crab Louis and drink ice-cold Heinekens on Jennifer's father's tab, then dive into the pool to clear their heads. Later they walked down the concrete steps, cool and gritty with sand, and walked the white sand of the beach to waded in the warm water.

The next evening they drove up to the 16th Street Drive-in movie. They smoked a couple of joints and drank several cans of Busch while they watched *The April Fools*. On the way home they could not stop repeating Jack Weston's drunken line, "This train doesn't go to cookie." They laughed so hard Mark thought he'd have to stop the car.

Most evenings, after the heat of the day had passed, they'd drive out to St. Pete Beach, park in Smolen's parking lot, get draft beers to go in plastic cups, and walk down to the beach. They would stand waist-deep in the bath-warm water, watching late afternoon thunderstorms on the Western horizon.

Haslam's bookstore was a favorite stop—a cool and inviting cave filled with comfortable silence and the scent of used books. Mark pulled out a worn volume of Blake's poetry and glanced inside, "...heaven in a wildflower..." then put the book back and stood watching Jennifer at the other end of the aisle, standing with her weight all on one leg the way she always did. Her long black hair fell forward, hiding her face as she leaned over a box of books. She brushed her hair back with an achingly familiar gesture and Mark felt his eyes welling up. She looked up and smiled at him across the room and he managed to put a smile on his face in return.

The last game of the World Series was on TV that evening, and to be polite they joined Mr. and Mrs. Campion in the living room in front of the TV. The Mets came from behind to win it. The evening felt comfortable and domestic. Mark had no interest in baseball, but the Campion's acceptance of him made the evening glow. They sat in a row on the big purple and yellow couch eating popcorn.

The day before he was to leave, Mark and Jennifer sat by the pool in the sun and humidity of late morning. WBAE was playing "The Girl from Ipanema."

"Remember the first time we spent the night together?" Mark's voice softened. "Keith loaned us his trailer. It was cold. You were wearing a blue turtleneck sweater and you'd brought one of your literature class books, Camus' *The Stranger*."

Jennifer smiled, pleased that he remembered. "I also remember our first date that spring. You took me to your trailer and we drank Busch beer and watched *Star Trek* with Bill stretched out on the floor in front of the TV."

Mark covered his face. "Sorry. I'm sure you thought I was a real geek."

"I didn't." She laughed and sat on his lap and kissed him. "You think you're the only one who remembers details. Let me tell you about that *Star Trek* episode we watched on our first date."

Mark grinned. "The best of times," he said.

She put her fingers on his lips. "No. The best times are now. Always will be."

He glanced up at the perfectly clear blue sky, then at the wavering rectangles of white light in blue water. "I want to think so. This last year has been 'the best of times, the worst of times.' Maybe it is always that way. And now, the Army, the war…I hate the thought of it, but I have to go. I can't take the easy way out. This war is useless, but…" his voice trailed off.

"All I want…" her voice broke. She hid her face for a moment, then whispered "…is for you to come back safe."

"I will." He hugged her. "I love you."

"I love you too."

They watched the shimmer of light in blue water. "I couldn't tell you that, not for a long time. I felt it, but…"

She put her arms around him and put her face right up to his. "For a long time I wondered if you felt as much for me as I felt for you."

"Sorry." He kissed her. "It was stupid for me not to tell you. And it was stupid of me not to tell you about my mother's illness." He paused. "Can I ask you something?" Exquisite white clouds had begun to drift across the sky, but the day remained bright. "What did my mother say that time she talked privately with you?"

Jennifer's face clouded. "Her words were, 'We each have only the time we have.' She felt like her life had been a good one. She regretted only that her illness was bringing pain into your father's life and yours and your sister's." Jennifer covered her face with her hands. Her narrow shoulders shook as she cried. Mark comforted her. And after a while the bright day worked its magic on their tears.

"Did you give up skydiving because of that near-death experience in Florida?" You were almost killed, skydiving," Jennifer said. "And you said nothing to me."

"No. This may sound strange, but I really don't think about that at all. Skydiving is about freedom, not defying death. The accident was my own fault." He paused for a moment then continued. "Two months later, in the midst of winter, I made a jump in bitter cold, alone, the highest altitude I could reach."

He looked her in the eye. "I felt like I was all alone, trying to deal with all kinds of problems. You and I weren't seeing each other. For a long time I had imagined there really was something, somewhere, deep in the country. But I was beginning to realize there is no idyllic place where nothing ever changes. No Shangri-La." He smiled at her. "You told me that and you were right. But you also told me that life is a journey, meant to be shared. You told me that once in a phone call just before you hung up on me."

"I'm sorry."

"No need to be. That's past, and you were right about that too. Now finish your story," he told her. "The *Star Trek* story we saw on our first date."

Jennifer beamed. "The crew beams down to explore Omicron Ceti five. Spock gets sprayed with alien spores that made him so emotional he falls in love with Leila Kalomi..."

"Played by Jill Ireland," Mark interjected. "I love trivia."

"Spock tells her, 'I love you. I can love you.' They kiss and lie on the grass on a hillside on a sunny day watching the clouds in the sky. Then Spock says, 'I never stopped to look at clouds before, or rainbows.'" Jennifer turned away for a moment. "And before I met you, I hadn't either, not really."

"Then Sandoval tells Kirk the effect of the spores gives them harmony, complete peace, paradise," Mark prompted. "I was looking for it deep in the country, but I think it actually existed when we sat in a circle in Dave's apartment—you, and me and Dave and Allison and Jeff and Steve. Friends. The best of times."

"I haven't finished my story," Jennifer pressed ahead. "The

effect of the spores wears off and as the *Enterprise* leaves orbit, Spock says wistfully, 'For the first time in my life I was happy…'" Jennifer stopped talking. Mark saw she was crying silently, her lips quivering. After a moment she said, "You've made me happier than I've ever been before."

The rains came and lingered into evening. After dinner, he and Jennifer drove around for a while trying to keep the moments from disappearing. They parked in the big empty parking lot of the Bayfront Center and watched the rain and wind whipping waves against the seawall. They held each other for a while, the radio playing softly, but when "Someday We'll Be Together" began, Mark turned it off.

After a while they drove back to her parents' house and each went to their own room.

* * *

The next morning Mark and Jennifer ate a silent breakfast with Mr. and Mrs. Campion at the kitchen table. Mr. Campion shook his hand; Mrs. Campion hugged him. Then they got in their white Vista Cruiser and drove off waving.

The house was silent. Mark took Jennifer in his arms. "Thank you," he whispered. "For everything."

She was crying and so was he. He caught a ragged breath. "I've got to go."

He got in his car, backed out of the driveway, and drove slowly away, watching Jennifer waving. She was dressed in a pink blouse and white pants, and seemed very small standing in front of the white door of the house.

He drove for twenty hours, memories moving slowly across his mind. It's all gone, he thought. My time with Jennifer, University days, the Columbia kids I grew up with, my mother, Dave, Columbia, the sixties themselves. The sky was beginning to turn blue with the coming day as he drove the last hundred miles. In that clear light he realized that despite all that time had taken away, love remained. In the rearview mirror he noticed he was smiling. "I have all I could ever want," he whispered.

The next morning, the horizon was a gold line under a black arch of sky at five AM. Mark filed onto the Greyhound bus with twenty five other conscripts, the door closed, and the bus turned East toward the military reception center in St. Louis.

www.ingramcontent.com/pod-product-compliance
Lightning Source LLC
Chambersburg PA
CBHW030757150426
42813CB00068B/3198/J
* 9 7 8 1 9 3 6 6 8 8 1 7 3 *